Spanish
Idioms

By
Eugene Savaiano, Ph.D.
Professor Emeritus of Spanish
Wichita State University, Wichita, Kansas
and
Lynn W. Winget, Ph.D.
Professor Emeritus of Spanish
Wichita State University, Wichita, Kansas

BARRON'S

© Copyright 1996 by Barron's Educational Series, Inc.
This book is also published as Part I of *2001 Spanish and English Idioms*, © Copyright 1995 by Barron's Educational Series, Inc.

All inquiries should be addressed to:
Barron's Educational Series, Inc.
250 Wireless Boulevard
Hauppauge, New York 11788

International Standard Book Number 0-8120-9027-6

Library of Congress Catalog Card Number 95-81411

PRINTED IN THE UNITED STATES OF AMERICA

19 18 17 16

Contents

Preface

This pocket edition is intended primarily for the use of North Americans and other English-speakers interested in Spanish for purposes of study or of travel in Spanish-speaking countries. It is also meant for Spanish-speakers who wish to learn English idiomatic expressions by looking up a Spanish idiom and then studying its translated form.

The body of the work consists of approximately 2500 Spanish idioms, arranged under their key words in alphabetical order. The idioms are for the most part accompanied by brief but complete illustrative sentences, and it is hoped that this procedure will help to eliminate the frustrations sometimes experienced by users of dictionaries in which idioms are simply listed in isolation, not in context.

For the purposes of this pocket edition, an "idiom" is understood to be almost any expression that (1) consists of at least two words in one or both of the languages involved, and (2) is expressed differently in the two languages (*"tener frío"*) = "to be cold" or *"tomarle el pelo"* = "to pull his leg"). We also have included a number of expressions that are the same in the two languages on the theory that the reader may need to be reassured that this is so. We refer to the "good" student who has learned that *"ser un pedazo de pan"* is not "to be a loaf of bread" and *"forrarse el riñón"* is not "to pad one's kidney," and who probably will hesitate to take for granted that *"tomar parte en"* is "to take part in" and may appreciate being explicitly told that it is.

The idioms come primarily from the contemporary spoken language and the Spanish used is more Latin American than peninsular. We have gathered material both from a variety of Spanish-European and Spanish-American sources which contain a considerable amount of colloquial language and from standard dictionaries, textbooks and idiom lists.

Parentheses indicate either optional or alternate material. For example, "it's (just) one of those things" implies that the expression can be either "it's one of those things" or "it's just one of those things," but "at (to) one side" implies that the expression can be either "at one side" or "to one side," but could scarcely be interpreted to mean that the idiom can be "at to one side."

To make the dictionary more practical for the traveler, we have included a Spanish-English index, lists of abbreviations, tables of weights and measures, and a list of common English idioms with the Spanish word in parentheses.

In conclusion we wish to express our sincere gratitude to all those who have in a variety of ways aided us in the preparation of this pocket edition, and in particular to our colleagues Kenneth Pettersen and John Koppenhaver whose help and advice have contributed significantly to the production of this volume.

Modismos Españoles (Spanish Idioms)

a — *to, at*

a la semana (al mes) — *a week, (a month).*
Le pagan dos veces a la semana. *They pay him twice a week.*

a + infinitive — *if.*
A haberlo comprado yo, lo hubiera devuelto. *If I had bought it, I would have returned it.*

al + infinitive — *upon.*
Al verla, la saludó. *Upon seeing her, he said hello (to her).*

uno a uno — *one by one.*
Entraron uno a uno. *They entered one by one.*

---

abajo — *down*

de abajo — *below.*
Vive en el piso de abajo. *He lives on the floor below.*

hacia abajo — *downward.*
Miró hacia abajo. *He looked down.*

venirse abajo (a tierra) — *to collapse.*
La muralla se vino abajo (a tierra). *The wall collapsed.*

---

el abril — *April*

tener . . . abriles — *to be . . . years old.*
Tenía veinte abriles. *She was twenty years old. [Said only of young people.]*

---

absoluto — *absolute*

en absoluto — *not at all.*
No dijo nada en absoluto. *He said nothing at all.*

---

la abuela — *grandmother*
  no necesitar abuela — *to toot one's own horn.*
  No necesita abuela. *He toots his own horn.*

No necesita abuela.
He toots his own horn.

---

abundar — *to abound*
  Lo que abunda no daña. *You can't have too much of a good thing.*

abusar — *to abuse*
  abusar de — *to take advantage of.*
  Abusan de su bondad. *They take advantage of his (her) kindness.*

acá — *here*
  por acá — *this way.*
  Por acá, por favor. *This way, please.*

acabar — *to finish*
  acabar de — *to have just.*
  Acaban de comer. *They have just eaten.*

  acabar por — *to end up by.*
  Acabó por creerlo. *He ended up believing it.*

---

acaso — *perhaps*
  por si acaso — *just in case.*
  Tome dos, por si acaso. *Take two just in case.*

la acción — *action*
  ganarle la acción — *to get the jump on someone.*
  Me ganó la acción. *He got the jump on me.*

  unir la acción a la palabra — *to suit the action to the word.*
  Unió la acción a la palabra. *He suited the action to the word.*

el aceite — *oil*
  echar aceite (leña) al fuego — *to add fuel to the flames (fire).*
  Echó aceite al fuego. *He added fuel to the flames (fire).*

la actividad — *activity*
  estar en plena actividad — *to be in full swing.*
  Está en plena actividad. *It's in full swing.*

el acto — *act*
  acto seguido (continuo) — *immediately afterwards.*
  Acto seguido (continuo) apareció mi hermano. *Immediately afterwards my brother appeared.*

  en el acto — *at once.*
  Dígale que venga en el acto. *Tell him to come at once.*

  hacer acto de presencia — *to put in an appearance.*
  Hizo acto de presencia. *He put in an appearance.*

la actualidad — *present time*
  en la actualidad — *at present; at the present time.*
  En la actualidad hay mucho desempleo. *At present (At the present time) there is much unemployment.*

  ser de actualidad — *to be important just now.*
  Es de gran actualidad. *It's very important just now.*

el acuerdo — *agreement*
  concertar un acuerdo — *to come to terms.*

Concertaron un acuerdo. *They came to terms.*

de acuerdo con (a) — *according to.*
Lo hizo de acuerdo con las instrucciones. *She did it according to the instructions.*

de común acuerdo — *by mutual agreement.*
Lo hicieron de común acuerdo. *They did it by mutual agreement.*

estar de acuerdo — *to agree.*
Estamos de acuerdo. *We agree.*

estar en (fuera de) su acuerdo — *to be in (out of) one's right mind.*
Está en su acuerdo. *He is in his right mind.*

llegar a un acuerdo — *to reach an agreement.*
Han llegado a un acuerdo. *They have reached an agreement.*

ponerse de acuerdo — *to come to an agreement.*
Nos pusimos de acuerdo. *We came to an agreement.*

---

adelante — *forward, ahead*
¡Adelante! — *Come in!*

(de hoy) en adelante — *from now on.*
(De hoy) En adelante compraremos menos. *From now on we'll buy less.*

hacia adelante — *forward.*
Va hacia adelante. *It's moving forward.*

más adelante — *farther on.*
La casa está más adelante. *The house is farther on.*

más adelante — *later on.*
Nos veremos más adelante. *We'll see each other later on.*

---

el ademán — *gesture*
hacer ademán de — *to make as if to.*
Hicieron ademán de disparar. *They made as if to shoot.*

---

además — *besides*

además de — *besides.*
Además de éste, tenemos otro. *Besides this one, we have another.*

---

adentro — *inside*
pensar para sus adentros — *to think to oneself.*
Pensé para mis adentros que no podía ser. *I thought to myself that it couldn't be.*

ser muy de adentro — *to be like one of the family.*
Es muy de adentro. *He's like one of the family.*

adiós — *goodbye*
decir adiós con la mano — *to wave goodbye.*
Les dijo adiós con la mano. *He waved goodbye to them.*

la afición — *fondness*
tener afición a — *to be fond of.*
Tienen afición al fútbol. *They are fond of football (soccer).*

el aficionado — *fan*
ser aficionado a — *to be a fan of.*
Es aficionado al béisbol. *He is a baseball fan.*

el agosto — *August*
hacer su agosto — *to make a killing.*
Hicieron su agosto. *They made a killing.*

agotado — *exhausted*
estar agotado — *to be out of print.*
La novela está agotada. *The novel is out of print.*

el agrado — *pleasure, liking*
ser de su agrado — *to be to one's liking.*
No es de mi agrado. *It's not to my liking.*

el agua — *water*
agua llovediza (lluvia) — *rainwater.*
Se lava el pelo en agua llovediza. *She washes her hair in rainwater.*

Agua pasada no mueve molino. — *That's (all) water over the dam.*
bailar el agua (delante) — *to dance attendance.*

Le bailan el agua (delante). *They dance attendance on him.*

Está tan claro como el agua. — *It's as plain as day.*

hacerse agua en la boca — *to melt in one's mouth.*
Estos bombones se hacen agua en la boca. *These chocolates melt in your mouth.*

hacérsele agua la boca — *to make one's mouth water.*
Se me hace agua la boca. *My mouth waters.*

ir agua(s) arriba (abajo) — *to move upstream (downstream).*
Ibamos aguas arriba. *We were moving upstream.*

nadar entre dos aguas — *to be on the fence.*
Nadan entre dos aguas. *They're on the fence.*

la aguja — *needle*

buscar una aguja en un pajar — *to look for a needle in a haystack.*
Es como buscar una aguja en un pajar. *It's like looking for a needle in a haystack.*

conocer la aguja de marear — *to know one's way around.*
Conoce la aguja de marear. *He knows his way around.*

meter aguja y sacar reja — *to do a small favor in order to receive a greater one.*
Metió aguja y sacó reja. *He did a small favor in order to receive a greater one.*

ahí — *there*

por ahí — *over there.*
Está por ahí. *It's over there.*

el ahinco — *earnestness, eagerness*

con mucho ahinco — *very diligently.*
Trabajó con mucho ahinco. *He worked very diligently.*

ahora — *now*

ahora bien — *now then.*
Ahora bien, ¿adónde vamos? *Now then, where are we going?*

Ahora es cuando — *Now's the time.*

ahora mismo — *right now.*
Venga ahora mismo. *Come right now.*

de ahora — *today's.*
Los niños de ahora son distintos. *Today's children are different.*

de ahora en adelante — *from now on.*
De ahora en adelante, no salga sola. *From now on, don't go out alone.*

desde ahora — *from now on.*
Me escucharás desde ahora. *You'll listen to me from now on.*

por ahora — *just now; for the present.*
Por ahora no necesito más. *I don't need any more just now (for the present).*

---

el aire — *air*

al aire libre — *in the open air.*
Comimos al aire libre. *We ate in the open air.*

darse aires — *to put on airs.*
Tiene fama de siempre darse aires. *She has the reputation of always putting on airs.*

tomar el aire — to take (go for) a walk.
Antes de acostarnos, vamos a tomar el aire. *Before we go to bed, let's take (go for) a walk.*

---

ajeno — *belonging to someone else, another's*

ajeno de cuidados — *free from care.*
Desea vivir ajeno de cuidados. *He wishes to live free from care.*

estar ajeno a — *to be unaware of.*
Está ajeno al problema. *He is unaware of the problem.*

---

el ala — *wing*

caérsele las alas (del corazón) — *to get discouraged.*
Se le cayeron las alas (del corazón). *He got discouraged.*

cortarle las alas — *to clip one's wings.*
Le cortaron las alas. *They clipped his wings.*

volar con las propias alas — *to stand on one's own (two) feet.*
Vuela con sus propias alas. *He stands on his own (two) feet.*

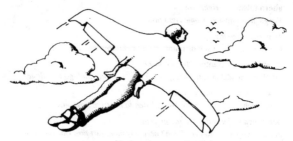

Vuela con sus propias alas.
He stands on his own (two) feet.

el alarde — *display, ostentation*
hacer alarde de — *to boast; to make a great show of.*
Hace alarde de su sabiduría. *He boasts (makes a great show) of his wisdom.*

el alba — *dawn*
al rayar (romper) el alba — *at the break of dawn.*
Salieron al rayar (romper) el alba. *They left at the break of dawn.*

el albedrío — *(free) will*
a su albedrío — *however one likes.*
Puede hacerlo a su albedrío. *You can do it however you like.*

el alboroto — *uproar, disturbance*
armar un alboroto — *to cause a commotion.*
Armaron un alboroto. *They caused a commotion.*

el alcance — *reach, range*
dar alcance a — *to catch up with.*
Me dieron alcance. *They caught up with me.*

estar a (estar fuera de) su alcance — *to be within (out of) one's reach.*
Está a (fuera de) mi alcance. *It's within (out of) my reach.*

alcanzar — *to reach, overtake*
  alcanzar el tiempo (dinero) — *to have enough time (money).*
  No alcanza el tiempo (dinero). *There isn't time (money) enough.*

la aldaba — *(door) knocker; bolt*
  echar (pasar) la aldaba — *to bolt the door.*
  Echó (Pasó) la aldaba. *He bolted the door.*

  tener buenas aldabas — *to have a lot of pull.*
  Tiene buenas aldabas. *He has lots of pull.*

el alfiler — *pin*
  estar de veinticinco alfileres — *to be all dolled up; dressed (fit) to kill; dressed to the teeth; dressed to the nines.*
  Está de veinticinco alfileres. *She's all dolled up (dressed fit to kill; . . . to the teeth; . . . to the nines).*

  estar prendido (pegado) con alfileres — *to be shakily put together (barely hanging together).*
  Está prendido con alfileres. *It's shakily put together (barely hanging together).*

  más flaco que un alfiler — *as thin as a rail.*
  ¿Qué tendrá Antonio? Está más flaco que un alfiler. *What do you suppose is the matter with Antonio? He's gotten as thin as a rail.*

algo — *something*
  Más vale algo que nada (algo es algo) — *It's better than nothing.*

  para algo — *for a purpose.*
  Para algo me está buscando. *He has a purpose in looking for me (He is looking for me for a purpose).*

  por algo — *not for nothing.*
  Por algo es el presidente. *He's not the president for nothing.*

el algodón — *cotton*
  ser criado entre algodones — *to be born with a silver spoon (in one's mouth); to have a pampered childhood.*

Fue criado entre algodones. *He was born with a silver spoon (in his mouth); (He had a pampered childhood).*

tener entre algodones — *to handle with kid gloves.*
Lo tienen entre algodones. *They handle him with kid gloves.*

alguno — *some*
alguno que otro — *occasional.*
Toma algún trago que otro. *He takes an occasional drink.*

la alhaja — *jewel*
¡Buena alhaja! — *He's a real gem! [Sarcastic.]*

el aliento — *breath*
cobrar aliento — *to take heart.*
Cobraron aliento. *They took heart.*

contener el aliento — *to hold one's breath.*
Contenía el aliento. *He was holding his breath.*

de un aliento — *in one breath.*
Lo dijo todo de un aliento. *He said it all in one breath.*

sin aliento — *out of breath.*
Estaba sin aliento. *He was out of breath.*

tomar aliento — *to catch one's breath.*
Tomó aliento. *He caught his breath.*

alimentar — *to feed, nourish*
alimentarse de — *to live on.*
Los carnívoros se alimentan de carne. *Carnivores live on meat.*

el alma — *soul*
Sale como alma que lleva el diablo. — *He takes off like a bat out of hell.*

sentir en el alma — *to be extremely sorry about.*
Siento en el alma no poderte ayudar. *I'm extremely sorry I can't help you.*

el almíbar — *syrup*
   estar hecho un almíbar — *to be especially nice.*
   Está hecho un almíbar hoy. *He's especially nice today.*

la almohada — *pillow*
   consultarlo con la almohada — *to sleep on it.*
   Lo tendré que consultar con la almohada. *I'll have to sleep on it.*

alrededor — *around*
   alrededor de — *around.*
   Están sentados alrededor de la mesa. *They are sitting around tthe table.*

alta — *certificate of discharge from a hospital or of induction into active service.*
   dar de alta — *to discharge.*
   El médico me dio de alta. *The doctor discharged me.*

   darse de alta — *to join the ranks.*
   Se dio de alta. *He joined the ranks.*

el altar — *altar*
   conducir al altar — *to marry.*
   La condujo al altar. *He led her to the altar (married her).*

   poner en un altar — *to put on a pedestal (idolize).*
   A su padre lo pone en un altar. *She puts her father on a pedestal (idolizes her father).*

alto — *halt*
   ¡Alto ahí! — *Stop right there!*

   hacer alto — *to halt.*
   Hizo alto. *He halted.*

alto — *high*
   en lo alto de — *at the top of.*
   En lo alto del cerro hay un restaurante. *At the top of the hill there is a restaurant.*

lo (más) alto — *the top.*
Llegamos a lo (más) alto. *We reached the top.*

la altura — *height*
a estas alturas — *at this point.*
¿Para qué hablar de eso a estas alturas? *Why talk about that at this point?*

estar a la altura de — *to be equal to (up to).*
No está a la altura de esa tarea. *He's not equal to (up to) that task.*

mostrarse a la altura de las circunstancias — *to rise to the occasion.*
Se mostró a la altura de las circunstancias. *He rose to the occasion.*

allá — *there*
allá arriba (abajo, dentro) — *up (down, in) there.*
Está allá arriba (abajo, dentro). *He's up (down, in) there.*

Allá él (ella, usted, etc.). — *That's his (her, your, etc.) affair.*

allá mismo — *right there.*
Lo encontraron allá mismo. *They found it right there.*

allá por — *about (around).*
Murió allá por 1936. *He died about (around) 1936.*

¡Allá voy! — *I'm coming!*

el más allá — *the great beyond.*
Se verán en el más allá. *They'll see each other in the great beyond.*

más allá de — *beyond.*
Está más allá del río. *It's beyond the river.*

más allá — *farther (further) on.*
Se encuentra más allá. *It's farther (further) on.*

por allá — *over there.*
Está por allá. *It's over there.*

amable — *kind*
ser amable con — *to be kind to.*
Son muy amables con él. *They're very kind to him.*

amanecer — *to dawn*
  al amanecer — *at dawn.*
  Salieron al amanecer. *They left at dawn.*
  ¿**Cómo amaneció?** — *How are you this morning?*

amén — *amen*
  amén de — *aside from.*
  Amén de lo dicho, no se le ocurrió nada. *Aside from what he had said,*
    nothing occurred to him.

  decir a todo amén — *to consent to everything.*
  Por ser tan bondadosa, dice a todo amén. *Because she is so kind she*
    consents to everything.

  en un decir amén — *in no time at all.*
  Terminaron el trabajo en un decir amén. *They finished the work in no time*
    at all.

el amigo — *friend*
  hacerse amigo de — *to make friends with.*
  Me hice amigo de ella. *I made friends with her.*

la amistad — *friendship*
  hacer las amistades — *to make up (to have a reconciliation).*
  Hicieron las amistades. *They made up (had a reconciliation).*

  llevar amistad con — *to be a friend of.*
  No lleva amistad íntima con nadie. *She's not an intimate friend of anyone.*

  romper las amistades — *to have a falling-out.*
  Rompieron las amistades. *They had a falling-out.*

  trabar amistad con — *to strike up a friendship with.*
  Trabé amistad con él. *I struck up a friendship with him.*

el amor — *love*
  hacer el amor — *to make love.*
  Le hacía el amor. *He was making love to her.*

ancho — *wide, broad*

estar a sus anchas — *to be comfortable.*
Están a sus anchas en el patio. *They are very comfortable on the patio.*

quedarse tan ancho — *not to get upset; to stay cool.*
Las noticias eran malísimas, pero Miguel se quedó tan ancho. *The news was terrible, but it didn't faze Miguel.*

---

las andadas — *(animal) tracks.*

volver a las andadas — *to go back to one's old ways.*
Volvió a las andadas. *He went back to his old ways.*

---

andar — *to go, walk*

a largo andar — *in the long run.*
A largo andar se arrepentirán. *In the long run they'll be sorry.*

a todo andar — *at top speed.*
Salió a todo andar. *He set off at top speed.*

andar en dimes y diretes — *to squabble (to bicker).*
Siempre anda en dimes y diretes con su tía. *She's always squabbling (bickering) with her aunt.*

andando los años (días, etc.) — *as the years (days, etc.) pass (go by).*
Andando los años (días, etc.), se quieren cada vez más. *As the years (days, etc.) pass (go by), they love each other more and more.*

subir (bajar) andando — *to walk up (down).*
Subimos (bajamos) andando la escalera. *We walked up (down) the stairs.*

---

las andas — *stretcher*

llevar en andas — *to carry on a stretcher.*
Lo llevaron en andas. *They carried him on a stretcher.*

---

el anillo — *ring*

venir como anillo al dedo — *to suit to a T.*
Me viene como anillo al dedo. *It suits me to a T.*

---

el ánimo — *spirit*

darle ánimo(s) — *to cheer up.*

Se lo dije para darle ánimo(s). *I said it to cheer him up.*

estar con ánimo de — *to have a notion to.*
La chica está con ánimo de irse. *The girl has a notion to leave.*

presencia de ánimo — *presence of mind.*
Afrentó la crisis con presencia de ánimo. *He faced the crisis with presence of mind.*

---

anochecer — *to get dark*
al anochecer — *at nightfall.*
Al anochecer se dirigieron a su casa. *At nightfall they made their way home.*

---

ansioso — *anxious, eager*
estar ansioso por (de) — *to be anxious to.*
Está ansioso por (de) verla. *He's anxious to see her.*

---

antemano — *beforehand*
de antemano — *ahead of time (in advance).*
Sacó las entradas de antemano. *He got the tickets ahead of time (in advance).*

---

la anterioridad — *anteriority, priority*
con anterioridad — *beforehand.*
Hicimos las reservaciones con anterioridad. *We made the reservations beforehand.*

con anterioridad a — *prior to.*
Lo terminé con anterioridad a su llegada. *I finished it prior to his arrival.*

---

antes — *before*
antes bien — *rather.*
No quería a su hija; antes bien la odiaba. *She didn't love her daughter; rather she hated her.*
Antes hoy que mañana. — *The sooner the better.*

la anticipación — *advance, anticipation.*
  con anticipación — *ahead of time.*
  El paquete llegó con anticipación. *The package arrived ahead of time.*

la antipatía — *dislike*
  tener antipatía — *to dislike.*
  Le tengo antipatía. *I dislike him.*

antojarse — *to fancy*
  antojarse — *to have a notion to.*
  Se me antoja invitarla. *I have a notion to invite her.*

el anzuelo — *fishhook*
  tragar el anzuelo — *to swallow it hook, line, and sinker.*
  Tragó el anzuelo. *He swallowed it hook, line, and sinker.*

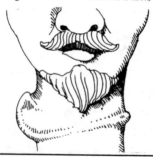

Tragó el anzuelo.
He swallowed it hook, line, and sinker.

la añadidura — *addition*
  por añadidura — *in addition.*
  Les dio el caballo y por añadidura la silla. *He gave them the horse and, in addition, the saddle.*

los añicos — *bits, fragments*
  hacer añicos — *to smash.*
  Hizo añicos el florero. *He smashed the vase.*

el año — *year*

en estos últimos años — *in recent years.*
En estos últimos años está de moda. *In recent years it has been in style.*

estar entrado (metido) en años — *to be well along in years.*
Ya está entrada (metida) en años. *She's well along in years.*

largos años — *(for) many years.*
Viví largos años en Río. *I lived (for) many years in Rio.*

por los años de — *around.*
Ocurrió por los años de 1890. *It occurred around 1890.*

quitarse años — *to lie about one's age.*
Se quita años. *She lies about her age.*

tener . . . años — *to be . . . years old.*
Tiene veintiún años. *She is twenty-one years old.*

apañar — *to seize, grasp*
apañarse — *to make do; to get by.*
Me apaño con poca cosa. *I can make do with very little.*

la apariencia — *appearance*
Las apariencias engañan. — *Appearances are deceiving.*

aparte — *apart, aside*
aparte de — *aside from.*
Aparte de su tía, no tiene parientes. *Aside from his aunt, he has no relatives.*

apenas — *scarcely.*
apenas ahora — *only now.*
Apenas ahora me han avisado. *Only now have they let me know.*

el apetito — *appetite*
abrirle el apetito — *to give one an appetite.*
Le abrió el apetito. *It gave him an appetite.*

apostar — *to bet*
  (apostar) a que — *to bet.*
  (Apuesto) a que no lo quiere. *I'll bet she doesn't want it.*

el aprendiz — *apprentice*
  Aprendiz de todo, oficial de nada. — *Jack of all trades, master of none.*

aprovechar — *to take advantage of*
  aprovechar(se) (de) — *to take advantage of.*
  (Se) aprovechan (de) la oportunidad. *They take advantage of the opportunity.*
  Que (le) aproveche. — *Enjoy your meal.*

apurado — *hard-pressed*
  verse apurado — *to be hard put.*
  Me veo muy apurado. *I'm very hard put.*

el apuro — *fix, predicament*
  pasar apuros — *to have a hard time.*
  Están pasando muchos apuros. *They're having a hard time of it.*
  sacar del apuro — *to get one out of a jam.*
  Me sacó del apuro. *He got me out of the jam.*

aquello — *that*
  aquello de — *that matter of.*
  Aquello del partido fue resuelto. *That matter of the game was resolved.*

aquí — *here*
  aquí dentro — *in here.*
  Pase aquí dentro. *Come in here.*
  aquí mismo — *right here.*
  Le esperaré aquí mismo. *I'll wait for you right here.*
  de aquí — *hence.*
  Ya no amaba a su mujer; de aquí su indiferencia a su infidelidad. *He no longer loved his wife; hence his indifference to her infidelity.*
  de aquí en adelante — *from now on.*

De aquí en adelante, llegue a tiempo. *From now on, arrive on time.*

por aquí — *this way.*
Se entra por aquí. *You enter this way.*

por aquí — *around here.*
Creo que viven por aquí. *I think they live around here.*

---

arder — *to burn*
estar que arde — *to come to a head.*
La cosa está que arde. *Things are coming to a head.*

---

la arena — *sand*
sembrar en arena — *to labor in vain.*
Sembraron en arena. *They labored in vain.*

---

el arma (f) — *weapon*
alzarse en armas — *to rise up in arms.*
Se alzaron en armas. *They rose up in arms.*

pasar por las armas — *to execute.*
Lo pasaron por las armas. *They executed him (by shooting).*

---

el aro — *hoop, ring*
entrar por el aro — *to fall into line; to yield.*
Por fin entró por el aro. *He finally fell into line (had to yield).*

---

arreglar — *to arrange*
arreglárselas (para) — *to manage (to).*
Se las arregla para llegar a tiempo. *He manages to arrive on time.*

---

el arreglo — *arrangement*
con arreglo a — *in accordance with.*
Lo prepararon con arreglo a las instrucciones. *They prepared it in accordance with the instructions.*

no tener arreglo — *not to be able to be helped.*
No tiene arreglo. *It can't be helped.*

---

arriba — *up*

  de arriba — *upstairs.*
  La familia de arriba es española. *The family upstairs is Spanish.*

  de arriba abajo — *from top to bottom.*
  Lo limpió de arriba abajo. *She cleaned it from top to bottom.*

  hacia arriba — *up.*
  Echó (Tiró) la pelota hacia arriba. *He threw the ball up.*

---

el arroz — *rice*

  haber arroz y gallo muerto — *to have a real feast.*
  Había arroz y gallo muerto. *It was a real feast.*

---

el arte — art

  no tener arte ni parte — *to have nothing to do with.*
  No tengo arte ni parte en eso. *I have nothing to do with that.*

---

ascender — *to ascend, to go up*

  ascender a — *to amount to.*
  Los gastos ascendieron a 500 dólares. *The expenses amounted to 500 dollars.*

---

el asco — *disgust*

  dar asco — *to disgust.*
  Me da asco. *It disgusts me.*

  estar hecho un asco — *to be filthy.*
  Está hecho un asco. *It's filthy.*

  hacer ascos a (de) — *to turn up one's nose at.*
  Hizo ascos a (de) la comida. *He turned up his nose at the meal.*

  ¡Qué asco de vida! — *What a rotten (sordid) life!*

---

el ascua — *live coal*

  estar sobre (en) ascuas — *to be on pins and needles.*
  Está sobre (en) ascuas. *He's on pins and needles.*

  sacar el ascua con la mano del gato — *to get someone else to pull one's chestnuts out of the fire.*

Sacó el ascua con la mano del gato. *He got someone else to pull his chestnuts out of the fire.*

---

así — *so, thus*

  así así — *so-so.*

  ¿Qué tal le gustó la comedia? Así así. *How did you like the play? (It was) so-so.*

  así como — *as well as.*

  Su padre, así como su madre, habla inglés. *His father, as well as his mother, speaks English.*

  así . . . como — *both . . . and.*

  Así los estudiantes como los profesores comieron en el comedor. *Both the students and the professors ate in the dining room.*

  así de — *that.*

  Son así de grandes. *They're that big.*

  así (es) que — *so.*

  Yo no traía dinero, así (es) que él tuvo que pagar. *I had no money with me, so he had to pay.*

  así que — *as soon as.*

  Comimos así que llegamos. *We ate as soon as we arrived.*

  y así sucesivamente — *and so on.*

  Uno para mí, otro para usted, y así sucesivamente. *One for me, another for you, and so on.*

---

el asiento — *seat*

  tomar asiento — *to sit down.*

  Tome asiento. *Sit down.*

---

asistir — *to attend*

  asistir a — *to attend.*

  Asistí a la conferencia. *I attended the lecture.*

---

asomar — *to show, appear*

  asomarse a — *to look out.*

  Se asoma a la ventana. *She looks out the window.*

---

asombrar — *to astonish*
  asombrarse de (con) — *to be astonished at.*
  Se asombraron de (con) mis relatos. *They were astonished at my stories.*

el asta — *shaft, staff; horn*
  a media asta — *at half mast.*
  La bandera estaba a media asta. *The flag was at half mast.*

  dejar en las astas del toro — *to leave in the lurch.*
  Me dejó en las astas del toro. *He left me in the lurch.*

el asunto — *matter, affair*
  ir al asunto — *to get down to the facts (to business).*
  Vamos al asunto. *Let's get down to the facts (to business).*

el atajo — *short cut*
  echar por el atajo — *to take the easiest way out.*
  Echó por el atajo. *He took the easiest way out.*

atardecer — *to draw towards evening*
  al atardecer — *at dusk (in the late afternoon).*
  Salimos al atardecer. *We left at dusk (in the late afternoon).*

la atención — *attention*
  llamar la atención — *to attract attention.*
  Llaman la atención. *They attract attention.*

  llamar la atención sobre — *to call one's attention to.*
  Me llamó la atención sobre el problema. *He called my attention to the problem.*

  prestar (poner) atención — *to pay attention.*
  Haga el favor de prestar (poner) atención. *Please pay attention.*

atenerse — *to abide*
  atenerse a — *to go by.*
  No sabía a qué atenerse. *He didn't know what to go by.*

atento — *attentive*
  ponerse atento — *to pay attention.*
  ¡Ponte atento! Esto es muy importante. *Pay attention! This is very important.*

atrás — *back*
  hacia atrás — *back.*
  Dio un paso hacia atrás. *He took a step back.*

la ausencia — *absence*
  brillar por la ausencia — *to be conspicuous by one's absence.*
  Brilla por su ausencia. *He is conspicuous by his absence.*

el avemaría — *Hail Mary*
  al avemaría — *at dusk.*
  Llegamos al avemaría. *We arrived at dusk.*

  en un avemaría — *in a jiffy.*
  Lo terminó en un avemaría. *He finished it in a jiffy.*

  saber como el avemaría — *to know backwards and forwards.*
  Lo sabían como el avemaría. *They knew it backwards and forwards.*

el avío — *preparation, provision*
  ¡Al avío! — *Hurry up! Get a move on!*

el aviso — *notice, warning*
  estar sobre aviso — *to be on (one's) guard.*
  Hay que estar sobre aviso. *You've got to be on (your) guard.*

ay — *alas*
  ¡Ay de mí! — *Woe is me!*

  ¡Ay del que los ofenda! — *Heaven help whoever offends them!*

ayuno — *fasting*
  estar en ayunas (en ayuno) — *to be fasting.*
  Estaban en ayunas (en ayuno). *They were fasting.*

quedarse en ayunas — *not to catch on.*
Se quedaron en ayunas. *They didn't catch on.*

---

el azar — *chance*
  al azar — *at random.*
  Los escogieron al azar. *They chose (picked) them at random.*

---

azogado — *affected by mercury, restless, trembling*
  temblar como un azogado — *to shake like a leaf.*
  Temblaba como un azogado. *He was shaking like a leaf.*

---

la baba — *slobber*
  caérsele la baba por — *to be wild about.*
  Se le cae la baba por las películas suecas. *He's just wild about Swedish movies.*

Babia — *proper name*
  estar en Babia — *to be up in the clouds; to daydream.*
  Está en Babia. *He's up in the clouds (He's daydreaming).*

---

la baja — *fall, drop; casualty*
  dar de baja — *to drop; to dismiss; to discharge.*
  Lo dieron de baja. *They dropped (dismissed; discharged) him.*

  darse de baja — *to drop out.*
  Se dio de baja. *He dropped out.*

---

bajar — *to go down, come down*
  bajarse en — *to stay (stop) at.*
  Se bajaron en el Hotel Ritz. *They stayed (stopped) at the Hotel Ritz.*

---

bajo — *low*
  por lo bajo — *in an undertone; under one's breath.*
  Lo dijo por lo bajo. *He said it in an undertone (under his breath).*

28

por lo bajo — *on the sly.*
Lo hizo por lo bajo. *He did it on the sly.*

la bala — *bullet*
matar a bala — *to shoot.*
Lo mataron a bala. *They shot him.*

salir como (una) bala — *to be off like a shot.*
Salió como (una) bala. *He was off like a shot.*

balde — *bucket*
de balde — *free.*
Se consiguen de balde. *You can get them free.*

en balde — *in vain.*
Fue en balde. *It was in vain.*

estar de balde — *to be superfluous.*
Está de balde. *It's superfluous.*

la banda — *band*
cerrarse a la banda — *to stand firm.*
Se cerraron a la banda. *They stood firm.*

la bandera — *flag*
con banderas desplegadas — *with flying colors.*
Entraron con banderas desplegadas. *They came in with flying colors.*

el baño — *bath*
darse un baño (una ducha) — *to take a bath (shower).*
Me di un baño. *I took a bath.*

la baraja — *pack, deck (of cards)*
jugar con dos barajas — *to be a double-crosser.*
Juega con dos barajas. *He is a double-crosser.*

la barba — *chin; beard*
en las barbas — *right to one's face.*
Me lo dijo en las barbas. *He told me right to my face.*

haberle salido la barba — *to be old enough to shave.*
Le ha salido la barba. *He's old enough to shave.*

hacerle la barba — *to butter up.*
Le hace la barba al profesor. *He butters up the professor.*

subirse a las barbas — *to be disrespectful.*
Se subió a las barbas de su padre. *He was disrespectful to his father.*

por barba — *apiece.*
Nos dieron uno por barba. *They gave us one apiece.*

barrer — *to sweep*
barrer hacia dentro — *to look out for oneself.*
Barre hacia dentro. *He looks out for himself.*

el barrio — *neighborhood*
pasar al otro barrio — *to pass on to the other world.*
Pasó al otro barrio. *He passed on to the other world.*

bartola — *paunch*
tenderse (tumbarse, echarse) a la bartola — *to take it easy.*
Se tiende (se tumba, se echa) a la bartola. *He takes it easy.*

los bártulos — *implements, tools*
liar los bártulos — *to pack up one's things.*
Vamos a liar los bártulos. *Let's pack up our things.*

preparar los bártulos — *to make preparations.*
Preparaban los bártulos. *They were making their preparations.*

el basilisco — *basilisk (a mythical monster)*
estar hecho un basilisco — *to be in a rage.*
Estaba hecho un basilisco. *He was in a rage.*

el bastidor — *frame; wing (of stage scenery)*
entre bastidores — *behind the scenes.*
Pasó entre bastidores. *It happened behind the scenes.*

bastar — *to be enough*
  bastar con — *to be enough.*
  Le bastaba con verla. *Just seeing her was enough for him.*
  Ya basta de disparates. — *That's enough nonsense.*

el bastón — *cane, staff (of office)*
  empuñar el bastón — *to take over.*
  Empuñó el bastón. *He took over.*

  meter el bastón — *to intercede.*
  Metieron el bastón. *They interceded.*

la batuta — *(conductor's) baton*
  llevar la batuta — *to run things (the show).*
  Les gusta llevar la batuta. *They like to run things (the show).*

el bautismo — *baptism*
  romperle el bautismo — *to break someone's neck.*
  Le romperemos el bautismo. *We'll break his neck.*

la baza — *trick (at cards)*
  meter baza — *to get a word in edgewise.*
  No nos dejó meter baza. *He didn't let us get a word in edgewise.*

Belén — *Bethlehem*
  estar (bailando) en Belén — *to be daydreaming; to be up in the clouds.*
  Estaban (bailando) en Belén. *They were daydreaming (were up in the clouds).*

el bemol — *flat (in music)*
  tener (muchos, tres) bemoles — *to be a tough job.*
  Tiene (muchos, tres) bemoles. *It's a tough job.*

la bendición — *blessing*
  echar la bendición — *to bless.*
  Les echó la bendición. *He blessed them.*

el beneficio — *benefit*

a beneficio de — *for the benefit of*
Se hizo a beneficio de los pobres. *It was done for the benefit of the poor.*

el berenjenal — *eggplant bed*

meterse en buen berenjenal — *to get oneself into a fine mess.*
En buen berenjenal se han metido. *They've gotten themselves into a fine mess.*

la berlina — *berlin*

estar en berlina — *to be in a ridiculous position.*
Estaban en berlina. *They were in a ridiculous position.*

el beso — *kiss*

dar un beso a la botella — *to take a (little) nip.*
Le gusta darle un beso a la botella de vez en cuando. *He likes to take a (little) nip once in a while.*

el bicho — *bug*

todo bicho viviente — *every living soul.*
Se lo dijo a todo bicho viviente. *She told every living soul.*

el bien — *good*

de bien — reputable.
Es un hombre de bien. *He's a reputable man.*

bien — *well*

no bien — *no sooner . . . than.*
No bien oyó la voz, reconoció a Pablo. *He no sooner heard the voice than he recognized Paul.*

o bien — *or else.*
Lo haré mañana, o bien el jueves. *I'll do it tomorrow, or else on Thursday.*

tener a bien — *to see fit to.*
Tuvo a bien ayudarnos. *He saw fit to help us.*

la bienvenida — *welcome*
   dar la bienvenida — *to welcome.*
   Nos dio la bienvenida. *He welcomed us.*

la blanca — *old coin*
   no tener (estar sin) blanca — *to be flat broke.*
   No tenía (Estaba sin) blanca. *I was flat broke.*

el blanco — *target*
   dar en el blanco — *to hit the mark.*
   Dio en el blanco. *He hit the mark.*

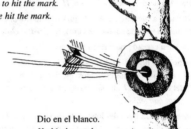

Dio en el blanco.
He hit the mark.

blanco — *white*
   en blanco — *blank.*
   La página estaba en blanco. *The page was blank.*

el bledo — *goosefoot (plant)*
   no importar un bledo — *not to give a damn about.*
   No me importan un bledo (no se me da un bledo de) sus problemas.
      I don't give a damn about his problems.

la boca — *mouth*
   a pedir de boca — *smoothly.*
   Todo salió a pedir de boca. *Everything went off smoothly.*

   andar de boca en boca — *to be generally known.*
   Anda de boca en boca. *It's generally known.*

   andar en boca de todos — *to have everyone talking about it.*

Anda en boca de todos. *Everybody's talking about it.*

boca abajo (arriba) — *face down (up).*
Lo encontraron boca abajo (arriba). *They found him face down (up).*

callarse la boca — *to keep one's mouth shut.*
Se calló la boca. *He kept his mouth shut.*

cerrarle la boca — *to shut someone up; to silence someone.*
Le cerraron la boca. *They shut him up (They silenced him).*

decir lo que se viene a la boca — *to say whatever comes into one's mind.*
Dice lo que se le viene a la boca. *He says whatever comes into his mind.*

disparar a boca de cañón (de jarro) — *to fire at close range.*
Disparó a boca de cañón (de jarro). *He fired at close range.*

En boca cerrada no entran moscas. — *Mum's the word.*

estar en la boca del lobo — *to be in great danger.*
Al ver a los soldados enemigos, me di cuenta de que estábamos en la boca del lobo. *When I saw the enemy soldiers, I realized that we were in great danger.*

meterse en la boca del lobo — *to stick one's head in the lion's mouth.*
Te meterás en la boca del lobo si te niegas a hacer lo que te pide tu tía. *You'll be sticking your head in the lion's mouth if you refuse to do what your aunt asks.*

sin decir esta boca es mía — *without saying a word.*
Se fue sin decir esta boca es mía. *He left without saying a word.*

quedarse con la boca abierta — *to be flabbergasted.*
Me quedé con la boca abierta. *I was flabbergasted.*

el bocado — *mouthful*
con el bocado en la boca — *just getting up from the table.*
Nos cogieron con el bocado en la boca. *They caught us just getting up from the table.*

el bofe — *lung*
echar los bofes — *to give something everything one's got.*
Echaba los bofes. *He was giving it everything he had.*

34

la bofetada — *slap in the face*
    arrimarle una bofetada — *to slap someone's face.*
    Le arrimó una bofetada. *She slapped his face.*

la boga — *vogue*
    estar en boga — *to be in vogue (in style; in fashion).*
    Ya no está en boga. *It's not in vogue (in style, in fashion) any more.*

la bola — *ball*
    hacerse uno bolas — *to get all balled up.*
    Se hace uno bolas. *You get all balled up.*

el bolsillo — *pocket*
    meterse en el bolsillo — *to wrap around one's little finger.*
    Se mete a las mujeres en el bolsillo. *He wraps the women around his little finger.*

    rascarse el bolsillo — *to cough up (the money).*
    Tuvo que rascarse el bolsillo. *He had to cough up.*

la bomba — *bomb*
    caer como una bomba — *to fall like a bombshell.*
    Cayó como una bomba. *It fell like a bombshell.*

la bondad — *goodness, kindness*
    tener la bondad — *please.*
    Tenga la bondad de acompañarme. *Please go with me.*

el borbotón — *bubbling, boiling*
    hablar a borbotones — *to talk a mile a minute.*
    Hablaba a borbotones. *He was talking a mile a minute.*

el borde — *edge*
    al borde del llanto — *on the verge of tears.*
    Está al borde del llanto. *She is on the verge of tears.*

la bota — *boot*

ponerse las botas — *to strike it rich.*
Se puso las botas con ese negocio. *He struck it rich with that deal.*

---

bote

(lleno) de bote en bote — *packed.*
El cuarto estaba (lleno) de bote en bote. *The room was packed.*

---

la brasa — *live coal*

en brasas — *on pins and needles.*
Estaban en brasas. *They were on pins and needles.*

estar hecho unas brasas — *to be red in the face.*
Estaba hecha unas brasas. *She was red in the face.*

---

el brazo — *arm*

a brazo partido — *in hand-to-hand combat.*
Pelearon a brazo partido. *They fought in hand-to-hand combat.*

con los brazos abiertos — *with open arms.*
Me recibieron con los brazos abiertos. *They received me with open arms.*

cruzarse de brazos — *to do nothing.*
No le interesó el proyecto y se cruzó de brazos. *The project did not interest him and he did nothing.*

el brazo derecho — *right-hand man.*
Es mi brazo derecho. *He's my right-hand man.*

en los brazos de Morfeo — *in the arms of Morpheus; asleep.*
Está en los brazos de Morfeo. *He is in the arms of Morpheus (asleep).*

estarse con los brazos cruzados — *to be doing nothing.*
Se está todo el día con los brazos cruzados. *He does nothing all day long.*

ir del brazo — *to walk arm in arm.*
Siempre iban del brazo. *They always walked arm in arm.*

no dar el brazo a torcer — *to stick to one's guns; not to give in.*
No da su brazo a torcer. *He sticks to his guns (won't give in).*

---

breve — *brief*
  en breve — *presently.*
  En breve sabremos. *Presently we'll know.*

---

la brevedad — *brevity*
  con la mayor brevedad — *as soon as possible.*
  Avíselo con la mayor brevedad. *Let him know as soon as possible.*

---

la brida — *bridle*
  a toda brida — *at top speed.*
  Iba a toda brida. *He was going at top speed.*

---

brindar — *to toast; offer*
  brindar con — *to offer.*
  Nos brindaron con muchas atenciones. *They offered us many courtesies.*

  brindarse a — *to offer.*
  Se brindó a hacerlo. *He offered to do it.*

---

la brocha — *brush*
  de brocha gorda — *poorly done.*
  Escribió unos cuantos versos de brocha gorda. *He wrote a few poorly
    done verses.*

  un pintor de brocha gorda — *a house painter.*
  Es un pintor de brocha gorda. *He's a house painter.*

---

la broma — *joke*
  bromas aparte — *all joking aside.*
  Bromas aparte, ¿qué quieren? *All joking aside, what do they want?*

  en (de) broma — *joking.*
  Lo dije en broma (de broma). *I didn't mean it (I was joking).*

  gastar bromas pesadas — *to play practical jokes.*
  Le gustaba gastar bromas pesadas. *He liked to play practical jokes.*

  hacer una broma — *to play a joke.*
  Me hizo una broma. *He played a joke on me.*

  no estar para bromas — *to be in no mood for jokes.*

37

Déjame en paz. No estoy para bromas. *Leave me alone. I'm in no mood for jokes.*

tomar a broma — to take lightly.

Lo tomó a broma. *He took it lightly.*

---

la bronca — *row, dispute*

armar una bronca — to start a fight.

Siempre arman una bronca cuando están en el bar. *They always start a fight when they are in the bar.*

---

bruces — *lips*

caer de bruces — to fall on one's face.

Cayó de bruces. *He fell on his face.*

---

el buche — *craw, crop*

sacarle el buche — to make someone tell everything they know.

Le sacaron el buche. *They made him tell everything he knew.*

---

bueno — *good*

¡Buena se va a armar! — *There's trouble brewing!*

¡Buenas! — *Hello!*

¡Bueno está! — *That will do!*

Bueno está lo bueno. — *Leave well enough alone.*

de buenas a primeras — *right off the bat.*

De buenas a primeras comenzó a hacer preguntas. *Right off the bat he started to ask questions.*

el bueno de . . . — *good old . . . .*

Así es el bueno de Juan. *That's the way good old John is.*

estar de buenas — *to be in a good mood.*

Está de buenas. *He's in a good mood.*

hacerla buena — *to make a fine mess of it.*

Buena la ha hecho. *He's made a fine mess of it.*

por las buenas — *on the up and up.*

Lo arreglaron por las buenas. *They settled it on the up and up.*

por las buenas o por las malas — *whether one likes it or not.*
Tendrá que asistir a la reunión por las buenas o por las malas. *He will have to attend the meeting whether he likes it or not.*

---

el buey — *ox*
¿Adónde irá el buey que no are? — *Where can the ox go that he won't have to plow? (Nothing is easy).*

El buey suelto bien se lame. — *The ox that's loose licks himself best. (He travels fastest who travels alone).*

trabajar como un buey — *to work like a horse.*
Trabaja como un buey. *He works like a horse.*

---

el bulto — *bulk, form, body*
buscarle el bulto — *to lie in wait (have it in) for someone.*
Le buscaban el bulto. *They were lying in wait (They had it in) for him.*

escurrir el bulto — *to slip away.*
Escurrió el bulto. *He slipped away.*

---

la burla — *mockery, ridicule; joke*
burlas aparte — *all joking aside.*
Burlas aparte, ¿qué piensas hacer? *All joking aside, what do you intend to do?*

hacer burla burlando — *to do unobtrusively.*
Lo hizo burla burlando. *He did it unobtrusively.*

---

burlar — *to ridicule, mock; trick, deceive*
burlarse de — *to make fun of.*
Se burla de ellos. *She makes fun of them.*

---

la busca — *search.*
salir en (a la) busca de — *to go out in search of.*
Salió en busca de sus padres. *He went out in search of his parents.*

---

buscar — *to look for*
buscárselo — *to ask for it.*

¿Tuviste problemas con tu jefe? Te los buscaste. *So you had problems with your boss? You asked for it.*

cabal — *exact, complete*

estar en los cabales — *to be in one's right mind (to be all there).*
No está en sus cabales. *He's not in his right mind (not all there).*

el caballero — *gentleman; knight*

armar caballero — *to knight.*
Lo armaron caballero. *They knighted him.*

caballero andante — *knight errant.*
Don Quijote fue el último caballero andante. *Don Quixote was the last knight errant.*

Poderoso caballero es Don Dinero. — *Money makes the world go round.*

el caballo — *horse*

A caballo regalado no hay que mirarle el diente. — *Don't look a gift horse in the mouth.*

a mata caballo — *at breakneck speed.*
Iban a mata caballo. *They were traveling at breakneck speed.*

montar a caballo — *to ride (on) horseback.*
Van montados a caballo. *They are riding (on) horseback.*

pasear a caballo — *to go horseback riding.*
La paseaba a caballo. *He used to take her horseback riding.*

el cabello — *hair*

asirse de un cabello — *to grasp at a straw.*
Se ase de un cabello. *He grasps at a straw.*

en cabello — *with one's hair down.*
La vimos en cabello. *We saw her with her hair down.*

40

en cabellos — *bareheaded.*
Estaba en cabellos. *She was bareheaded.*

estar pendiente de un cabello — *to be hanging by a hair.*
Estaba pendiente de un cabello. *It was hanging by a hair.*

ponérsele los cabellos de punta — *to have one's hair stand on end.*
Se me pusieron los cabellos de punta. *My hair stood on end.*

---

caber — *to fit, be contained*
  caber todo en — *to (be able to) expect anything of.*
  Todo cabe en él. *You can expect anything of him.*

  no caber de contento — *not to be able to be any happier.*
  No cabe de contento. *He couldn't be any happier.*

---

la cabeza — *head*
  asentir (afirmar) con la cabeza — *to nod (yes).*
  Asintió (afirmó) con la cabeza. *He nodded (yes).*

  de cabeza — *head first.*
  Se cayó de cabeza. *He fell head first.*

  doblar la cabeza — *to bow one's head.*
  Dobló la cabeza y se puso a llorar. *He bowed his head and began to cry.*

  levantar cabeza — *to get on one's feet.*
  Por fin está levantando cabeza. *He's finally getting on his feet.*

  metérsele en la cabeza — *to get it into one's head.*
  Se le metió en la cabeza que estaban enfermos. *He got it into his head that they were sick.*

  perder la cabeza — *to lose one's head.*
  A pesar del insulto no perdió la cabeza. *In spite of the insult, he didn't lose his head.*

  romperse (calentarse) la cabeza — *to rack one's brains.*
  Se rompía (Se calentaba) la cabeza. *He was racking his brains.*

  subírsele a la cabeza — *to go to one's head.*
  La fortuna se le subió a la cabeza. *Success went to his head.*

---

la cabezada — *nod*

   dar cabezadas — *to nod (with drowsiness).*

   Daba cabezadas. *He was nodding (with drowsiness).*

la cabida — *space, capacity*

   tener (gran) cabida — *to have (a lot of) pull.*

   Tiene (gran) cabida con el gobernador. *He has (a lot of) pull with the governor.*

el cable — *cable*

   cruzársele los cables — *to get confused.*

   Se me cruzaron los cables y lo hice al revés. *I got confused and did it backward.*

el cabo — *end*

   al cabo — *at last.*

   Al cabo llegó. *At last he arrived.*

   al cabo de un rato — *after a while.*

   Al cabo de un rato regresó. *After a while he returned.*

   atar cabos — *to put two and two together.*

   Ataron cabos. *They put two and two together.*

   cabos sueltos — *loose ends.*

   Todavía hay algunos cabos sueltos. *There are still a few loose ends.*

   de cabo a rabo (de cabo a cabo) — *from one end to the other.*

   Lo leímos de cabo a rabo (de cabo a cabo). *We read it from one end to the other.*

   el cabo del mundo — *the ends of the earth.*

   La seguiré hasta el cabo del mundo. *I'll follow her to the ends of the earth.*

   llevar a cabo — *to carry out.*

   Llevó a cabo sus planes. *He carried out his plans.*

la cabra — *goat*

   estar más loco que una cabra — *to be as crazy as a loon (as nutty as a fruitcake).*

No le hagas caso. Está más loco que una cabra. *Don't pay any attention to him. He's as crazy as a loon (as nutty as a fruitcake).*

cada — *each*
   A cada cual lo suyo. — *To each his own.*

   cada cuánto (tiempo) — *how often.*
   ¿Cada cuánto (tiempo) pasa? *How often does it go by?*

   cada poco — *every so often; every once in a while.*
   Toma uno cada poco. *He takes one every so often (every once in a while).*

caer — *to fall*
   caerle bien — *to like someone.*
   No me cae bien. *I don't like him.*

   caer enfermo — *to fall ill.*
   Cayó enferma. *She fell ill.*

   caer redondo — *to fall flat.*
   Cayó redondo al suelo. *He fell flat on the floor.*

la caída — *fall*
   a la caída del sol — *at sundown.*
   Llegué a la caída del sol. *I arrived at sundown.*

   a la caída de la tarde — *late in the afternoon.*
   Nos encontramos a la caída de la tarde. *We met late in the afternoon.*

Caín — *Cain*
   pasar las de Caín — *to go through hell.*
   Pasaron las de Caín. *They went through hell.*

la caja — *box; drum*
   despedir con cajas destempladas — *to send packing.*
   Lo despidieron con cajas destempladas. *They sent him packing.*

la cal — *lime*
   ser de cal y canto — *to be as solid as a rock.*
   Es de cal y canto. *It's as solid as a rock.*

la calabaza — *pumpkin, squash*
    dar calabazas — *to flunk.*
    El profesor le dio calabazas. *The professor flunked him.*

    dar calabazas — *to jilt.*
    Su novia le dio calabazas. *His girlfriend jilted him.*

la calada — *soaking*
    darle una calada — *to give someone a dressing down.*
    Le dieron una calada. *They gave him a dressing down.*

el caldo — *broth*
    hacerle el caldo gordo — *to play into someone's hands.*
    Le hacían el caldo gordo. *They were playing into his hands.*

la calidad — *quality*
    en calidad de — *in one's capacity as.*
    Lo hizo en calidad de alcalde. *He did it in his capacity as mayor.*

la calma — *calm*
    con calma — *calmly.*
    Se lo tomó con calma. *He accepted it calmly.*

    estar en calma — *to be calm.*
    El mar estaba en calma. *The sea was calm.*

    una calma chicha — *a dead calm.*
    Reinaba una calma chicha. *A dead calm prevailed.*

el calor — *heat*
    Hace calor. — *It's hot.*

    ir entrando en calor — *to be warming up.*
    Van entrando en calor. *They're getting warmed up.*

    tener calor — *to be warm.*
    Tengo calor. *I'm warm.*

las calzas — *hose, tights, stockings*
    en calzas prietas — *in a tight spot (fix).*

Se encontraba en calzas prietas. *He was in a tight spot (fix).*

tomar las (calzas) de Villadiego — *to beat it (to take off, to run away).*
Tomó las (calzas) de Villadiego. *He beat it (took off, ran away).*

---

los calzones — *breeches, shorts, trousers*
llevar los calzones — *to wear the pants.*
Lleva los calzones en su familia. *She wears the pants in her family.*

---

callar — *to be silent*
Quien calla, otorga. — *Silence gives (means) consent.*

ser mejor para callado — *to be better left unsaid.*
Sería mejor para callado. *It would be better left unsaid.*

---

la calle — *street*
calle abajo (arriba) — *down (up) the street.*
Vienen calle abajo (arriba). *They are coming down (up) the street.*

dejar en la calle — *to leave destitute.*
Lo dejaron en la calle. *They left him destitute.*

poner en (echar a, plantar en) la calle — *to throw out.*
La puso en (echó a, plantó en) la calle. *He threw her out.*

quedar en la calle — *to be left without a penny to one's name.*
Quedó en la calle. *He was left without a penny to his name.*

traer por la calle de la amargura — *to make someone suffer.*
Su hijo la trae por la calle de la amargura. *She's suffering a lot on account of her son.*

---

el callejón — *alley, lane*
un callejón sin salida — *a blind alley (dead end).*
Es un callejón sin salida. *It's a blind alley (dead end).*

---

la cama — *bed*
caer en cama — *to fall ill.*
Cayó en cama. *He fell ill.*

estar en cama — *to be sick in bed.*

Está en cama. *He's sick in bed.*

guardar cama — *to stay in bed.*
Tuvo que guardar cama. *He had to stay in bed.*

hacer (arreglar) la cama — *to make the bed.*
Hizo (Arregló) la cama. *She made the bed.*

reducir a cama — *to put in bed.*
La gripe lo redujo a cama. *The flu put him in bed.*

cambiar — *change*
cambiar de tren — *to change trains.*
Hay que cambiar de tren. *You've got to change trains.*

el cambio — *change*
a cambio de — *in exchange for.*
Lo aceptó a cambio del libro. *He accepted it in exchange for the book.*

en cambio — *on the other hand.*
Su padre, en cambio, no quería ir. *His father, on the other hand, wouldn't go.*

el camino — *road, way*
a medio camino — *halfway.*
Nos encontramos a medio camino. *We met halfway.*

abrirse camino — *to make one's way.*
Se abrió camino por la multitud. *He made his way through the crowd.*

allanar el camino — *to smooth the way.*
Nos allana el camino. *He smooths the way for us.*

apartarse del camino — *to get off the track.*
Se ha apartado del camino. *He's gotten off the track.*

camino de — *on the way to.*
Los visitamos camino de México. *We visited them on the way to Mexico.*

de camino — *on the way.*
De camino, deje el recado. *On the way, leave the message.*

el camino trillado — *the beaten path.*
No salen del camino trillado. *They don't leave the beaten path.*

ponerse en camino — *to start out.*
Se puso en camino. *He started out.*

la camisa — *shirt*

dejar sin camisa — *to clean out.*
Lo dejaron sin camisa. *They cleaned him out.*

meterse en camisa de once varas — *to get into trouble.*
No quería meterme en camisa de once varas. *I didn't want to get into trouble.*

el campo — *field; country(side)*

a campo raso — *out in the open.*
Trabajaban a campo raso. *They were working out in the open.*

a campo travieso (traviesa) — *across country.*
Partieron a campo travieso (traviesa). *They set out across country.*

la cana — *gray hair*

echar una cana al aire — *to have a little fling.*
Vamos a echar una cana al aire. *Let's have a little fling.*

el candado — *padlock*

echar candado a la puerta — *to padlock the door.*
Echó candado a la puerta. *He padlocked the door.*

el candelero — *candlestick*
  estar en el candelero — *to be in the limelight (in the public eye).*
  Le encanta estar en el candelero. *He loves being in the limelight (in the public eye).*

el cantar — *song*
  ser otro cantar — *to be another story (to be a horse of another color).*
  Ese es otro cantar. *That's another story (a horse of another color).*

cantar — *to sing*
  cantar de plano — *to make a full confession.*
  Cantó de plano. *He made a full confession.*

  cantarlas claras (cantar claro) — *to speak out plainly.*
  Las canta claras (Canta claro). *He speaks out plainly.*

el cántaro — *jug*
  llover a cántaros — *to rain cats and dogs (pitchforks).*
  Está lloviendo a cántaros. *It's raining cats and dogs (pitchforks).*
  Tanto va el cántaro a la fuente que alguna vez se quiebra. — *Don't press your luck.*

el canto — *edge*
  estar de canto — *to be on edge.*
  Está de canto. *It's on edge.*

la cara — *face*
  cara a cara — *right to someone's face.*
  Se lo dije cara a cara. *I said it right to his face.*

  cara a cara con — *face to face with.*
  Se encontró cara a cara con su papá. *He found himself face to face with his father.*

  cara dura — *shamelessness.*
  ¡Qué cara más dura tiene ese tipo! *What a nerve that guy has!*

  Cara o cruz — *Heads or tails.*

  cruzarle la cara — *to slap someone's face.*

Le cruzaron le cara. *They slapped his face.*

dar la cara a — *to face up to.*
Se resiste a dar la cara a sus problemas. *She's unwilling to face up to her problems.*

echar en cara — *to throw up to.*
Me echaron en cara mi extravagancia. *They threw my extravagance up to me.*

lucir cara de — *to act.*
Ella luce cara de inocente, pero yo tengo mis dudas. *She acts very innocent, but I have my doubts.*

mirarse a la cara — *to look each other in the face.*
Se miraron a la cara. *They looked each other in the face.*

poner cara de circunstancias — *to put on a sad face.*
Puso cara de circunstancias. *He put on a sad face.*

poner mala cara — *to show discontent.*
Puso mala cara. *His face showed discontent.*

tener cara de enfado — *to look mad.*
Tiene cara de enfado. *He looks mad.*

tener cara de pocos amigos — *to look cross (sour).*
El tenía cara de pocos amigos. *He was looking cross.*

tener cara de sueño — *to look sleepy.*
Tienes cara de sueño. ¿Por qué no te acuestas? *You look sleepy. Why don't you go to bed?*

tener cara de tonto — *to look stupid.*
¿Es que tengo cara de tonto, o qué? *Do I look stupid or something?*

tener mala cara — *to look mean.*
Tiene mala cara. *He looks mean.*

tener mala cara — *to look bad (ill).*
Pablo tiene muy mala cara hoy. *Pablo is looking really sick today.*

---

carecer — *to lack*
  carecer de — *to lack.*
  Carece de valor. *He lacks courage.*

---

cargar — *to load*
    cargar con — *to carry off.*
    Cargó con el dinero. *He carried off the money.*

---

el cargo — *burden, load, responsibility*
    desempeñar el cargo de — *to hold the position of.*
    Desempeña el cargo de profesor. *He holds the position of professor.*

    estar a cargo de — *to be in charge of.*
    Está a cargo del baile. *He is in charge of the dance.*

    estar a cargo de — *to be the responsibility of (to be entrusted to).*
    El dinero está a su cargo. *The money is his responsibility (entrusted to him).*

    hacerse cargo de — *to take charge of.*
    Se hizo cargo de la tripulación. *He took charge of the crew.*

---

la caridad — *charity*
    hacer la caridad de — *to do the favor of.*
    Les hizo la caridad de decírselo. *He did them the favor of telling them.*
    La caridad empieza por uno mismo. — *Charity begins at home.*

---

la carne — *meat, flesh*
    de carne y hueso — *flesh and blood.*
    Ese novelista crea personajes de carne y hueso. *That novelist creates flesh and blood characters.*

    ponérsele a uno la carne de gallina — *to get (to give one) gooseflesh (goose-bumps; goose-pimples).*
    Como hacía tanto frío se me puso la carne de gallina. *Since it was so cold, I got gooseflesh.*

---

la carrera — *race; career*
    a la carrera — *at full speed; hastily.*
    Salió a la carrera. *He took off at full speed (hastily).*

    dar una carrera — *to run fast.*
    Dando una carrera, llegó a tiempo. *By running fast, he arrived on time.*

---

la carta — *letter; (playing) card*

echar una carta — *to mail a letter.*

Eché la carta. *I mailed the letter.*

no saber a qué carta quedarse — *not to be able to make up one's mind (to be at a loss).*

No sabe a qué carta quedarse. *He can't make up his mind (he's at a loss).*

poner las cartas sobre la mesa — *to put one's cards on the table.*

Puso las cartas sobre la mesa. *He put his cards on the table.*

saber jugar a las cartas — *to know how to play one's cards.*

Ellos han sabido jugar a las cartas, y por eso han ganado. *They knew how to play their cards, and that's why they won.*

---

el cartucho — *cartridge*

quemar el último cartucho — *to play one's last trump (card); to use up one's last resource.*

Hemos quemado el último cartucho. *We've played our last trump (card) (used up our last resource).*

---

la casa — *house*

en casa — *(at) home.*

Estaremos en casa mañana. *We will be (at) home tomorrow.*

echar la casa por la ventana — *to go overboard.*

Echaron la casa por la ventana. *They really went overboard.*

estar en casa de . . . — *to be at . . .'s house.*

Está en casa de los Centeno. *He's at the Centenos'.*

nunca volver a pisar la casa — *never to set foot in the house again.*

Nunca volvió a pisar la casa. *He never set foot in the house again.*

pagar la casa — *to pay the rent.*

No puede pagar la casa. *He can't pay the rent.*

poner casa — *to set up housekeeping.*

Van a poner casa. *They're going to set up housekeeping.*

quedarse en casa — *to stay (at) home.*

Nos quedaremos en casa. *We'll stay (at) home.*

ser muy de casa — *to be like one of the family; to be very much at home.*

Es muy de casa aquí. *He's like one of the family (He's very much at home here).*

---

casar — *to marry*

Antes que te cases, mira lo que haces. — *Look before you leap.*

casar con — *to marry to.*
El sacerdote la casó con Roberto. *The priest married her to Robert.*

casarse con — *to marry.*
Juan se casó con Alicia. *John married Alice.*

no casarse con nadie — *not to get tied up (involved) with anybody.*
No se casa con nadie. *He doesn't get tied up (involved) with anybody.*

---

el casco — *head, skull*

romperse (calentarse) los cascos — *to rack one's brains.*
Se rompía (se calentaba) los cascos. *He was racking his brains.*

---

la casilla — *cabin, hut; pigeonhole; square (of a chessboard, etc.)*

sacar de las casillas — *to drive crazy.*
El ruido lo saca de sus casillas. *The noise drives him crazy.*

---

el caso — *case*

el caso es — *the fact is.*
El caso es que estaban cansados. *The fact is that they were tired.*

en caso contrario — *otherwise.*
En caso contrario, vendrán mañana. *Otherwise, they'll come tomorrow.*

en caso de — *in case.*
En caso de no entender, avíseme. *In case you don't understand, let me know.*

en cualquier (todo) caso — *in any case.*
En cualquier (todo) caso, voy. *In any case, I'm going.*

en el peor de los casos — *if worst comes to worst.*
En el peor de los casos, puede llevar el mío. *If worst comes to worst, you can take mine.*

en último caso — *as a last resort.*
En último caso iré a pie. *As a last resort I'll walk.*

en uno u otro caso — *one way or the other.*
En uno u otro caso lo compraré. *One way or the other I'll buy it.*

estar en el caso de — *to be obligated to.*
Está en el caso de hacerlo. *He's obligated to do it.*

hacer caso a (de) — *to pay attention to.*
No me hizo caso. *She paid no attention to me.*

hacer caso omiso — *to disregard.*
Hizo caso omiso de las instrucciones. *He disregarded the instructions.*

ir al caso — *to get to the point.*
Vamos al caso. *Let's get to the point.*

poner por caso — *to assume.*
Pongamos por caso que no vuelve. *Let's assume he doesn't return.*

según el caso — *as the case may be.*
Escríbales en español o en inglés según el caso. *Write to them in Spanish or in English as the case may be.*

venir al caso — *to be to the point (relevant).*
No viene al caso. *It's not to the point (not relevant).*

---

la castaña — *chestnut*
   sacarle las castañas del fuego — *to pull someone's chestnuts out of the fire.*
   Le saqué las castañas del fuego. *I pulled his chestnuts out of the fire.*

---

castaño — *brown, chestnut-colored*
   pasar de castaño oscuro — *to be too much (to be the absolute limit).*
   Eso pasa de castaño oscuro. *That's too much (the absolute limit).*

---

el castillo — *castle*
   hacer castillos en el aire — *to build castles in the air (castles in Spain).*
   Le gusta hacer castillos en el aire. *He likes to build castles in the air (castles in Spain).*

   un castillo de naipes — *a house of cards.*
   Su gran proyecto no es más que un castillo de naipes. *His great plan is only a house of cards.*

la casualidad — *chance, coincidence*

da la casualidad de que — *it so happens that.*

Da la casualidad de que mañana no vienen. *It so happens that tomorrow they're not coming.*

por (de) (pura) casualidad — *by (pure; mere) chance.*

Lo supo por pura casualidad. *He found out by (pure; mere) chance.*

la categoría — *category*

de categoría — *of importance.*

Es una persona de categoría. *He's a person of importance.*

la causa — *cause*

a causa de — *because of.*

No vamos a causa de la lluvia. *We're not going because of the rain.*

hacer causa común — *to make common cause.*

Hizo causa común con los revolucionarios. *He made common cause with the revolutionaries.*

la caza — *hunting*

andar a caza (de) — *to go (out) hunting (for).*

Andaban a caza de patos. *They were out hunting for ducks.*

la ceja — *eyebrow*

arquear las cejas — *to raise one's eyebrows.*

Arqueó las cejas. *He raised his eyebrows.*

quemarse las cejas — *to burn the midnight oil.*

Cuando estudia para sus exámenes, se quema las cejas. *When he studies for his exams, he burns the midnight oil.*

tener entre ceja y ceja — *to be set on.*

Lo tiene entre ceja y ceja. *He's set on it.*

tomar entre cejas — *to take a dislike to.*

Lo tomó entre cejas y no quiso contratarlo. *He took a dislike to him and wouldn't hire him.*

s celos — *jealousy*

dar celos — *to make jealous.*
Lo hizo para darme celos. *She did it to make me jealous.*

tener celos — *to be jealous.*
Tiene celos. *He's jealous.*

---

centenar — *hundred*

a centenares — *by the hundreds.*
A causa de la peste murieron a centenares. *Because of the plague, they died by the hundreds.*

---

centro — *center*

estar en su centro — *to be right where one belongs.*
Estoy en mi centro. *I'm right where I belong.*

---

erca — *near*

de cerca — *at close range.*
Lo observó de cerca. *He observed it at close range.*

---

cero — *zero*

ser un cero a la izquierda — *not to amount to anything.*
Es un cero a la izquierda. *He doesn't amount to anything.*

---

iego — *blind*

a ciegas — *blindly.*
Me obedece a ciegas. *He obeys me blindly.*

comprar a ciegas — *to buy a pig in a poke.*
Siempre es peligroso comprar a ciegas. *It's always dangerous to buy a pig in a poke.*

Un ciego mal guía a otro ciego. — *The blind leading the blind.*

---

l cielo — *sky, heaven*

como llovido del cielo — *Like manna from heaven.*
El premio llegó como llovido del cielo. *The prize came like manna from heaven.*

    mover cielo y tierra — *to move heaven and earth.*
    Movieron cielo y tierra. *They moved heaven and earth.*

la ciencia — *science, knowledge*
    a ciencia cierta — *for sure.*
    No se sabe a ciencia cierta. *It's not known for sure.*

cierto — *certain*
    dar por cierto (seguro) — *to be certain (sure).*
    Daba por cierto (seguro) que nadie lo sabía. *He was certain (sure) that no one knew it.*

    estar en lo cierto — *to be right.*
    Está en lo cierto. *He's right.*

    por cierto — *certainly.*
    Por cierto trabaja diez horas diarias. *Certainly he works ten hours a day.*

    ser cierto — *to be true.*
    Es cierto. *It's true.*

    un cierto — *a certain.*
    Me habló con un cierto temor. *He spoke to me with a certain fear.*

cinco — *five*
    decirle cuántas son cinco — *to tell someone what's what.*
    Voy a decirle cuántas son cinco. *I'm going to tell him what's what.*

la cintura — *waist*
    meter en cintura — *to make (someone) toe the line; to discipline; to hold back.*
    Va a ser difícil meterlos en cintura. *It's going to be hard to make them toe the line (to discipline them; to hold them back).*

citar — *to make an appointment with*
    citarse con — *to make an appointment with.*
    Me cité con Juan. *I made an appointment with John.*

claro — *clear*
    claro — *of course.*

Claro que es ésta la calle. *Of course this is the street.*

sacar (poner) en claro — *to make clear; to clear up.*

Sacó (Puso) en claro los detalles. *He made the details clear (He cleared up the details).*

---

la clase — *class*

fumarse la clase — *to cut class (to play hooky).*

Se fumó la clase. *He cut class (played hooky).*

toda clase de — *all kinds of.*

Hay toda clase de gente. *There are all kinds of people.*

---

la clavija — *peg, pin*

apretarle las clavijas — *to put the screws on someone.*

Le apretaron las clavijas. *They put the screws on him.*

---

el clavo — *nail*

dar en el clavo — *to hit the nail on the head.*

Su descripción dio en el clavo. *His description hit the nail on the head.*

---

el claxon — *(automobile) horn*

tocar el claxon (la bocina) — *to blow one's horn.*

No toque el claxon (la bocina). *Don't blow your horn.*

---

la coba — *trick, fraud; cajolery, flattery*

darle coba — *to soft-soap someone.*

Me daban coba. *They were soft-soaping me.*

---

el coco — *coconut; head, brain*

comerse el coco — *to worry a lot.*

¡No te comas el coco por eso! *Don't worry so much about that!*

---

el codo — *elbow*

dar con el codo — *to nudge.*

Le di con el codo. *I nudged him.*

empinar el codo — *to bend an elbow.*

Le gusta empinar el codo con sus amigos. *He enjoys bending an elbow with his friends.*

hablar hasta por los codos — *to talk one's ear off; chatter.*
Habla hasta por los codos. *He'll talk your ear off (He's a chatterbox).*

coincidir — *to coincide*
coincidir con — *to be somewhere at the same time as.*
Coincidimos con él en la fábrica. *We were at the factory at the same time he was.*

la cola — *tail*
hacer cola — *to stand in line.*
Tuvieron que hacer cola. *They had to stand in line.*

la colada — *washing, bleaching*
Todo saldrá en la colada. — *It'll all come out in the wash.*

colado — *cast (metal)*
estar colado por — *to be infatuated with.*
Juan está colado por Paula. *Juan is head over heels in love with Paula.*

colmar — *to fill (to overflowing)*
colmarle de — *to shower someone with.*
La colmaron de elogios. *They showered her with praise.*

el colmillo — *eyetooth, canine tooth*
enseñar los colmillos — *to show one's teeth.*
Enseña los colmillos. *He shows his teeth.*

tener (mucho) colmillo — *to have been around; to know a thing or two.*
Tiene (mucho) colmillo. *He's been around (knows a thing or two).*

el colmo — *fill, completion*
ser el colmo — *to be the limit.*
Es el colmo. *It's the limit.*

el color — *color*

  dar color — *to lend color.*

  La actuación de los bailarines dio color a la fiesta. *The performance of the dancers lent color to the fiesta.*

  verlo todo de color de rosa — *to look at everything through rose-colored glasses.*

  Lo ve todo de color de rosa. *He looks at everything through rose-colored glasses.*

colorado — *red*

  ponerse colorado — *to blush.*

  Ella se puso colorada. *She blushed.*

la coma — *comma*

  sin faltar una coma — *down to the last detail.*

  Nos lo contó sin faltar una coma. *He told us about it down to the last detail.*

el comino — *cumin (seed)*

  no valer un comino — *not to be worth a damn (thing).*

  No vale un comino. *It isn't worth a damn (thing).*

como — *as, like*

  como quiera — *as (any way) one likes.*

  Puede hacerlo como quiera. *You may do it as (any way) you like.*

cómo — *how*

  ¿A cómo se vende? — *How much does it sell for?*

  ¡Cómo no! — *Of course!*

  ¿Le gusta? ¡Cómo no! *Do you like it? Of course!*

  ¿Cómo que . . .? — *What do you mean . . .?*

  ¿Cómo que no lo tiene? *What do you mean you don't have it?*

el compás — *time, beat (in music)*

  al compás de — *in time to.*

59

Bailaban al compás de la música. *They were dancing in time to the music.*

fuera de compás — *off beat (out of time).*
Tocaba fuera de compás. *He was playing off beat (out of time).*

llevar el compás — *to keep time.*
Llevaban el compás. *They were keeping time.*

---

completo — *complete*
  por completo — *completely.*
  Lo ignoraba por completo. *He was completely unaware of it.*

la compra — *purchase*
  ir (salir) de compras — *to go (out) shopping.*
  Van (Salen) de compras. *They go (out) shopping.*

el compromiso — *commitment*
  ponerle en un compromiso — *to put someone in a difficult situation.*
  Me puso en un compromiso. *He put me in a difficult situation.*

común — *common*
  común y corriente — *common, ordinary.*
  Busco una caja de cartón común y corriente. *I'm looking for a common, ordinary cardboard box.*

  el común de la(s) gente(s) — *most people (the majority of people).*
  Así lo cree el común de la(s) gente(s). *That's what most people (the majority of people) think.*

  en común — *in common.*
  No tienen nada en común. *They have nothing in common.*

  por lo común — *usually.*
  Por lo común se llama Pepe. *He's usually called Joe.*

concentrado — *concentrated*
  estar concentrado en los pensamientos — *to be absorbed in one's thoughts.*

Estaba concentrado en sus pensamientos. *He was absorbed in his
   thoughts.*

---

el concepto — *concept*
   en concepto de — *for.*
   Me cobró mil pesos en concepto de alojamiento. *He charged me a
      thousand pesos for lodging.*

---

la conciencia — *conscience; consciousness*
   a conciencia — *conscientiously.*
   La secretaria hace su trabajo a conciencia. *The secretary does her work
      conscientiously.*

   conciencia de culpa — *guilty conscience.*
   Lo aceptó con conciencia de culpa. *She accepted it with a guilty
      conscience.*

---

la conclusión — *conclusion*
   precipitarse en sus conclusiones — *to jump to conclusions.*
   Me parece que te estás precipitando en tus conclusiones. *I think you're
      jumping to conclusions.*

---

concreto — *concrete, definite*
   en concreto — *definite.*
   No dijeron nada en concreto. *They didn't say anything definite.*

   en concreto — *to sum up.*
   En concreto, no vale nada. *To sum up, it's not worth anything.*

---

la condición — *condition*
   a condición de que — *on the condition that.*
   Lo aceptaré a condición de que usted cambie el título. *I'll accept it on the
      condition that you change the title.*

   en (buenas) condiciones — *in (good) shape; up to par.*
   No estaba en (buenas) condiciones. *He wasn't in (good) shape (up to par).*

   en condiciones de — *in a position to.*

No estaba en condiciones de ayudarme. *He wasn't in a position to help me.*

---

el conejillo — *(small) rabbit*
conejillo de Indias — *guinea pig.*
Necesitamos un conejillo de Indias para el experimento. *We need a guinea pig for the experiment.*

---

confesar — *to confess*
confesar de plano — *to make a clean breast of it.*
Confesó de plano. *He made a clean breast of it.*

---

la confianza — *confidence*
con toda confianza — *feel free.*
Pregúntemelo con toda confianza. *Feel free to ask me about it.*

(digno) de confianza — *reliable, trustworthy; private.*
(1) Aurelio es (digno) de confianza. *Aurelio is reliable (trustworthy).*
(2) Se trata de una conversacíon de confianza. *It is a private conversation.*

en confianza — *in confidence.*
Me lo dijo en confianza. *He told (it to) me in confidence.*

un amigo de confianza — *an intimate friend.*
Es un amigo de confianza. *He's an intimate friend.*

---

confiar — *to trust*
confiar en — *to trust.*
Confían en ella. *They trust her.*

---

la confidencia — *confidence*
en confidencia — *in confidence.*
Me lo dijeron en confidencia. *They told (it to) me in confidence.*

hacer una confidencia — *to confide in.*
Nunca me hacía una confidencia. *She never confided in me.*

el confite — *(type of) candy*
  morder en un confite — *to be very close.*
  Muerden en un confite. *They're very close.*

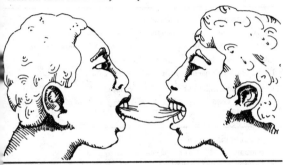

conformar — *to conform*
  conformarse con — *to resign oneself to.*
  Se conformaron con recibir sólo la mitad. *They resigned themselves to getting only half.*

  conformarse con — *to put up with.*
  Se conforma con todo. *He puts up with everything.*

conforme — *conformable, consistent, according*
  conforme a — *in accordance with.*
  Conforme a sus instrucciones, despedí a ese empleado. *In accordance with your instructions, I fired that employee.*

  estar conforme — *to agree.*
  Está conforme. *He agrees.*

la conformidad — *conformity*
  de conformidad con — *in conformity with.*
  Lo haré de conformidad con la ley. *I'll do it in conformity with the law.*

conocer — *to know*
  se conoce — *it is obvious.*
  Se conoce que no vienen. *It's obvious that they're not coming.*

el conocimiento — *knowledge, cognizance*
  obrar con conocimiento de causa — *to know what one is doing.*
  Obraron con conocimiento de causa. *They knew what they were doing.*

  perder el conocimiento — *to lose consciousness.*
  Perdió el conocimiento. *He lost consciousness.*

  venir en conocimiento de — *to find out about.*
  Vinimos en conocimiento de lo ocurrido. *We found out about what had occurred.*

la consecuencia — *consequence*
  a consecuencia de — *as a consequence of.*
  A consecuencia de la muerte de su tío, se hizo rico. *As a consequence of his uncle's death, he became rich.*

  de consecuencia — *important.*
  El asunto es de consecuencia. *It's an important matter.*

  en (por) consecuencia — *as a result.*
  En (por) consecuencia no pudimos ir. *As a result, we weren't able to go.*

  tener (mayores) consecuencias — *to have (great) consequences.*
  La cosa no ha tenido (mayores) consecuencias. *The matter has had no (great) consequences.*

consentir — *to consent*
  consentir en — *to consent to.*
  Consintieron en vernos. *They consented to see us.*

conservar — *to keep, preserve*
  estar bien conservado — *to be well preserved.*
  Está bien conservada. *She's well preserved.*

la consideración — *consideration*
  por consideración a — *out of consideration for.*
  Lo hago por consideración a ella. *I'm doing it out of consideration for her.*

---

consiguiente — *consequent*
  por consiguiente — *consequently.*
  Por consiguiente tuve que volver. *Consequently I had to return.*

---

constar — *to be clear; to consist, be composed*
  constar de — *to consist of.*
  La obra consta de tres actos. *The work consists of three acts.*

  constarle (a uno) — *to seem evident (to one).*
  Me consta que es un buen maestro. *It seems evident to me that he is a good teacher.*

---

el consuelo — *consolation*
  sin consuelo — *hopeless.*
  Gastaba sin consuelo. *He was a hopeless spendthrift.*

---

el contacto — *contact*
  perder el contacto con — *to lose touch with.*
  No quiero perder el contacto con ella. *I don't want to lose touch with her.*

  ponerse en contacto con — *to get in touch with.*
  Se puso en contacto conmigo. *He got in touch with me.*

---

contado — *counted, numbered*
  pagar al contado — *to pay cash.*
  Siempre pagamos al contado. *We always pay cash.*

---

contante — *ready (money)*
  dinero contante y sonante — *hard cash.*
  Pagó con dinero contante y sonante. *He paid hard cash.*

---

contar — *to count; to tell*
  contar con — *to count on.*
  Cuento con usted. *I'm counting on you.*

contar con — *to have.*
No cuenta con suficiente dinero. *He doesn't have enough money.*
¡Cuénteme a ver! — *Tell me!*

la continuación — *continuation*
   a continuación — *following.*
   A continuación se ve la lista de jugadores. *The list of players follows.*

continuo — *continuous*
   de continuo — *continually.*
   Llovió de continuo. *It rained continually.*

contra — *against*
   en contra de — *against.*
   Está en contra de las manifestaciones. *He's against the demonstrations.*

la contra — *trouble, inconvenience*
   llevar la contra a — *to disagree with (to oppose).*
   Siempre insiste en llevarme la contra. *He always insists on disagreeing with (opposing) me.*

contrario — *contrary*
   al contrario — *on the contrary.*
   Yo, al contrario, no sé nada. *I, on the contrary, know nothing.*

   de lo contrario — *otherwise.*
   Vaya con ella. De lo contrario, tendré que ir yo. *Go with her. Otherwise, I'll have to go.*

   llevar la contraria (la contra) — *to contradict.*
   Siempre me lleva la contraria (la contra). *He always contradicts me.*

la contraseña — *countersign; check (for baggage, etc.)*
   una contraseña de salida — *a re-entry pass.*
   Me dieron una contraseña de salida. *They gave me a re-entry pass.*

la conversación — *conversation*
   dejar caer en la conversación — *to let (it) drop.*

Dejó caer en la conversación que iba a casarse. *She let it drop that she was going to get married.*

---

convertir — *to convert*

convertirse en — *to turn into.*

Su dolor de cabeza se convirtío en un resfriado. *Her headache turned into a cold.*

---

convidar — *to invite*

convidar con — *to treat to.*

Me convidó con una copa de coñac. *He treated me to a glass of brandy.*

---

copa — *glass, goblet; drink*

pasársele las copas — *to have too much to drink.*

Anoche salí con unos amigos y se me pasaron las copas. *I went out with some friends last night and had too much to drink.*

---

la copia — *copy*

sacar una copia — *to make a copy.*

Sáqueme una copia de esta carta. *Make me a copy of this letter.*

---

el corazón — *heart*

¡Arriba los corazones! — *(Keep your) chin up!*

con el corazón en la mano — *in all frankness.*

Le digo esto con el corazón en la mano. *I'm telling you this in all frankness.*

llevar el corazón en la mano — *to wear one's heart on one's sleeve.*

Lleva el corazón en la mano. *He wears his heart on his sleeve.*

no tener corazón para — *not to have the heart to.*

No tengo corazón para decírselo. *I haven't the heart to tell him.*

partirle el corazón — *to break someone's heart.*

Me partió el corazón. *It broke my heart.*

querer de todo corazón — *to love with all one's heart.*

La quiero de todo corazón. *I love her with all my heart.*

ser blando de corazón — *to be soft-hearted.*

Soy muy blando de corazón. *I am very soft-hearted.*

tener corazón de piedra — *to be very hard-hearted.*
Tiene corazón de piedra. *He is very hard-hearted.*

el coro — *chorus, choir*
  brindar a coro — *to drink a toast together.*
  Brindaron a coro. *They all drank a toast together.*

  hacerle coro — *to echo (to second) someone's opinion.*
  Me hicieron coro. *They echoed (seconded) my opinion.*

  recitar a coro — *to recite in chorus.*
  Lo recitaron a coro. *They recited it in chorus.*

  rezar a coros — *to pray alternately (responsively).*
  Rezaban a coros. *They were praying alternately (responsively).*

la coronilla — *crown (of the head)*
  estar hasta la coronilla (de) — *to be fed up (with).*
  Estoy hasta la coronilla de mi trabajo. *I'm fed up with my work.*

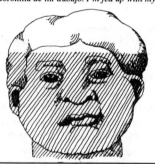

el correo — *mail*
  echar al correo — *to mail.*
  Escribió la carta y la echó al correo. *He wrote the letter and mailed it.*

correr — *to run*
  a todo correr — *at top speed.*
  Salieron a todo correr. *They set off at top speed.*

corresponder — *to correspond*

A quien le corresponda. — *To whom it may concern.*

corresponderle — *to be one's affair.*
Eso no me corresponde. *That's not my affair.*

corresponderle — *to be one's turn.*
A mí me corresponde ganar el premio. *It's my turn to win the prize.*

---

la corriente — *current, stream*

dejarse llevar de la corriente — *to follow the crowd.*
Se deja llevar de la corriente. *He follows the crowd.*

llevarle la corriente — *to humor someone.*
Sólo lo hice por llevarles la corriente. *I only did it to humor them.*

---

corriente — *current*

estar al corriente (al tanto) de — *to be up-to-date on.*
Está al corriente (al tanto) de lo que pasa. *He's up-to-date on what's
happening.*

(man)tener al corriente (de) — *to keep posted (informed, up-to-date on).*
La (man)tenía al corriente. *He was keeping her posted (informed, up-to-date).*

poner (a uno) al corriente (de) — *to bring (someone) up-to-date (on).*
Me puso al corriente. *He brought me up-to-date.*

---

corto — *short*

a la corta o a la larga — *sooner or later.*
A la corta o a la larga se arrepentirán. *Sooner or later they'll be sorry.*

quedarse corto — *not to have enough (left).*
Me quedé corto de café. *I didn't have enough coffee (left).*

---

la cosa — *thing*

como quien no quiere la cosa — *casually (with pretended indifference).*
Lo hace como quien no quiere la cosa. *He does it casually (with pretended
indifference).*

como si tal cosa — *as if nothing had happened.*

Seguí trabajando como si tal cosa. *I went on working as if nothing had happened.*

cosa de — *about; more or less.*
Estuvo allí cosa de dos meses. *He was there about two months (two months, more or less).*

cosa de ver — *something to see.*
Su actuación era cosa de ver. *Her performance was something to see.*

(ser) cosas de . . . — *to be the way . . . is.*
(Esas son) Cosas de Pablo. *Oh, that's just the way Paul is.*

creerse la gran cosa — *to think one is really something (someone).*
Andrés se cree la gran cosa, pero yo no me explico por qué. *Andrew thinks he's really something (someone), but I don't understand why.*

dejar las cosas a medias — *to leave things half done.*
Dejó las cosas a medias. *He left things half done.*

Eso ya es otra cosa. — *That's quite another matter.*

No hay tal cosa. — *That's not true at all (It's not like that at all).*

no ser de morirse — *not to be fatal (not all that serious).*
La enfermedad no es de morirse. *The disease is not fatal (not all that serious).*

otra cosa — *something else.*
¿No desea otra cosa? *Don't you want something else?*

poner las cosas en su punto — *to set things straight.*
Puso las cosas en su punto. *He set things straight.*

por cualquier cosa — *on the slightest provocation.*
Llora por cualquier cosa. *She cries on the slightest provocation.*

ser cosa del otro mundo — *to be out of the ordinary; special; something to write home about.*
No es cosa del otro mundo. *It's nothing out of the ordinary (nothing special; nothing to write home about).*

ser cosa suya — *to be one's business (one's affair).*
Eso es cosa mía. *That's my business (my affair).*

tomar las cosas con calma — *to take things calmly.*
Siempre toma las cosas con calma. *He always takes things calmly.*

la cosecha — *harvest, crop*

  ser de la propia cosecha — *to be something one thought up oneself (out of one's own head); brainchild.*

  Eso es de su propia cosecha. *That's something he thought up himself (out of his own head); That's his brainchild.*

---

coser — *to sew*

  ser coser y cantar — *(to have) nothing to it; to be child's play.*

  Esto es coser y cantar. *There's nothing to this (This is child's play).*

---

las cosquillas — *tickling, ticklishness*

  buscarle las cosquillas — *to try to get someone irritated; to tease.*

  Le buscaban las cosquillas. *They were trying to get him irritated (teasing him).*

  hacerle cosquillas — *to tickle someone.*

  Le hizo cosquillas. *She tickled him.*

---

la costa — *cost*

  a costa de — *at the expense of.*

  Se divierten a costa de su primo. *They amuse themselves at their cousin's expense.*

  a toda costa — *at all costs.*

  Lo haré a toda costa. *I'll do it at all costs.*

---

el costado — *side*

  por los cuatro costados — *on both sides.*

  Es noble por los cuatro costados. *He's of noble blood on both sides.*

---

el costal — *sack, bag*

  estar hecho un costal de huesos — *to be nothing but skin and bones.*

  Está hecho un costal de huesos. *He's nothing but skin and bones.*

---

costar — *to cost*

  costarle caro — *to cost one dearly.*

  Les costó caro. *It cost them dearly.*

cueste lo que cueste — *cost what it may.*
Encontrémoslo, cueste lo que cueste. *Let's find it, cost what it may.*

el coste — *cost*
a coste y costa(s) — *at cost.*
Me lo vendió a coste y costa(s). *He sold it to me at cost.*

la costumbre — *custom*
como de costumbre — *as usual.*
Empezaremos a las ocho como de costumbre. *We will begin at eight as usual.*

de costumbre — *usual.*
Me habló con su cortesía de costumbre. *She spoke to me with her usual courtesy.*

tener la costumbre de (tener por costumbre) — *to be in the habit of.*
Tiene la costumbre de (tiene por costumbre) llegar tarde. *He is in the habit of arriving late.*

la cotorra — *parrot*
hablar como una cotorra — *to be a chatterbox.*
Nunca le faltan palabras. Habla como una cotorra. *He's never at a loss for words. He's a chatterbox.*

la coz — *kick*
dar (tirar) coces — *to kick.*
El asno daba (tiraba) coces. *The donkey was kicking.*

las creces — *increase, excess*
con creces — *and then some.*
Se lo pagué con creces. *I paid him back and then some.*

el crédito — *credit*
a crédito — *on credit.*
Allí no se vende a crédito. *They don't sell on credit there.*

dar crédito a — *to believe (to give credence to).*

Nunca da crédito a lo que oye. *He never believes (gives credence to) what he hears.*

---

creer — *to believe*

creer que sí (no) — *to think so (not).*
Creemos que sí (no). *We think so (not).*

no crea — *don't get the wrong idea.*
No crea, es muy inteligente. *Don't get the wrong idea, he's very intelligent.*

¡Quién había de creerlo! — *Who would have thought it!*

¡Ya lo creo! — *Yes indeed! (I should say so!)*

---

el/la crisma — *chrism*

romperle la crisma — *to break someone's neck.*
Le voy a romper la crisma. *I'm going to break his neck.*

---

cristiano — *Christian*

hablar en cristiano — *to talk plain Spanish [English].*
¿Por qué no hablan en cristiano? *Why don't they talk plain Spanish [English]?*

---

la cruz — *cross*

hacerse cruces — *to show great astonishment.*
Se hizo cruces. *He showed great astonishment.*

---

cuál — *which (one)*

a cuál más ... — *each one more ... than the last.*
Tienen cinco hijas, a cuál más bonita. *They have five daughters, each one prettier than the last (other).*

---

cualquiera — *any (whatsoever)*

ser un cualquiera — *to be just run of the mill (to be of no account).*
Es un cualquiera. *He's just run of the mill (of no account).*

---

cuando — *when*

cuando más — *at most.*
Debe de tener cincuenta años cuando más. *He must be fifty at most.*

cuando menos — *at least.*

Se llevó cuando menos diez. *He carried off at least ten.*

de cuando en cuando (de vez en cuando) — *from time to time.*
Me acompaña de cuando en cuando (de vez en cuando). *He accompanies me from time to time.*

---

cuanto — *as much as, however much*
  cuanto antes — *as soon as possible.*
  Se lo devolveré cuanto antes. *I will return it to her as soon as possible.*

  cuanto más (menos) — *the more (less).*
  Cuanto más (menos) se estudia, (tanto) más (menos) se aprende. *The more (less) one studies, the more (less) one learns.*

  cuanto más que — *especially since.*
  La quiero mucho, cuanto más que es mi prima. *I'm very fond of her, especially since she's my cousin.*

  en cuanto — *as soon as.*
  En cuanto salgan, venga a vernos. *As soon as they leave, come see us.*

  en cuanto a — *as for.*
  En cuanto a mi profesor, es de España. *As for my professor, he's from Spain.*

  todo cuanto — *everything.*
  Cree todo cuanto le dicen. *He believes everything they tell him.*

  unos cuantos — *a few.*
  Me trajo unos cuantos libros. *He brought me a few books.*

---

cuánto — *how much*
  ¿A cuántos estamos? — *What is the date?*

---

cuarenta — *forty*
  cantarle las cuarenta — *to tell someone off.*
  Le cantaron las cuarenta. *They told him off.*

---

el cuarto — *old coin*
  no tener un cuarto — *not to have a penny to one's name.*
  No tiene un cuarto. *He hasn't got a penny to his name.*

cuatro — *four*
  más de cuatro — *quite a few.*
  Me lo han dicho más de cuatro. *Quite a few people have told me so.*

---

la cuba — *cask, vat*
  estar hecho una cuba — *to be drunk as a lord.*
  Andaba por la calle hecho una cuba. *He was walking down the street drunk as a lord.*

---

cuclillas
  en cuclillas — *squatting.*
  Estaban en cuclillas. *They were squatting.*

---

la cuchara — *spoon*
  meter la cuchara — *to butt in.*
  Siempre tiene que meter su cuchara. *He always has to butt in.*

  metérselo con cuchara (de palo) — *to spoon-feed someone.*
  Hay que metérselo con cuchara (de palo). *You have to spoon-feed it to him.*

---

la cuenta — *account*
  ajustar (arreglar) cuentas — *to settle accounts.*
  ¡Ya ajustaré (arreglaré) cuentas con ellos! *I'll settle accounts with them!*

  caer en la cuenta (de) — *to catch on (to); realize; see the point of.*
  No cae en la cuenta de la historia. *He doesn't catch on to (see the point of) the story.*

  correr por la cuenta — *to see to; to be one's affair; to be up to one.*
  Eso corre por mi cuenta. *I'll see to that (That's my affair; That's up to me).*

  dar cuenta de — *to report on; to give an account of.*
  Dio cuenta de su visita a los Estados Unidos. *He reported on (gave an account of) his visit to the United States.*

  darse cuenta de — *to realize.*
  Me doy cuenta de ello. *I realize it.*

  echar la cuenta — *to balance the account.*

Echó la cuenta. *He balanced the account.*

en resumidas cuentas — *in short; to sum up.*
En resumidas cuentas, no vale nada. *In short (To sum up), it's not worth anything.*

hacerse cuenta (que) — *to imagine; to pretend (that).*
Hágase cuenta que aquí hay un árbol. *Imagine (Pretend) that there's a tree right here.*

ir a cuentas — *to settle something.*
¡Vamos a cuentas! *Let's settle this!*

rendir cuentas a (ante) — *to explain oneself.*
Tendrás que rendir cuentas a (ante) tu patrón. *You will have to explain yourself to your boss.*

ir por cuenta de la casa — *to be on the house.*
Va por cuenta de la casa. *It's on the house.*

llevar bien las cuentas — *to keep careful track.*
Tiene que llevar bien sus cuentas. *He has to keep careful track.*

más de la cuenta — *too much; to excess.*
Comió más de la cuenta. *He ate too much (to excess).*

no entrar en la cuenta — *not to count.*
No entra en la cuenta. *It doesn't count.*

pedirle cuentas — *to ask someone for an explanation.*
Nadie le pedía cuentas. *No one asked him for an explanation.*

perder la cuenta — *to lose count (track).*
Perdió la cuenta de su edad. *She lost count (track) of her age.*

poner las cuentas claras — *to tell it like it is.*
Te voy a poner las cuentas claras. *I'm going to tell it (to you) like it is.*

por cuenta y riesgo — *at one's own risk.*
Ese viaje lo hará usted por su cuenta y riesgo. *You will make that trip at your own risk.*

por su cuenta — *on one's own.*
Lo compró por su cuenta. *He bought it on his own.*

tener en cuenta — *to bear (keep) in mind.*
Tenga en cuenta que es necesario. *Bear (Keep) in mind that it is necessary.*

tomar en cuenta — *to take into account.*

Tome en cuenta todo lo que ha hecho por usted. *Take into account
everything he has done for you.*

---

el cuento — *tale, story*

cuento chino — *cock and bull story.*

No me venga con esos cuentos chinos. *Don't tell me any of those cock and
bull stories.*

cuento de viejas — *old wives' tale.*

Lo que nos dijo parece un cuento de viejas. *What he told us sounds like
an old wives' tale.*

¡Déjese de cuentos! — *Oh, come on now!; Get to the point!*

ir de cuento — *to be said.*

Va de cuento que aquella reina era bruja. *It is said that that queen was a
witch.*

venir a cuento — *to be to the point.*

No viene a cuento. *It's not to the point.*

sin cuento — *endless.*

Ha tenido problemas sin cuento. *He has had endless problems.*

---

la cuerda — *rope, cord, string*

dar cuerda (a) — *to wind.*

Cada noche da cuerda al reloj. *Each night he winds the clock.*

---

el cuero — *hide, leather*

en cueros (vivos) — *stark naked.*

Salió a la calle en cueros (vivos). *He went out on the street stark naked.*

---

el cuerpo — *body*

luchar cuerpo a cuerpo — *to fight in hand-to-hand combat.*

Lucharon cuerpo a cuerpo. *They fought in hand-to-hand combat.*

---

el cuervo — *crow, raven*

Cría cuervos y te sacarán los ojos. — *That's the thanks you get!; to
bite the hand that feeds one; to nurse a viper in one's bosom.*

---

la cuesta — *slope*

a cuestas — *on one's back.*
Llevaba el baúl a cuestas. *He was carrying the trunk on his back.*

cuesta abajo — *downhill; easy going.*
Iba cuesta abajo. *He was going downhill.*

cuesta arriba — *uphill; heavy going.*
Se me hace cuesta arriba. *It's uphill (heavy going) for me.*

la cuestión — *question*

ser cuestión de — *to be a question of.*
Es cuestión de demasiado dinero. *It's a question of too much money.*

el cuidado — *care*

al cuidado de — *to the care of.*
Dejó la venta de la casa al cuidado de un agente. *He left the sale of the house to the care of an agent.*

andar con mucho cuidado — *to proceed very carefully (cautiously).*
Si quieres poner un negocio allí, tendrás que andar con mucho cuidado. *If you want to start a business there, you'll have to proceed very cautiously.*

cuidado — *be careful.*
¡Cuidado con quemarse! *Be careful not to burn yourself!*

cuidado — *look out.*
¡Cuidado con el ganado! *Look out for the cattle!*

estar (enfermo) de cuidado — *to be seriously ill.*
Está (enfermo) de cuidado. *He is seriously ill.*

no tener cuidado — *not to worry.*
No tenga cuidado. *Don't worry.*

perder cuidado — *not to worry.*
¡Pierda cuidado! *Don't worry!*

poner cuidado — *to be careful.*
Pone mucho cuidado en su trabajo. *He is very careful in his work.*

sin cuidado — *indifferent.*

Sus problemas me tienen sin cuidado. *His problems are a matter of indifference to me.*

tener cuidado — *to be careful.*
Tenga cuidado de no resbalar. *Be careful not to slip.*

tener sin cuidado — *not to bother.*
Eso me tiene sin cuidado. *That doesn't bother me at all.*

---

cuidar — *to care for*
  cuidar de (a) — *to take care of.*
La emplearon para cuidar de (a) los niños. *They hired her to take care of the children.*

  cuidarse de — *to care about.*
No se cuida de mi opinión. *He doesn't care about my opinion.*

---

la culpa — *guilt, blame*
  echar la culpa a — *to blame.*
Le echan la culpa a Juan. *They are blaming John.*

  por culpa de — *to be the fault of.*
No recibió el puesto por culpa del jefe. *It was the boss's fault that he didn't get the job.*

  tener la culpa de — *to be to blame for.*
Tiene la culpa del accidente. *She is to blame for the accident.*

---

cumplir — *to perform, fulfill*
  cumplir años — *to have a birthday.*
Mañana cumple tres años. *Tomorrow he'll be three.*

  por cumplir — *for form's sake; as a formality.*
Sólo lo hizo por cumplir. *He did it for form's sake (as a formality).*

---

el chance — *chance*
  darle chance — *to give someone a chance.*

¿Por qué no le damos chance? *Why don't we let him have a try (give him a chance)?*

---

la chancla — *old shoe; slipper*

estar hasta las chanclas — *to be fed up.*

Estoy hasta las chanclas con mi primo. *I'm fed up with my cousin. (I've had it with my cousin.)*

---

el chasco — *trick; disappointment*

llevarse (un) chasco — *to have a disappointment.*

¡Qué chasco se llevó! *What a disappointment he had!*

---

la chinche — *bedbug*

morir como chinches — *to die like flies.*

Morían como chinches. *They were dying like flies.*

---

la chispa — *spark*

estar echando (estar que echa) chispas — *to be hopping mad (fit to be tied).*

Estaban echando (Estaban que echaban) chispas. *They were hopping mad (fit to be tied).*

---

chistar — *to speak*

no chistar — *not to say a word.*

No chistó. *He didn't say a word.*

sin chistar ni mistar — *without saying a word.*

Lo aceptaron sin chistar ni mistar. *They accepted it without saying a word.*

---

el chiste — *joke*

hacerle chiste (gracia) — *to strike one as being funny.*

No me hizo chiste (gracia). *It didn't strike me as funny.*

---

la chita — *ankle bone*

a la chita callando (a la chiticallando) — *stealthily; on the sly.*

Salieron a la chita callando (a la chiticallando). *They left stealthily (on the sly).*

---

el chorro — *jet, spurt*
  a chorros — *profusely.*
  Estaban sudando a chorros. *They were sweating profusely.*

daño — *harm, damage*
  hacerle daño (a) — *to harm one; to disagree (physically) with one.*
  No le hará daño. *It won't hurt (disagree with) you.*

  hacerse daño — *to get hurt.*
  Se hizo daño. *He got hurt.*

dar — *to give*
  ¡Dale que dale! — *That's right, just keep it up! (Sarcastic.)*

  dar a — *to face.*
  La universidad da al hotel. *The university faces the hotel.*

  dar a (de) beber — *to give a drink.*
  Le dieron a (de) beber. *They gave him a drink.*

  dar a conocer — *to make known.*
  Dio a conocer que no aceptaría. *He made it known that he would not
    accept.*

  dar a entender — *to give to understand.*
  Le di a entender que no quería ir. *I gave him to understand that I didn't
    want to go.*

  dar con — *to find.*
  No pudo dar con el motivo del crimen. *He couldn't find the reason for the
    crime.*

  dar con — *to run into.*
  Di con Juan en la calle. *I ran into John on the street.*

  dar de comer — *to feed.*
  Tengo que dar de comer al perro. *I have to feed the dog.*

  dar de sí — *to stretch.*

La tela da de sí. *The cloth stretches.*

dar en — *to hit.*
Me dio en la cabeza con una piedra. *He hit me in the head with a stone.*

dar las . . . — *to strike. . . .*
Dieron las cuatro. *The clock struck four.*

dar por — *to consider.*
Lo doy por perdido. *I consider it lost.*

dar que decir — *to cause a lot of talk.*
Dio que decir. *It caused a lot of talk.*

dar (mucho) que hacer — *to cause (a lot of) bother.*
Esto da (mucho) que hacer. *This is causing (a lot of) bother.*

dar que pensar — *to make think.*
Me da que pensar. *It makes me think.*

darle — *to hit someone.*
Le dieron con un palo en la cabeza. *They hit him on the head with a stick.*

darle a — *to reach down to.*
El cabello le daba a las espaldas. *Her hair reached down to her back.*

darle a cada cual lo suyo — *to give each one his just deserts.*
Le da a cada cual lo suyo. *He gives each one his just deserts.*

darle por — *to take it into one's head.*
Le dio por hacerle el amor a María Elena. *He took it into his head to make love to Mary Ellen.*

darle por — *to take to.*
Le dio por tocar la guitarra. *He took to playing the guitar.*

Lo mismo (Igual) da. — *It's all the same.*

no darse por entendido — *to pretend not to understand.*
No se dio por entendido. *He pretended not to understand.*

¿Qué más da? — *What difference does it make?*

de — *of, from*
  de — *as.*
Terminó trabajando de sirvienta. *She ended up working as a servant.*

  de + infinitive — *if.*

De (A) haberlo sabido, no hubieran ido. *If they had known, they wouldn't have gone.*

de día (noche) — *in the daytime (at night).*
Estudia sólo de día (noche). *He studies only in the daytime (at night).*

de dos en dos (dos a dos) — *two by two.*
Entraban de dos en dos (dos a dos). *They were going in two by two.*

de ... en ... — *from ... to ....*
Fuimos de tienda en tienda. *We went from store to store.*

de joven — *as a youth.*
De joven le gustaba nadar. *As a young man he liked to swim.*

de la mañana (noche) — *in the morning (evening).*
Llegó a las ocho de la mañana (noche). *He arrived at eight in the morning (evening).*

más (menos) de — *more (less) than.*
Asistieron más (menos) de cien. *More (Less) than a hundred attended.*

decidir — *to decide*

estar decidido a — *to be determined to.*
Estoy decidido a ir. *I'm determined to go.*

decir — *to say, tell*

como dijo el otro — *as the saying goes (as they say).*
Más vale tarde que nunca, como dijo el otro. *Better late than never, as the saying goes (as they say).*

como quien dice — *as if to say.*
Hizo una mueca, como quien dice. — No me gusta. *He made a face, as if to say, "I don't like it."*

decir bien — *to be right.*
Es un hombre que siempre dice bien. *He's a man who is always right.*

Dicho y hecho. — *No sooner said than done.*

diciendo y haciendo — *and so doing.*
Diciendo y haciendo, renunció el puesto. *And so doing, he resigned his job.*

el qué dirán — *what people may say.*

No le importa el qué dirán. *She doesn't care about what people may say.*

es decir — *that is to say.*

La viejita, es decir, mi abuela, no oyó nada. *The little old lady, that is to say, my grandmother, didn't hear anything.*

Lo dicho, dicho. — *What I've said stands (I mean what I say).*

mejor dicho — *rather.*

Vamos mañana, o mejor dicho pasado mañana. *We're going tomorrow, or rather the day after tomorrow.*

ni que decir tiene (va sin decir) — *to go without saying.*

Ni que decir tiene (Va sin decir) que es una buena idea. *It goes without saying that it's a good idea.*

no decir de — *not to mention; to say nothing of.*

Tiene cinco perros, y no digamos de sus gatos. *She has five dogs, not to mention (to say nothing of) her cats.*

por decirlo así — *so to speak.*

Es nuestra ama de llaves, por decirlo así. *She's our housekeeper, so to speak.*

que digamos — *to speak of.*

No es muy inteligente que digamos. *He's not really very intelligent (not very intelligent to speak of).*

ser un decir — *to be a saying.*

Es un decir en esta región. *It is a saying in this region.*

---

la decisión — *decision*

    tomar una decisión — *to make a decision.*

    ¿Cuándo va usted a tomar una decisión? *When are you going to make a decision?*

---

dedicar — *to dedicate*

    dedicarse a — *to devote oneself to.*

    Se dedicó a la enseñanza. *She devoted herself to teaching.*

---

el dedillo — *little finger*

    saber al dedillo — *to know backwards and forwards; to have at one's fingertips.*

Lo sabe todo al dedillo. *He knows it all backwards and forwards (has it all at his fingertips).*

el dedo — *finger*

a dos dedos de — *within an inch of; on the verge of.*
Estaba a dos dedos de ahogarse. *He came within an inch of (was on the verge of) drowning.*

contar por los dedos — *to count on one's fingers.*
Cuenta por los dedos. *He counts on his fingers.*

no tener dos dedos de frente — *to be really stupid.*
Ese no tiene ni dos dedos de frente. *That guy's a real idiot.*

poner el dedo en la llaga — *to hit the sore spot.*
Ha puesto el dedo en la llaga. *You've hit the sore spot.*

señalarle con el dedo — *to point the finger at someone.*
La señalaron con el dedo. *They pointed a finger at her.*

ser para chuparse los dedos — *to taste delicious.*
Este postre es para chuparse los dedos. *This dessert tastes delicious.*

Un dedo no hace mano, ni una golondrina verano. *One swallow doesn't make a summer.*

defender — *to defend*
defenderse — *to get along.*
Se defiende bien en español. *He gets along well in Spanish.*

la defensiva — *defensive*
  a la defensiva — *on the defensive.*
  Estábamos a la defensiva. *We were on the defensive.*

dejar — *to let, leave*
  dejar caer — *to drop.*
  Dejó caer su cartera. *He dropped his billfold.*

  dejar de — *to fail to.*
  No deje de leerlo. *Don't fail to read it.*

  dejar de — *to stop.*
  Dejó de ser mi enemigo. *He stopped being my enemy.*

delante — *in front, ahead*
  por delante — *at the head.*
  Una mujer iba por delante de la banda. *There was a woman at the head of the band.*

la delantera — *front; lead, advantage*
  tomar (coger; llevar) la delantera — *to get ahead of.*
  Me tomó (cogió; llevó) la delantera. *He got ahead of me.*

demás — *other(s), rest*
  estar por demás — *to be useless (superfluous).*
  Está por demás. *It's useless (superfluous).*

  por demás — *excessively.*
  Es por demás orgulloso. *He's excessively proud.*

  por lo demás — *furthermore; aside from this.*
  Por lo demás, está lloviendo. *Furthermore (Aside from this), it's raining.*

la demasía — *excess*
  en demasía — *to excess.*
  Comió en demasía. *He ate to excess.*

la demostración — *demonstration*
  hacer una demostración — *to give a demonstration.*
  Nos hizo una demostración. *He gave us a demonstration.*

dentellada — *bite, toothmark*

romper a dentelladas — *to chew up.*
El perro lo rompió a dentelladas. *The dog chewed it up.*

---

dentro — *inside*

por dentro y por fuera — *inside and out.*
Lo pintaron por dentro y por fuera. *They painted it inside and out.*

---

depender — *to depend*

depender de — *to depend on.*
Depende del tiempo. *It depends on the weather.*

---

derecho — *right*

tener derecho a — *to have a right to.*
Todos tenemos derecho a votar. *We all have a right to vote.*

---

derecho — *right, straight*

a (la) derecha — *to the right.*
La salida está a (la) derecha. *The exit is to the right.*

a derechas — *right; correctly.*
No sabe hacer nada a derechas. *He can't do anything right (correctly).*

guardar la derecha — *to keep to the right.*
Guarde la derecha. *Keep to the right.*

---

deriva — *drift*

ir a la deriva — *to drift.*
El bote iba a la deriva. *The boat was drifting.*

---

desbandada — *disbandment*

a la desbandada — *in confusion; in disorder.*
Huyeron a la desbandada. *They fled in confusion (in disorder).*

---

escampado — *open, clear*

en descampado — *in the open country.*
Pasamos la noche en descampado. *We spent the night in the open country.*

---

el descaro — *effrontery, impudence*
  tener el descaro de — *to have the nerve (audacity) to.*
  Tuvo el descaro de decirme que el dinero era suyo. *He had the nerve (audacity) to tell me that the money belonged to him.*

descosido — *imprudent, indiscreet*
  gritar como un descosido — *to shout at the top of one's lungs.*
  Gritaba como un descosido. *He was shouting at the top of his lungs.*

descubrir — *to discover, uncover*
  a(l) descubierto — *(out) in the open.*
  Se batían a(l) descubierto. *They were fighting (out) in the open.*

  descubrirse — *to take off one's hat.*
  Todos se descubrieron al ver pasar la bandera. *They all took off their ha when they saw the flag go by.*

descuidar — *to be careless*
  a poco que se descuide — *if one isn't careful (if one doesn't watch out*
  A poco que nos descuidemos, nos van a robar el coche. *If we aren't careful (if we don't watch out), they're going to steal our car.*

el descuido — *neglect, carelessness*
  como al descuido — *as if by accident.*
  Se acercó como al descuido. *He approached as if by accident.*

  por (en un) descuido — *inadvertently; carelessly.*
  Tropezó por (en un) descuido con una estatua. *He inadvertently (carelessly) bumped into a statue.*

  tener el descuido de no — *to neglect to.*
  Tuvo el descuido de no apagar la luz. *He neglected to turn out the light*

desde — *from, since*
  desde antes — *before.*
  Se habían casado desde mucho antes. *They had gotten married a long time before.*

  desde niño — *from childhood on.*

Desde niño recibió una educación clásica. *From childhood on he received a classical education.*

desentenderse — *to take no part (in); to have nothing to do (with)*
hacerse el desentendido — *to pretend not to notice (understand).*
Se hizo el desentendido. *He pretended not to notice (understand).*

el deseo — *desire*
tener deseos de — *to want to.*
Tiene deseos de ver la comedia. *He wants to see the play.*

la desesperación — *desperation, despair*
echarse a la desesperación — *to sink into despair.*
Se echó a la desesperación. *He sank into despair.*

desesperado — *desperate*
a la desesperada — *in desperation; as a last resort.*
A la desesperada se lo pidió a su padre. *In desperation (As a last resort) he asked his father for it.*

la desgracia — *misfortune*
por desgracia — *unfortunately.*
Por desgracia no puedo. *Unfortunately I can't.*

deshacer — *to undo*
deshacerse — *to put oneself out.*
Se deshace por complacerme. *He puts himself out to please me.*

deshacerse de — *to get rid of.*
Va a deshacerse de su coche. *She is going to get rid of her car.*

deshacerse en — *to break out in.*
Se deshizo en sudor (lágrimas). *He broke out in a sweat (tears).*

la deshecha — *pretense, dissembling*
hacer la deshecha — *to dissemble; to pretend.*

Hacía la deshecha cuando me dijo que era inocente. *He was dissembling (pretending) when he told me he was innocent.*

---

la deshonra — *dishonor*
  tener a deshonra — *to consider dishonorable.*
  No lo tiene a deshonra. *He doesn't consider it dishonorable.*

---

el desierto — *desert*
  en (el) desierto — *to deaf ears.*
  Predicaba en (el) desierto. *He was preaching to deaf ears.*

---

el despecho — *spite*
  a despecho de — *in spite of; despite.*
  A despecho de su mala suerte, siguió jugando. *In spite of (despite) his bad luck, he went on gambling.*

  por despecho — *out of spite.*
  Lo hicieron por despecho. *They did it out of spite.*

---

desprender — *to detach, loosen*
  desprenderse de — *to give away.*
  El rico se desprendió de su fortuna. *The rich man gave away his fortune.*

---

el destino — *fate, destiny*
  con destino a — *bound for.*
  Se embarcó el gerente en Hamburgo con destino a Londres. *The manager boarded the ship in Hamburg bound for London.*

---

desvivirse — *to be very much interested, very eager*
  desvivirse por — *to do one's utmost to.*
  Se han desvivido por ayudarnos. *They have done their utmost to help us.*

---

la determinación — *determination, decision*
  tomar una determinación (decisión) — *to make a decision.*
  Tomó una determinación (decisión). *He made a decision.*

detrás — *behind*
  por detrás — *(from) behind.*
  Venía por detrás. *He was coming along (from) behind.*

---

el día — *day*
  de día en día — *by the day.*
  Crece de día en día. *He grows by the day.*

  de hoy en ocho (quince) días — *a week (two weeks) from today.*
  Empieza de hoy en ocho (quince) días. *It starts a week (two weeks) from today.*

  del día — *today's.*
  Los coches del día son muy costosos. *Today's cars are very expensive.*

  día por día — *by the day.*
  Día por día se va enriqueciendo. *He's getting richer by the day.*

  el día menos pensado — *when least expected.*
  Vendrán el día menos pensado. *They will come when least expected.*

  estar al día — *to be up-to-date.*
  Está al día. *It's up-to-date.*

  poner al día — *to bring up-to-date.*
  Me puso al día. *He brought me up-to-date.*

  por (al) día — *a day.*
  Recibe cinco cartas por (al) día. *He receives five letters a day.*

  por esos días — *around that time.*
  Por esos días volvió José. *Around that time Joe came back.*

  quedarse con el día y la noche — *to be left penniless.*
  Se quedaron con el día y la noche. *They were left penniless.*

  todo el santo día — *all day long; all the livelong day.*
  Trabajan todo el santo día. *They work all day long (all the livelong day).*

  al romper el día — *at dawn; at daybreak.*
  Salieron al romper el día. *They left at dawn (at daybreak).*

  un día de éstos — *one of these days.*
  Nos veremos un día de éstos. *We'll see each other one of these days.*

  vivir al día — *to live from hand to mouth.*
  Vive al día. *He lives from hand to mouth.*

el diamante — *diamond*
   un diamante en bruto — *a diamond in the rough.*
   Es un diamante en bruto. *He's a diamond in the rough.*

diario — *daily*
   a diario — *daily.*
   Nos visitan a diario. *They visit us daily.*

el dicho — *saying*
   dejar dicho — *to leave word.*
   Deje dicho si piensa acompañarnos. *Leave word if you intend to go with us.*

   Del dicho al hecho hay mucho trecho. — *It's easier said than done.*

el diente — *tooth*
   armar hasta los dientes — *to arm to the teeth.*
   Iba armado hasta los dientes. *He was armed to the teeth.*

   enseñar (mostrar) los dientes — *to show one's teeth.*
   Enseñó (mostró) los dientes. *He showed his teeth.*

   hablar entre dientes — *to mumble.*
   Habla entre dientes. *He mumbles.*

   ponérsele los dientes largos — *to get envious.*
   Cuando me contó lo de su viaje a Bali, se me pusieron los dientes largos.
   When she told me about her trip to Bali, I felt really envious.

diestro — *right*
   a diestra y siniestra — *right and left.*
   Caían bombas a diestra y siniestra. *Bombs were falling right and left.*

la dieta — *diet*
   estar a dieta — *to be on a diet.*
   Está a dieta. *She's on a diet.*

la diferencia — *difference*
   a diferencia de — *unlike.*

María, a diferencia de su prima, es muy inteligente. *Mary, unlike her cousin, is very intelligent.*

partir la diferencia — *to split the difference.*
Vamos a partir la diferencia. *Let's split the difference.*

difícil — *difficult*
ser difícil que — *to be unlikely that.*
Es difícil que vengan. *It's unlikely that they'll come.*

el dinero — *money*
hacer dinero — *to make money.*
Han hecho mucho dinero. *They've made a lot of money.*

nadar en dinero (la abundancia) — *to be rolling in money.*
Dicen que el gerente de esa compañía nada en dinero (la abundancia). *They say that the manager of that company is rolling in money.*

Dios — *God*
A Dios gracias. — *Thank heaven.*

A Dios rogando y con el mazo dando (Ayúdate, que Dios te ayudará). — *Heaven (God) helps those who help themselves.*

a la buena de Dios — *haphazardly; (just) any old way.*
Contestó las preguntas a la buena de Dios. *He answered the questions haphazardly (just any old way).*

Al que madruga Dios le ayuda. — *The early bird catches the worm.*

como Dios manda — *the way one is supposed to.*
¿Por qué no trabajan de día como Dios manda? *Why don't they work in the daytime the way one is (you're) supposed to?*

Digan, que de Dios dijeron. — *Let them talk.*

Dios los cría y ellos se juntan. — *Birds of a feather flock together.*

¡Dios me libre! — *Heaven forbid! (Far be it from me!)*

¡Dios mío! — *Good heavens!*

estar de Dios — *to be meant to be; to be fated.*
Estaba de Dios. *It was meant to be (was fated).*

¡Por Dios! — *For heaven's sake!*

sabe Dios — *heaven only knows; there's no telling.*

Está aquí desde hace sabe Dios cuándo. *Heaven only knows (There's no telling) how long he's been here.*

Se va a armar la de Dios es Cristo. — *All hell is (really) going to break loose; the fur is (really) going to fly.*

¡Válgame Dios! — *Good heavens!*

la dirección — *direction*

calle de dirección única — *one-way street.*

Es una calle de dirección única. *It's a one-way street.*

el disgusto — *unpleasantness, annoyance*

a disgusto — *against one's will.*

Lo hicieron a disgusto. *They did it against their will.*

dar(le) disgustos (a) — *to worry (someone).*

Su manera de comportarse me da disgustos. *His behavior worries me.*

estar a disgusto — *to be ill at ease.*

Está a disgusto entre tantas personas. *She is ill at ease among so many people.*

tener un disgusto — *to have a falling out.*

Ha tenido un disgusto con su hijo. *He's had a falling out with his son.*

disparar — *to fire, shoot*

disparar sobre (contra) — *to fire on.*

Los soldados dispararon sobre (contra) los manifestantes. *The soldiers fired on the demonstrators.*

dispararle — *to shoot at someone.*

Le disparamos. *We shot at him.*

disponer — *to dispose*

disponer de — *to have (at one's disposal).*

No dispongo de dinero. *I don't have any money (at my disposal).*

disponerse a (para) — *to get ready to.*

Se disponen a (para) comer. *They're getting ready to eat.*

estar dispuesto a — *to be willing to.*
Está dispuesto a ayudarnos. *He's willing to help us.*

la disposición — *disposal, disposition*
a la disposición de . . . — *at . . . 's disposal.*
Se puso a la disposición de Enrique. *He put (placed) himself at Henry's disposal.*

estar a la disposición de — *to be at one's service.*
Estoy a su disposición. *I am at your service.*

por disposición de — *by arrangement of.*
Trabajaba por disposición de su padre. *His father arranged for him to work.*

la disputa — *dispute*
entrar en disputas — *to get into arguments.*
Siempre entra en disputas. *He is always getting into arguments.*

la distancia — *distance*
mantenerse a prudente distancia — *to keep (at) a safe distance.*
¡Manténgase a prudente distancia! *Keep (at) a safe distance!*

la distinción — *distinction*
a distinción de — *as distinguished from.*
Estudió los síntomas a distinción de las causas. *He studied the symptoms as distinguished from the causes.*

la distracción — *distraction*
por distracción — *absent-mindedly.*
Lo rompió por distracción. *He absent-mindedly broke it.*

doble — *double*
al doble — *double.*
Me lo pagó al doble. *He paid me double for it.*

la docena — *dozen*
la docena del fraile — *a baker's dozen.*

Siempre me dan la docena del fraile. *They always give me a baker's dozen.*

el dogal — *halter, (hangman's) rope*
estar con el dogal a la garganta — *to be in a terrible fix (jam).*
Estaba con el dogal a la garganta. *He was in a terrible fix (jam).*

doler — *to ache, hurt*
dolerle — *to hurt one.*
Le duele la cabeza (garganta, etc.). *His head (throat, etc.) hurts (him).*

el dolor — *pain*
tener dolor de . . . — *to have a . . . ache.*
Tengo dolor de cabeza. *I have a headache.*

el don — *gift*
tener don de gentes — *to have winning ways; to have a way with people.*
Tiene don de gentes. *He has winning ways (a way with people).*

tener el don de mando — *to be a born leader.*
Tiene el don de mando. *He's a born leader.*

dos — *two*
en un dos por tres — *in a flash (jiffy).*
Terminó la carta en un dos por tres. *He finished the letter in a flash (jiffy).*

los dos — *both; both of them.*
Los dos lo hicieron. *They both (Both of them) did it.*

la duda — *doubt*
estar en duda — *to be in doubt.*
Los resultados están en duda. *The results are in doubt.*

no cabe duda (de que) — *there's no doubt (that).*
No cabe duda de que es verdad. *There's no doubt that it's true.*

poner en duda — *to cast doubt on.*
Puso en duda su proposición. *She cast doubt on his proposal.*

sin duda — *no doubt.*

Sin duda es verdad. *No doubt it's true.*

---

dudar — *to doubt*

  no dudar — *not to hesitate.*

  No dude en preguntárselo. *Don't hesitate to ask him.*

---

el dueño — *owner*

  ser dueño de sí mismo — *to have self-control.*

  Es muy dueño de sí mismo. *He has great self-control.*

echar — *to throw*

  echar(se) a — *to burst out.*

  (Se) Echó a reír (llorar). *He burst out laughing (crying).*

  echar a perder — *to ruin; to spoil.*

  Todo se echó a perder. *Everything was ruined (spoiled).*

  echar chispas — *to be hopping mad.*

  Está echando chispas. *He is hopping mad.*

  echar de ver — *to notice.*

  Eché de ver que estaba muy pálida. *I noticed that she was very pale.*

echar (todo) a rodar — *to spoil (everything).*

Su llegada echó a rodar nuestros planes (echó todo a rodar). *His arrival spoiled our plans (spoiled everything).*

echarse a la calle — *to go out on the street.*

Me eché a la calle. *I went out on the street.*

echarse atrás — *to back out.*

Temiendo el resultado, se echó atrás. *Fearing the outcome, he backed out.*

echarse en la cama — *to lie down on the bed.*

Se echó en la cama. *He lay down on the bed.*

echarse encima (echarse sobre las espaldas) — *to take on; to take upon oneself.*

Se echó encima (sobre las espaldas) la responsabilidad. *She took on (took upon herself) the responsibility.*

echarse hacia atrás — *to lean back.*

Se echó hacia atrás. *He leaned back.*

echárselas de — *to fancy oneself (as); to boast of being.*

Se las echa de poeta. *He fancies himself (as) (boasts of being) a poet.*

---

la edad — *age*

de corta edad — *of tender years.*

La acompañaba un niño de corta edad. *She was accompanied by a child of tender years.*

ser mayor de edad — *to be of age.*

Es mayor de edad. *He's of age.*

ser menor de edad — *to be a minor.*

Es menor de edad. *He's a minor.*

tener edad — *to be . . . years old.*

¿Qué edad tiene? *How old is he?*

---

efectivo — *real, actual*

(dinero) efectivo — *cash.*

Pagó con (dinero) efectivo. *He paid cash.*

---

el efecto — *effect*

en efecto — *as a matter of fact; in fact.*

En efecto, son amigos. *As a matter of fact (In fact), they're friends.*

hacer mal efecto — *to have a bad effect.*

Me hizo mal efecto. *It had a bad effect on me.*

---

el ejemplo — *example*

por ejemplo — *for example (instance).*

Me gusta la comida española, por ejemplo, la paella. *I like Spanish food, for example (instance), paella.*

servir de ejemplo — *to set an example.*

Sirve de ejemplo a sus colegas. *He sets an example for his colleagues.*

sin ejemplo — *unparalleled; without precedent.*

Fue una cosa sin ejemplo. *It was something unparalleled (without precedent).*

---

el elefante — *elephant*

un elefante blanco — *a white elephant.*

Es un elefante blanco. *It's a white elephant.*

---

el elemento — *element*

estar en su elemento — *to be in one's element.*

Está en su elemento. *He's in his element.*

---

el embargo — *embargo*

sin embargo — *nevertheless.*

Sin embargo, tiene sus defectos. *Nevertheless, it has its defects.*

---

el embozo — *part of cloak used to cover the face*

quitarse el embozo — *to drop one's mask; to show (tip) one's hand.*

Se quitó el embozo. *He dropped his mask (showed [tipped] his hand).*

---

el empellón — *push*

abrirse paso a empellones — *to push one's way through.*

Se abrió paso a empellones. *She pushed her way through.*

entrar a empellones — *to push one's way in.*

Oyeron el ruido y entraron a empellones. *They heard the noise and pushed their way in.*

empeñar — *to pledge, pawn*
empeñarse en — *to insist on; to persist in.*
Se empeña en cantar. *He insists on (persists in) singing.*

el empeño — *pledge, obligation, determination*
tener empeño en — *to be eager to.*
Tiene empeño en educarse. *He is eager to become educated.*

emplear — *to use, employ*
dar por bien empleado — *to consider well worth the trouble.*
Lo doy por bien empleado. *I consider it well worth the trouble.*

estarle bien empleado (empleársele bien) — *to serve someone right.*
Le está bien empleado (Se le emplea bien). *It serves him right.*

emprender — *to undertake*
emprenderla — *to get into it.*
Había considerado el problema, y anoche la emprendí con mi primo. *I had considered the problem, and last night I got into it with my cousin.*

emprenderla — *to set out.*
La emprendimos para la ciudad. *We set out for the city.*

el empujón — *push*
abrirse paso a empujones — *to push one's way through.*
Se abrió paso a empujones. *She pushed her way through.*

encarar — *to face*
encararse con — *to come face to face with; to face.*
Di la vuelta y me encaré con él. *I turned around and came face to face with (faced) him.*

encararse con — *to face (up to).*
No puede encararse con la realidad. *He can't face (up to) reality.*

encargar — *to entrust*
  encargarse de — *to take charge of.*
  Se encargó de los preparativos. *He took charge of the preparations.*

el encargo — *commission, job*
  por encargo — *to (on) order.*
  Hacía el vestido por encargo. *She made the dress to (on) order.*

encima — *above, at the top*
  encima de todo — *on top of everything else.*
  Encima de todo, perdió su dinero. *On top of everything else, he lost his money.*

la encorvada — *stooping, bending*
  hacer la encorvada — *to malinger.*
  Hacía la encorvada. *He was malingering.*

el encuentro — *encounter, meeting*
  salir al encuentro (a; de) — *to go (out) to meet someone.*
  Le salí al encuentro. *I went (out) to meet him.*

ende
  por ende — *therefore.*
  Está en casa; por ende no está aquí. *He's at home; therefore he's not here.*

la encuesta — *poll*
  hacer una encuesta — *to take a poll.*
  El alcalde hizo una encuesta para medir su popularidad. *The mayor took a poll to measure his popularity.*

enfermo — *sick, ill*
  caer enfermo — *to fall ill.*
  Cayó enfermo. *He fell ill.*

enfrentar — *to face, confront*
  enfrentarse con — *to stand up to; to confront.*
  Se enfrenta con ellos. *She stands up to (confronts) them.*

enfrente — *opposite, in front*

  de enfrente — *across the street; directly opposite.*

  La casa de enfrente es de ellos. *The house across the street (directly opposite) is theirs.*

---

engaño — *deceit, deception*

  llamarse a engaño — *to call foul; allege fraud.*

  Cuando rompieron el contrato, se llamó a engaño. *When they broke the contract, he called foul (alleged fraud).*

---

la enhorabuena — *congratulations*

  dar la enhorabuena — *to offer congratulations.*

  Le doy mi más sincera enhorabuena. *I offer you my heartiest congratulations.*

---

el entendedor — *one who understands*

  A(l) buen entendedor, pocas palabras. — *A word to the wise is suffcient.*

---

entender — *to understand*

  a (según) su entender — *in one's opinion; to one's way of thinking.*

  A (según) mi entender, el cuadro no vale nada. *In my opinion (To my way of thinking), the picture isn't worth anything.*

---

enterar — *to inform*

  enterarse de — *to find out about; to learn of.*

  Se enteró de mi llegada. *He found out about (learned of) my arrival.*

---

entero — *whole, entire*

  por entero — *completely.*

  La gasolina se agotó por entero. *The gas(oline) was completely used up.*

---

entonces — *then*

  de entonces — *of that time.*

  Los vestidos de entonces eran largos. *The dresses of that time were long.*

  desde entonces — *(ever) since then.*

Desde entonces la vemos raras veces. *(Ever) Since then we rarely see her.*

para entonces — *by that time.*
Para entonces llovía. *By that time it was raining.*

por (en) aquel entonces — *at that time.*
Por (En) aquel entonces no había televisión. *At that time there was no television.*

---

entrar — *to enter*

entrar en (a) — *to enter.*
Entraron en el (al) café. *They entered the cafe.*

muy entrada la mañana (noche) — *well along in the morning (night).*
Esperamos hasta muy entrada la mañana (noche). *We waited until well along in the morning (night).*

---

entre — *between, among*

entre . . . y . . . — *half . . . and half . . . .*
Es una obra entre trágica y cómica. *It's a work half tragic and half comic.*

por entre — *among.*
Se paseaba por entre los niños. *He was walking around among the children.*

---

la envidia — *envy*

comerse de envidia — *to be eaten up with envy.*
Se comían de envidia. *They were eaten up with envy.*

---

la época — *epoch, period*

hacer época — *to make quite a splash; to be an epoch-making element.*
Hizo época. *It made quite a splash (was an epoch-making event).*

para esa época — *by that time.*
Para esa época se había terminado. *By that time it was over.*

por esa (la) época — *around that time.*
Por esa (la) época les nació la hija. *Around that time, their daughter was born.*

el equipaje — *baggage*
   hacer el equipaje — *to pack one's bags.*
   Hizo su equipaje. *He packed his bags.*

la equivocación — *mistake*
   por equivocación — *by mistake.*
   Por equivocación me llevé su libro. *By mistake I carried off his book.*

equivocar — *to mistake*
   equivocarse de — *to be wrong about; to make a mistake about.*
   Me equivoqué de cuarto. *I went to the wrong room (I made a mistake about the room).*

la escala — *ladder; scale; port of call*
   en gran escala — *on a large scale.*
   Se fabrican en gran escala. *They are manufactured on a large scale.*

   hacer escala — *to put in; make a stop.*
   El barco no hace escala en Barcelona. *The ship doesn't put in (make a stop) at Barcelona.*

la escalera — *stairs*
   tomar por la escalera arriba — *to start upstairs.*
   Tomó por la escalera arriba. *He started upstairs.*

el escándalo — *scandal*
   armar un escándalo — *to make a scene.*
   Pedro armó un escándalo cuando vio a su novia en la fiesta con otro hombre. *Pedro made a scene when he saw his girlfriend at the party with another man.*

escapar — *to escape*
   escapar a — *to escape from.*
   Escapó al policía. *He escaped from the policeman.*

el escape — *escape, flight*
  salir a escape — *to go off in great haste (on the run).*
  Salió a escape. *He went off in great haste (on the run).*

escaso — *scarce, scant*
  estar escaso de — *to be short of.*
  Están escasos de fondos. *They are short of money.*

la escena — *scene; stage*
  estar en escena — *to be on stage.*
  Está en escena. *He's on stage.*

  poner en escena — *to stage (put on).*
  Pusieron la obra en escena. *They staged (put on) the play.*

escondido — *hidden*
  a escondidas — *on the sly; secretly.*
  Lo practicaba a escondidas. *She practiced it on the sly (secretly).*

  a escondidas de — *without the knowledge of.*
  Fue a escondidas de su madre. *She went without the knowledge of her mother.*

el escote — *neckline (of a garment); quota, share (of an expense)*
  pagar a escote — *to go Dutch.*
  Pagaron a escote. *They went Dutch.*

escrito — *written*
  estar escrito — *to be fate(d); to be meant to be; to be written (in the stars).*
  Estaba escrito. *It was fate(d) (was meant to be; was written in the stars).*

  por escrito — *in writing.*
  Hizo la solicitud por escrito. *He applied in writing.*

escupir — *to spit*
  ser escupido su ... — *to be the spitting image (spit and image) of one's ....*
  Es escupida su madre. *She's the spitting image (spit and image) of her mother.*

el esfuerzo — *effort*

no omitir esfuerzos — *to spare no effort.*

No omitimos esfuerzos para obtenerlo. *We spared no effort to obtain it.*

eso — *that*

a eso de — *at about.*

Empieza a eso de las cuatro. *It's beginning at about four.*

eso de — *that business (matter) about.*

Me contó eso de la huelga. *He told me that business (matter) about the strike.*

¡Eso es! — *That's right!*

¡Eso sí que es! — *Yes indeed!*

¡Eso sí que no! — *No indeed!*

ir a eso — *to come to that.*

A eso voy. *I'm coming to that.*

por eso — *that's why; for that reason; therefore.*

Por eso tuvimos que esperar. *That's why (for that reason; therefore) we had to wait.*

y eso que — *in spite of (despite) the fact that.*

Se viste muy mal, y eso que tiene mucho dinero. *She dresses very poorly, in spite of (despite) the fact that she has a lot of money.*

la espada — *sword*

Entre la espada y la pared. — *Between the devil and the deep blue sea.*

la espalda — *back*

a espaldas de . . . — *behind . . . 's back.*

¿Por qué lo hicieron a espaldas de su padre? *Why did they do it behind their father's back?*

darle (volverle) la espalda — *to turn one's back on someone.*

Me dio (volvió) la espalda. *He turned his back on me.*

de espaldas — *from behind.*

Fue atacado de espaldas. *He was attacked from behind.*

de espaldas — *on one's back.*

Lo tiraron de espaldas. *They threw him on his back.*

de espaldas a — *with one's back up against.*

Lo pusieron de espaldas al muro. *They put him with his back up against the wall.*

estar de espaldas — *to have one's back turned.*

Estaba de espaldas. *He had his back turned.*

---

el espárrago — *asparagus*

mandar a freír espárragos — *to tell (someone) to go jump in the lake (to go fly a kite).*

Lo mandé a freír espárragos. *I told him to go jump in the lake (to go fly a kite).*

---

especial — *special*

en especial — *especially.*

Me gustó la comedia, en especial el último acto. *I liked the play, especially the last act.*

---

la especie — *sort, kind*

pagar en especie — *to pay in kind.*

Me pagaron en especie. *They paid me in kind.*

---

la espera — *wait(ing)*

en espera de — *waiting for.*

Pasó dos horas en espera del tren. *He spent two hours waiting for the train.*

---

esperar — *to hope; expect; wait*

ser de esperar — *to be to be hoped.*

Es de esperar que venga. *It is to be hoped that she'll come.*

---

la espina — *thorn, spine*

darle mala espina — *to worry one (arouse one's suspicions).*

Me da mala espina. *He worries me (arouses my suspicions).*

---

el espinazo — *backbone*
 partirse el espinazo — *to break one's back.*
 Se partían el espinazo trabajando. *They were breaking their backs working.*

el espíritu — *spirit*
 exhalar (despedir) el espíritu — *to give up the ghost.*
 Exhaló (despidío) el espíritu. *He gave up the ghost.*

la esponja — *sponge*
 beber como una esponja — *to drink like a fish.*
 Tiene un tío que bebe como una esponja. *She has an uncle who drinks like a fish.*
 tirar (arrojar) la esponja — *to throw in the towel (sponge).*
 Discutió con ella por una hora pero por fin tiró (arrojó) la esponja. *He argued with her for an hour but finally threw in the towel (sponge).*

el espumarajo — *froth*
 echar espumarajos por la boca — *to foam at the mouth.*
 Echaba espumarajos por la boca. *He was foaming at the mouth.*

el estado — *state*
 estar en estado interesante — *to be in the family way (to be in an interesting condition).*
 Estaba en estado interesante. *She was in the family way (in an interesting condition).*

estar — *to be*
 estamos a . . . — *today is . . . .*
 Estamos a 20 de agosto. *Today is August 20.*
 estar bien — *to be all right (OK).*
 Está bien. *(That's) all right (OK).*
 estar bien — *to be comfortable.*
 Está bien en el sofá. *He is comfortable on the sofa.*
 estar bien con — *to be on good terms with.*
 Estoy bien con él. *I'm on good terms with him.*

estar con — *to have.*
Estoy con la gripe. *I have the flu.*

estar con — *to agree with.*
Estamos con usted. *We agree with you.*

estar para (por) — *to be about to.*
Están para (por) aceptar. *They are about to accept.*

estar por — *to be in favor of.*
No está por decírselo ahora. *He isn't in favor of telling them (about it) now.*

---

el estilo — *style*

algo por el estilo — *something like that.*
Me dijo que estaba agotado o algo por el estilo. *He told me he was exhausted, or something like that.*

cosas por el estilo — *things of that sort.*
Tenía pulseras, aretes, y cosas por el estilo. *She had bracelets, earrings, and things of that sort.*

---

esto — *this*

con esto — *with this.*
Con esto se despidió. *With this she left.*

esto de — *this business (matter) about.*
Esto de los impuestos no me gusta. *I don't like this business (matter) about the taxes.*

por esto — *for this reason.*
Por esto más vale esperar. *For this reason it's better to wait.*

---

el estómago — *stomach*

revolverle el estómago — *to turn one's stomach.*
Me revuelve el estómago. *It turns my stomach.*

---

la estrella — *star*

ver las estrellas — *to see stars.*
El golpe me hizo ver las estrellas. *The blow made me see stars.*

poner sobre (por) las estrellas — *to praise to the skies.*
La pusieron sobre (por) las estrellas. *They praised her to the skies.*

estrenar — *to use (wear, show, perform, etc.) for the first time*
estrenarse — *to open.*
La obra se estrenó anoche. *The play opened last night.*

el estribo — *stirrup*
    estar con (tener) un pie en el estribo — *to have one foot in the grave.*
    Su pobre abuelo ya está con un pie en el estribo (la sepultura). *His poor grandfather already has one foot in the grave.*

    estar con (tener) un pie en el estribo — *to be about to leave (on the point of leaving).*
    Lo encontré con un pie en el estribo y no pude hablar con él. *I found him about to leave (on the point of leaving) and I couldn't talk to him.*

    perder los estribos — *to lose one's head; to get rattled.*
    Perdió los estribos. *He lost his head (got rattled).*

el estudio — *study*
    plan de estudios — *curriculum.*
    Hay que estudiar bien el plan de estudios. *You have to study the curriculum carefully.*

la etiqueta — *etiquette*
  de etiqueta — *formally.*
  Vinieron vestidos de etiqueta. *They came dressed formally.*

  con etiqueta — *formally.*
  Nos recibieron con mucha etiqueta. *They received us very formally.*

la evidencia — *evidence*
  ponerle en evidencia — *to show someone up.*
  Lo hicieron para ponerla en evidencia. *They did it in order to show her up.*

  tener la evidencia — *to be obvious to one.*
  Tengo la evidencia de que Juan no estuvo. *It's obvious to me that John wasn't there.*

el examen — *examination*
  salir bien en (aprobar) un examen — *to pass an exam.*
  Salió bien en (Aprobó) su examen. *He passed his exam.*

  sufrir (presentar) un examen — *to take an exam.*
  Sufrió (Presentó) dos exámenes. *He took two exams.*

exceder — *to exceed*
  excederse a sí mismo — *to outdo oneself.*
  Se ha excedido a sí mismo. *He has outdone himself.*

la excelencia — *excellence*
  por excelencia — *par excellence.*
  Es un tenorio por excelencia. *He's a Don Juan par excellence.*

la excepción — *exception*
  a excepción de — *with the exception of.*
  Vinieron todos a excepción de Felipe. *They all came with the exception of Philip.*

el éxito — *success*
  con (buen) éxito — *successfully.*

Terminó sus estudios con (buen) éxito. *He finished his studies successfully.*

---

la expectativa — *expectation*

estar a la expectativa de — *to be on the lookout for.*

Estamos a la expectativa de nuestros amigos. *We are on the lookout for our friends.*

---

las expensas — *expenses*

a expensas de — *at the expense of.*

Trabajaba quince horas diarias a expensas de su salud. *He was working fifteen hours a day at the expense of his health.*

---

explicar — *to explain*

explicar clases — *to teach.*

Explica clases de francés. *She teaches French.*

explicarse — *to understand.*

No me explico por qué es así. *I can't understand why it's that way.*

---

extranjero — *foreign*

en el extranjero — *abroad.*

Están pasando el verano en el extranjero. *They are spending the summer abroad.*

ir al extranjero — *to go abroad.*

Todos los años van al extranjero. *Every year they go abroad.*

---

el extremo — *end, extreme*

en extremo — *a very great deal.*

Me gusta en extremo. *I like it a very great deal.*

llegar al extremo de — *to reach the point of.*

Llegó al extremo de darle una bofetada. *He reached the point of slapping him.*

pasar de un extremo a otro — *to go from one extreme to the other.*

Han pasado de un extremo a otro. *They have gone from one extreme to the other.*

---

fácil — *easy*
  es fácil — *it is likely.*
  Es fácil que lo hagan. *It's likely that they'll do it.*

  lo más fácil — *the most likely.*
  Lo más fácil es que se haya dormido. *The most likely is that he's fallen asleep.*

la facilidad — *ease, facility*
  dar (toda clase de) facilidades — *to facilitate; to offer every assistance; to make everything very easy.*
  Me dieron toda clase de facilidades. *They made everything very easy for me (They facilitated things for me; They offered me every assistance).*

facilitar — *to facilitate*
  facilitar — *to make available.*
  Me facilitó su coche. *He made his car available to me.*

la falda — *skirt*
  cosido a las faldas de — *tied to the apron strings of.*
  Anda cosido a las faldas de su mamá. *He is tied to his mother's apron strings.*

la falta — *lack*
  a falta de — *for lack of.*
  Lo coció en manteca a falta de aceite. *She cooked it in lard for lack of oil.*

  hacer falta — *to (be) need(ed).*
  Le hace falta dinero. *He needs money.*

  sin falta — *without fail.*
  Se lo daré sin falta. *I will give it to you without fail.*

faltar — *to be lacking, be missing*
  faltar a — *to fail to show up for.*

113

Faltó a la cita. *He failed to show up for the appointment.*

faltar a clase — *to cut class.*

Faltó a dos clases. *He cut two classes.*

faltar ... para ... — *to be ... off.*

Faltaba menos de un mes para la boda. *The wedding was less than a month off.*

faltar ... para ... — *to be... till (of) ....*

Faltan diez para las ocho. *It is ten till (of) eight.*

faltar poco — *to be almost ready.*

Falta poco para que empiece la comedia. *The play is almost ready to begin.*

faltarle experiencia — *to lack experience.*

Le falta experiencia. *He lacks experience.*

¡No faltaba más! — Claro que estoy enojado. ¡No faltaba más! *Of course I'm mad. The very idea (That's the last straw)!*

¡No faltaba más! — ¡No faltaba más! Lo haré con mucho gusto. *Why, of course! I'll be glad to do it.*

no faltar quien — *to be those who.*

No faltaba quien lo considerara avaro. *There were those who considered him miserly.*

---

la fama — *fame*

correr (ser) fama (que) — *to be rumored that.*

Corre (Es) fama que no están casados. *It's rumored that they're not married.*

tener fama de — *to have a reputation for.*

La tienda tiene fama de dar buen servicio. *The store has a reputation for giving good service.*

---

la familia — *family*

en familia — *within the family; in the family circle.*

Trataron el asunto en familia. *They discussed the matter within the family (in the family circle).*

---

fas

    por fas o por nefas — *by hook or by crook.*

    Por fas o por nefas lo conseguirán. *They'll get it by hook or by crook.*

---

el favor — *favor*

    a (en) favor de — *in favor of.*

    Juanita rehusó la presidencia a (en) favor de Consuelo. *Juanita declined the presidency in favor of Consuelo.*

    a su favor — *in one's favor.*

    Decidió a mi favor. *He decided in my favor.*

    hacer el favor de — *please.*

    Haga el favor de firmar. *Please sign.*

    por favor — *please.*

    Pase, por favor. *Come in, please.*

---

la fe — *faith*

    dar fe — *to certify.*

    El documento da fe de que murió ayer. *The document certifies that he died yesterday.*

    de buena (mala) fe — *in good (bad) faith.*

    Obraba de buena (mala) fe. *He was acting in good (bad) faith.*

---

la fecha — *date*

    hasta la fecha — *to date.*

    Hasta la fecha no he recibido nada. *To date I haven't received anything.*

---

la feria — *fair*

    Cada uno cuenta de la feria según le va en ella. — *Everyone gives his own account of an event.*

---

fiar — *to trust*

    al fiado — *on credit.*

    Nunca compro al fiado. *I never buy on credit.*

    fiarse de — *to trust (in); to rely on.*

    No nos fiamos de ella. *We don't trust (rely on) her.*

la fiera — *wild animal*
  como una fiera — *furiously.*
  Reaccionó como una fiera. *He reacted furiously.*

  ser una fiera para — *to be a fiend for.*
  Es una fiera para el estudio. *He's a fiend for study.*

  trabajar como una fiera — *to work like a dog.*
  José trabaja como una fiera. *Joe works like a dog.*

la fiesta — *festivity, celebration; (religious) feast, holiday*
  aguar la fiesta — *to be a wet blanket (kill-joy).*
  Siempre nos agua la fiesta. *He's always a wet blanket (kill-joy).*

  dar una fiesta — *to throw (give) a party.*
  Van a darnos una fiesta. *They're going to throw (give) a party for us.*

  estar de fiesta — *to be in a holiday mood.*
  Están de fiesta. *They're in a holiday mood.*

  no estar para fiestas — *to be in no mood for joking.*
  No estoy para fiestas. *I'm in no mood for joking.*

figurar — *to figure*
  ¡Figúrese! — *Just imagine!*

fijar — *to fix, set, establish*
  fijarse en — *to notice.*
  Fíjese en aquel edificio. *Notice that building.*

fijo — *fixed, firm*
  de fijo — *for sure.*
  No lo sé de fijo. *I don't know for sure.*

la fila — *row, file, rank*
  en fila india — *in single (Indian) file.*
  Pasaron en fila india. *They went by in single (Indian) file.*

  incorporarse a filas — *to join the army.*
  Se incorporó a filas. *He joined the army.*

llamar a filas — *to call to the colors.*
Fueron llamados a filas. *They were called to the colors.*

---

el fin — *end*

a fin de — *at the end of.*
A fin de año me voy. *I'm leaving at the end of the year.*

a (en) fin de cuentas — *after all.*
A (En) fin de cuentas, son mis padres. *After all, they are my parents.*

a fines de — *around (toward) the end of.*
Nació a fines del siglo XIX. *He was born around (toward) the end of the nineteenth century.*

al fin — *finally.*
Al fin se marcharon. *Finally they left.*

al fin y al cabo — *after all.*
Al fin y al cabo no se casaron. *They didn't get married after all.*

dar fin a — *to complete.*
Dio fin a su obra maestra. *He completed his masterpiece.*

en fin — *in short.*
En fin, es todo lo que tengo. *In short, it's all I have.*

llevar mal fin — *to have bad intentions.*
Lleva mal fin. *He has bad intentions.*

poner (dar) fin a — *to put a stop (an end) to.*
Puso (Dio) fin al ruido. *She put a stop (an end) to the noise.*

por fin — *at last.*
Por fin llegó. *At last he arrived.*

(un) sin fin de — *no end of.*
La dejó con un sin fin de deudas. *He left her with no end of debts.*

---

el final — *end*

al final — *at the end.*
Al final de la comedia, murió el protagonista. *At the end of the play, the protagonist died.*

al final de la página — *at the bottom of the page.*

117

Lo apunté al final de la página. *I made a note of it at the bottom of the page.*

firme — *firm, solid*
estar en lo firme — *to be on firm ground; to be in the right.*
Está en lo firme. *He's on firm ground (in the right).*

trabajar de firme — *to work very hard.*
Voy a trabajar de firme. *I'm going to work very hard.*

flagrante — *blazing, flaming*
coger (pescar, pillar) en flagrante — *to catch in the act (red-handed).*
Lo cogieron (pescaron, pillaron) en flagrante. *They caught him in the act (red-handed).*

el flechazo — *arrow wound (love's)*
tener un flechazo — *to become infatuated; to fall in love at first sight.*
Cuando vio a Raúl en el bar, tuvo un flechazo. *When she saw Raúl in the bar, she was smitten instantly (it was love at first sight).*

la flor — *flower*
a flor de agua (tierra) — *at water (ground) level.*
Esas plantas crecen a flor de agua (tierra). *Those plants grow at water (ground) level.*

a flor de labio — *on the tip of one's tongue.*
Tenía la respuesta a flor de labio. *He had the answer on the tip of his tongue.*

decir (echar) flores — *to flatter (sweet-talk).*
Le gusta decir (echar) flores a las señoritas. *He likes to flatter (sweet-talk) the young ladies.*

la flor y nata — *the cream (flower).*
En la guerra perdimos la flor y nata de nuestra juventud. *In the war we lost the cream (flower) of our youth.*

el flote — *floating*
mantenerse a flote — *to stay afloat.*
No puede mantenerse a flote. *He can't stay afloat.*

118

ponerse a flote — *to get on one's feet again; to get out of the jam.*
Por fin pudimos ponernos a flote. *We finally succeeded in getting on our feet again (getting out of the jam).*

el fondo — *bottom; fund*
  a fondo — *thoroughly.*
Lo aprendió a fondo. *She learned it thoroughly.*

  andar escaso de fondos — *to be short of money.*
Ando escaso de fondos. *I'm short of money.*

  del fondo — *back.*
Está en la pared del fondo. *It's on the back wall.*

  dormir a fondo — *to sleep soundly.*
Durmieron a fondo. *They slept soundly.*

  en el fondo — *at heart.*
En el fondo es una buena persona. *At heart he is a good person.*

  entrar en el fondo del asunto — *to get to the bottom of the matter.*
Tenemos que entrar en el fondo del asunto. *We have to get to the bottom of the matter.*

  sin fondo — *bottomless.*
Es un lago sin fondo. *It's a bottomless lake.*

la forma — *form*
  de todas formas — *in any case.*
De todas formas viene mañana. *In any case he's coming tomorrow.*

  en forma de — *in the shape of.*
Me mandó un prendedor en forma de sombrero. *He sent me a pin in the shape of a hat.*

  en la misma forma — *the same way.*
Contestó en la misma forma. *She answered the same way.*

la fortuna — *fortune*
  por fortuna — *fortunately.*
Por fortuna puede venir. *Fortunately he can come.*

probar fortuna — *to try one's luck.*

Voy a probar fortuna. *I'm going to try my luck.*

francés — *French*

despedirse (irse) a la francesa — *to take French leave.*

Se despidió (Se fue) a la francesa. *He took French leave.*

la frecuencia — *frequency*

con frecuencia — *frequently.*

Nos visita con frecuencia. *He visits us frequently.*

freír — *to fry*

Al freír será el reír. — *We'll see when the time comes; time will tell.*

el frente — *front*

al frente de — *in charge of.*

Vino aquí al frente de un grupo de estudiantes. *He came here in charge of a group of students.*

dar frente a — *to face.*

Nuestra casa da frente a la iglesia. *Our house faces the church.*

en frente de (frente a) — *in front of.*

Nos veremos en frente del (frente al) hotel. *We'll meet in front of the hotel.*

frente a — *across from.*

Frente a la fábrica hay una carnicería. *Across from the factory there is a butcher shop.*

frente a — *in the face of.*

Se mostró muy valiente frente al peligro. *He was very brave in the face of (the) danger.*

frente a frente — *face to face.*

Los dos enemigos se encontraron frente a frente. *The two enemies met face to face.*

hacer frente a — *to face up to.*

No pudo hacer frente a sus problemas personales. *She couldn't face up to her personal problems.*

ponerse al frente — *to head.*
Se puso al frente de la rebelión. *He headed the rebellion.*

---

la frente — *forehead*
  traer escrito en la frente — *to be written all over one's face.*
  Lo trae escrito en la frente. *It's written all over his face.*

---

fresco — *cool, fresh*
  quedarse tan fresco — *to stay cool; to be as cool as a cucumber.*
  Se quedó tan fresco. *He stayed cool (was as cool as a cucumber).*

  tomar el fresco — *to get a breath of (fresh) air.*
  Tomaban el fresco. *They were getting a breath of (fresh) air.*

---

frío — *cold*
  hacer frío — *to be cold.*
  Hace frío hoy. *It's cold today.*

  tener frío — *to be (feel) cold.*
  Tiene frío. *She's cold.*

---

frisar — *to near, approach*
  frisar en — *to get close to.*
  Frisaba en los cuarenta años. *She was getting close to forty.*

---

frito — *fried*
  estar frito — *to have had it.*
  ¡Estamos fritos! *We've had it!*

---

el fruto — *fruit*
  dar fruto — *to bear fruit.*
  Esas plantas no darán fruto. *Those plants will not bear fruit.*

  sin fruto — *fruitlessly; in vain.*
  Se esforzó sin fruto. *He exerted himself fruitlessly (in vain).*

---

el fuego — *fire*
  a fuego vivo (lento) — *over a high (low) flame.*
  Se cuecen a fuego vivo (lento). *You cook them over a high (low) flame.*

darle fuego (lumbre) — *to give someone a light.*
Le di fuego (lumbre). *I gave her a light.*

hacer fuego — *to (open) fire.*
Hicieron fuego al gentío. *They fired (opened fire) on the crowd.*

jugar con fuego — *to play with fire.*
Está jugando con fuego. *He's playing with fire.*

pegar (prender) fuego a — *to set fire to.*
Pegó (Prendió) fuego al documento. *He set fire to the document.*

poner a fuego y sangre — *to lay waste.*
Los invasores pusieron a fuego y sangre toda la comarca. *The invaders laid waste the whole district.*

---

fuera — *out(side)*

estar fuera de sí — *to be beside oneself.*
Estaba fuera de sí. *He was beside himself.*

por fuera — *(on the) outside.*
Pintó la casa por fuera. *He painted the outside of the house. (He painted the house on the outside).*

---

la fuerza — *strength, force*

a fuerza de — *by dint of.*
Se hizo rico a fuerza de su propio trabajo. *He got rich by dint of his own work.*

a la fuerza — *against one's will.*
Lo hizo a la fuerza. *He did it against his will.*

a la fuerza — *by force; forcibly.*
Los soldados entraron a la fuerza. *The soldiers entered by force (forcibly).*

a viva fuerza — *by pure (sheer) force.*
Alcanzó a hacerlo a viva fuerza. *He managed to do it by pure (sheer) force.*

sacar fuerzas de flaqueza — *to make a tremendous effort; to summon up one's courage.*
Sacando fuerzas de flaqueza, le dije que se marchara. *Making a tremendous effort (Summoning up my courage), I told him to leave.*

ser superior a sus fuerzas — *to be too much for one.*
Esto es superior a mis fuerzas. *This is too much for me.*

el furor — *furor*
hacer furor — *to make a hit.*
El mono hizo furor en el circo. *The monkey made a hit at the circus.*

la furia — *fury*
hecho una furia — *mad as a hornet.*
Se veía que estaba hecho una furia. *You could see that he was mad as a hornet.*

el futuro — *future*
en lo futuro — *in the future.*
En lo futuro pórtate bien. *In the future, behave properly.*

en un futuro próximo — *in the near future.*
Haremos el viaje en un futuro próximo. *We will make the trip in the near future.*

el galgo — *greyhound*
De casta le viene al galgo ser rabilargo. — *Like father, like son; A chip off the old block; He comes by it honestly.*

el galope — *gallop*
a galope (a galope tendido) — *at a gallop; at full speed.*
Salió a galope (a galope tendido). *He set off at a gallop (at full speed).*

la gallina — *hen*
acostarse con las gallinas — *to go to bed with the chickens [early].*
Se acuestan con las gallinas. *They go to bed with the chickens.*

como gallina en corral ajeno — *like a fish out of water.*
Estoy como gallina en corral ajeno. *I feel like a fish out of water.*

    matar la gallina de los huevos de oro — *to kill the goose that laid the golden eggs.*

    Mató la gallina de los huevos de oro. *He killed the goose that laid the golden eggs.*

el gallito — *small rooster*

    el gallito del lugar — *the cock of the walk.*

    Le gusta ser el gallito del lugar. *He likes to be the cock of the walk.*

el gallo — *rooster*

    en menos que canta un gallo — *as quick as a wink; in the twinkling of an eye.*

    Se escapó en menos que canta un gallo. *He escaped as quick as a wink (in the twinkling of an eye).*

la gana — *desire*

    darle la gana — *to feel like.*

    No me da la gana. *I don't feel like it.*

    Harán lo que les dé la (real) gana. *They'll do whatever they feel like.*

    de buena (mala) gana — *willingly (unwillingly).*

    Lo aceptó de buena (mala) gana. *She accepted it willingly (unwillingly).*

    reventar de ganas de — *to be dying to.*

    Reventaba de ganas de reír. *He was dying to laugh.*

    tener ganas de — *to feel like.*

    Tiene ganas de trabajar. *He feels like working.*

la garra — *claw*

    caer en las garras de — *to fall into the clutches of.*

    Cayó en las garras de su enemigo. *He fell into the clutches of his enemy.*

    sacar de las garras de — *to free from someone's clutches.*

    La sacaron de nuestras garras. *They freed her from our clutches.*

el gasto — *expense*

    meterse en gastos — *to go to the expense.*

    Se metió en gastos de componerlo. *He went to the expense of repairing it.*

sufragar (pagar) los gastos — *to pay (the expenses) for; to foot the bill.*
Sufragó los gastos de mi educación. *He paid (footed the bill) for my education.*

---

el gato — *cat*
  (Aquí) hay gato encerrado. — *There's something fishy (here); There's more (here) than meets the eye.*

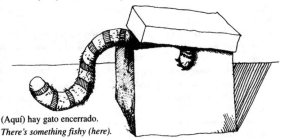

(Aquí) hay gato encerrado.
There's something fishy (here).

  dar gato por liebre — *to put something over; deceive.*
  No se deje dar gato por liebre. *Don't let them put anything over on you (deceive you).*
  ponerle el cascabel al gato — *to bell the cat.*

---

gatas
  a gatas — *crawling (on all fours).*
  Tuvimos que entrar a gatas. *We had to crawl in (go in on all fours).*

---

general — *general*
  en (por lo) general — *in general.*
  En (Por lo) general se come muy poco aquí. *In general they eat very little here.*

---

el genio — *disposition, character; genius*
  Genio y figura, hasta la sepultura. — *You can't make a silk purse out of a sow's ear; The leopard can't change his spots.*

tener mal (buen) genio — *to be bad (good)-tempered.*
Tiene mal (buen) genio. *He's bad (good)-tempered.*

la gente — *people*
la gente de bien — *decent (nice) people.*
La gente de bien no va allí. *Decent (Nice) people don't go there.*

el gesto — *face; gesture*
hacer gestos — *to make faces.*
A ese niño le encanta hacer gestos. *That child loves making faces.*

el giro — *turn*
tomar un giro favorable — *to take a turn for the better.*
Cuando ya estábamos casi desesperados, las cosas tomaron un giro
favorable. *When we were almost in despair, things took a turn for the
better.*

el globo — *globe*
en globo — *as a whole; all together.*
Hay que ver las cosas en globo. *You have to look at things as a whole (all
together).*

la gloria — *glory*
estar en la gloria (en sus glorias) — *to be in one's glory; to be in
seventh heaven.*
Estaban en la gloria (en sus glorias). *They were in their glory (in seventh
heaven).*

saber (oler) a gloria — *to taste (smell) heavenly.*
Sabe (Huele) a gloria. *It tastes (smells) heavenly.*

el golpe — *blow, stroke*
a puros golpes de suerte — *through sheer (strokes of) luck.*
Acumuló una fortuna a puros golpes de suerte. *He accumulated a fortune
through sheer (strokes of) luck.*

al primer golpe de vista — *at first glance.*

Descubrieron al primer golpe de vista que no era verdad. *They discovered at first glance that it wasn't true.*

cerrar de golpe — *to slam.*
Cerró de golpe la puerta. *She slammed the door.*

dar golpes — *to beat.*
Daba golpes al burro. *He was beating the burro.*

de golpe (y porrazo) — *all of a sudden.*
De golpe (y porrazo) se desmayó. *All of a sudden she fainted.*

de un golpe — *in one gulp.*
Tomó de un golpe la medicina. *He took the medicine in one gulp.*

el golpe de gracia — *the coup de grâce.*
Le dieron el golpe de gracia. *They gave him the coup de grâce.*

no dar golpe — *not to lift a finger.*
No da golpe. *He doesn't lift a finger.*

---

gordo — *fat*
Se armó la gorda. — *There was a terrible row.*

---

la gorra — *cap*
vivir de gorra — *to live (to sponge) off other people; to live at other people's expense.*
Vive de gorra. *He lives (sponges) off other people (He lives at other people's expense).*

---

la gota — *drop*
gota a gota — *drop by drop.*
El agua salía gota a gota. *The water was coming out drop by drop.*

no ver gota — *not to be able to see a thing.*
No veo gota. *I can't see a thing.*

sudar la gota gorda — *to sweat blood; to make a superhuman effort.*
Tuvimos que sudar la gota gorda para contentar a nuestro padre. *We had to sweat blood (to make a superhuman effort) to satisfy our father.*

---

gozar — *to enjoy*
    gozar de — *to enjoy.*
    Goza de buena salud. *She enjoys good health.*

el gozo — *joy*
    El gozo en el pozo. — *It's all fallen through; it's gone down the drain.*
    no caber en sí de gozo — *to be beside oneself with joy.*
    María no cabe en sí de gozo. *Mary is beside herself with joy.*
    saltar (brincar) de gozo — *to jump for joy.*
    Saltaba (Brincaba) de gozo. *He was jumping for joy.*

la gracia — *grace; pleasantry, witticism*
    caer de la gracia de — *to fall out of favor (to fall in disfavor) with.*
    Cayó de la gracia del gerente y lo despidieron. *He fell out of favor (fell into disfavor) with the manager and they fired him.*
    caerle en gracia — *to take a liking to.*
    Me cayó en gracia. *I took a liking to her.*
    causar gracia — *to make laugh.*
    Sus chistes me causan gracia. *His jokes make me laugh.*
    dar las gracias — *to thank.*
    Le dieron las gracias. *They thanked him.*
    gracias a — *thanks to.*
    Todo ha salido bien, gracias a su ayuda. *Everything has turned out well, thanks to your help.*
    tener (hacer) (mucha) gracia — *to be (very) funny.*
    Tiene (Hace) (mucha) gracia. *It's (very) funny.*

el grado — *will*
    de (buen) grado — *willingly.*
    Lo hizo de (buen) grado. *He did it willingly.*
    mal de su grado (de mal grado) — *against one's will.*
    Lo hizo mal de su grado (de mal grado). *He did it against his will.*

el grado — *degree*
   de grado en grado — *by degrees.*
   Se acercaban de grado en grado. *They were drawing nearer by degrees.*

grande — *large, great*
   en grande — *as a whole.*
   Debemos considerar el asunto en grande. *We must consider the matter as a whole.*

   a lo (en) grande — *grandly; on a grand scale.*
   Le gusta vivir a lo (en) grande. *He likes to live grandly (on a grand scale).*

el grano — *grain*
   apartar el grano de la paja — *to separate the wheat from the chaff.*
   Es difícil apartar el grano de la paja. *It's hard to separate the wheat from the chaff.*

   con un (con su) grano de sal — *with a grain of salt.*
   Hay que tomar lo que dice con un (con su) grano de sal. *You have to take what he says with a grain of salt.*

   ir al grano — *to get to the point.*
   Siempre va al grano. *He always gets to the point.*

el grito — *cry, shout*
   a gritos — *at the top of one's voice.*
   Nos llamó a gritos. *He called (to) us at the top of his voice.*

   dar gritos — *to shout.*
   Daba gritos. *He was shouting.*

   lanzar un grito — *to cry out.*
   Lanzó un grito. *She cried out.*

   poner el grito en el cielo — *to hit the ceiling; to raise a big howl.*
   Puso el grito en el cielo. *He hit the ceiling (raised a big howl).*

el guante — *glove*
   arrojar el guante — *to throw down the gauntlet.*
   Arrojó el guante. *He threw down the gauntlet.*

   con guante blanco — *with kid gloves.*

A ese señor hay que tratarlo con guante blanco. *You have to handle that gentleman with kid gloves.*

---

guardar — *to keep, guard*
guardarse de — *to refrain from.*
Guárdese de hacer comentarios. *Refrain from making comments.*

---

la guardia — *guard*
de guardia — *on duty.*
¿Quién está de guardia esta noche? *Who is on duty tonight?*

en guardia — *on (one's) guard.*
Estaba en guardia. *He was on (his) guard.*

Guatemala — *Guatemala*
salir de Guatemala y entrar (dar) en Guatepeor — *to jump out of the frying pan and into the fire.*
Cuidado, que así vas a salir de Guatemala y dar en Guatepeor. *Be careful, because that way you're just going to jump out of the frying pan and into the fire.*

---

la guerra — *war*
dar guerra — *to cause (make) trouble.*
Siempre daban guerra. *They were always causing (making) trouble.*

hacer (la) guerra — *to wage war.*
Hicieron (la) guerra. *They waged war.*

una guerra de nervios — *a war of nerves.*
Nos sometieron a una guerra de nervios. *They subjected us to a war of nerves.*

---

la guisa — *way, manner*
a guisa de — *as; by way of.*
Me lo dijo a guisa de disculpa. *He told it to me as (by way of) an excuse.*

---

gustar — *to please*
gustarle — *to like.*
Le gusta manejar (conducir). *He likes to drive.*

    gustarle más — *to like better.*
    Me gustan más las rubias. *I like blondes better.*

el gusto — *taste; pleasure, liking*
    con mucho gusto — *gladly.*
    Le dije que le haría el trabajo con mucho gusto. *I told him I'd gladly do the job for him.*

    dar gusto — *to be a pleasure.*
    Da gusto oírla tocar. *It's a pleasure to hear her play.*

    darse el gusto — *to treat oneself.*
    Se dio el gusto de hacer un viaje a Europa. *He treated himself to a trip to Europe.*

    de buen (mal) gusto — *in good (bad) taste.*
    No es de buen (mal) gusto. *It's not in good (bad) taste.*

    Eso va en gustos. — *That's a matter of taste.*

    estar a gusto — *to be comfortable.*
    Estamos muy a gusto aquí. *We are very comfortable here.*

    Sobre gustos no hay nada escrito. — *Everyone to his (own) taste; to each his own.*

    tener gusto — *to be glad.*
    Tengo (mucho) gusto en conocerlo. *I'm (very) glad to meet you.*

    tomar(le) (el) gusto — *to take a liking to; to acquire a liking for.*
    Le tomó (el) gusto. *He took a liking to it (acquired a liking for it).*

haber — *to have; (for) there to be*
    Allá se las haya. — *That's his problem (worry); let him take the consequences.*

    ¿Cuánto hay? — *How far is it?*
    ¿Cuánto hay de aquí al banco? *How far is it (from here) to the bank?*

    haber de — *to be (expected; suppposed) to.*

Ha de llegar mañana. *He is (expected) to arrive tomorrow.*

habérselas con — *to have it out with; deal with.*
Tendré que habérmelas con ellos. *I'll have to have it out with (deal with) them.*

hay — *there is (are).*
Hay tantos problemas que resolver. *There are so many problems to (be) solve(d).*

hay que — *it is necessary to; one must.*
Hay que comer. *It is necessary to (One must) eat.*

No hay de qué. — *Don't mention it; you're welcome.*

poco (tiempo) ha — *a short time ago.*
Murieron poco (tiempo) ha. *They died a short time ago.*

¿Qué hay? — *What's the matter?; What's up?*

si los hay — *if there ever was one.*
Es inteligente, si los hay. *He's an intelligent man if there ever was one.*

---

el hábito — *habit*
El hábito no hace al monje. — *Clothes don't make the man.*

---

el habla — *speech, language*
¡Al habla! — *Speaking! [on the telephone]*

estar al habla — *to be within hailing distance.*
El otro barco estaba al habla. *The other ship was within hailing distance.*

perder el habla — *to be speechless.*
Cuando vio el incendio perdió el habla. *When he saw the fire he was speechless.*

ponerse al habla con — *to get in communication with.*
Me puse al habla con él. *I got in communication with him.*

---

hablar — *to speak, talk*
hablar por hablar — *to talk for the sake of talking.*
Habla por hablar. *He talks for the sake of talking.*

hablar solo — *to talk to oneself.*
Mi abuelo hablaba solo. *My grandfather used to talk to himself.*

no hablarse — *not to be on speaking terms.*
Ya no nos hablamos. *We're not on speaking terms any more.*

ser mal hablado — *to be ill-spoken (foul-mouthed).*
Es muy mal hablado. *He's very ill-spoken (foul-mouthed).*

---

hacer — *to make, do*
  desde hace (hacía) — *for.*
  Estoy (Estaba) leyendo desde hace (hacía) una hora. *I have (had) been reading for an hour.*

  hace poco — *a short time ago.*
  Lo vendió hace poco. *He sold it a short time ago.*

  hacer — *to make; to have.*
  Hace estudiar a los niños. *He makes (has) the children study.*

  hacer de — *to act as.*
  Hacía de presidente. *He was acting as president.*

  hacer resaltar — *to emphasize; to bring out.*
  Hace resaltar el problema del indio. *He emphasizes (brings out) the problem of the Indian.*

  hacerse — *to become.*
  Se hizo médico. *He became a doctor.*

  hacerse a — *to get used to.*
  No se hace a trabajar de noche. *He can't get used to working at night.*

  hacerse con (de) — *to get hold of.*
  Se hizo con (de) los documentos. *He got hold of the documents.*

  hacerse de rogar — *to have to be coaxed; to play hard to get.*
  No se hace de rogar. *He doesn't have to be coaxed (doesn't play hard to get).*

---

el hambre — *hunger*
  morirse de hambre — *to starve to death.*
  Se murió de hambre. *She starved to death.*

  pasar hambre — *to go hungry.*
  Muchas veces han pasado hambre. *They have often gone hungry.*

tener hambre — *to be hungry.*
No tengo hambre. *I'm not hungry.*

la harina — *flour*
    ser harina de otro costal — *to be a horse of another (a different) color.*
    Eso es harina de otro costal. *That's a horse of another (a different) color.*

harto — *satiated*
    estar harto de — *to be fed up with; to be sick and tired of.*
    Estoy harto de sus quejas. *I'm fed up with (sick and tired of) his complaints.*

hasta — *until*
    hasta ahora (aquí) — *up to now; so far.*
    Hasta ahora (Hasta aquí) no han llegado. *They haven't arrived up to now (so far).*
    hasta entonces — *up to that time.*
    Hasta entonces no había tenido novio. *Up to that time she hadn't had a boyfriend (sweetheart).*

he
    he aquí — *here is.*
    He aquí su respuesta. *Here is his answer.*

el hecho — *fact; act, deed*
    de hecho — *actually; in fact.*
    De hecho no sabe nada. *Actually (In fact) he doesn't know anything.*

hecho — *finished, done*
    hecho y derecho — *every inch; grown; mature.*
    Es un hombre hecho y derecho. *He's every inch a (He's a grown) man.*

el hielo — *ice*
    romper el hielo — *to break the ice.*
    Su comentario rompió el hielo. *His comment broke the ice.*

---

la hierba — *grass*
  Hierba mala nunca muere. — *A bad penny always turns up.*

---

el hierro — *iron*
  El que a hierro mata a hierro muere. — *They that take the sword shall perish by (with) the sword.*

  Es como llevar hierro a Vizcaya. — *It's like carrying coals to Newcastle.*

  machacar en hierro frío — *to labor in vain.*
  Machacaban en hierro frío. *They were laboring in vain.*

---

el higo — *fig*
  de higos a brevas — *every once in a while.*
  De higos a brevas les hago una visita. *I visit them every once in a while.*

---

la higuera — *fig tree*
  estar en la higuera — *to be daydreaming; to have one's head in the clouds.*
  Está en la higuera. *He's daydreaming (got his head in the clouds).*

---

el hijo — *son*
  como cualquier (cada) hijo de vecino — *just like everybody else.*
  Trabaja como cualquier (cada) hijo de vecino. *He works just like everybody else.*

---

el hilo — *thread*
  cortar el hilo — *to interrupt.*
  Le cortó el hilo en lo mejor del cuento. *She interrupted him in the best part of the story.*

  estar pendiente de un hilo — *to be hanging by a thread.*
  Está pendiente de un hilo. *It's hanging by a thread.*

  perder el hilo (de la conversación) — *to lose the thread (of the conversation).*
  Perdieron el hilo (de la conversación). *They lost the thread (of the conversation).*

---

el hincapié — *act of getting a firm footing*
hacer hincapié en — *to put special emphasis (stress) on.*
Hizo hincapié en los defectos de nuestro plan. *He put special emphasis (stress) on the shortcomings of our plan.*

el hinojo — *knee*
estar de hinojos — *to be kneeling.*
Estaban de hinojos. *They were kneeling.*

la historia — *history, story*
dejarse de historias — *to get to the point.*
¡Déjese de historias! *Get to the point!*

el hito — *landmark; target*
mirar de hito en hito — *to stare at.*
Me miró de hito en hito. *He stared at me.*

el hombre — *man*
El hombre propone y Dios dispone. — *Man proposes, God disposes.*

¡Hombre! — *Man alive!*

¡Hombre al agua! — *Man overboard!*

Hombre prevenido vale por dos. — *Forewarned is forearmed.*

el hombro — *shoulder*
arrimar el hombro — *to put one's shoulder to the wheel; to lend a hand.*
Arrimaron el hombro. *They put their shoulder to the wheel (lent a hand).*

encogerse de hombros — *to shrug one's shoulders.*
Se encogió de hombros. *He shrugged his shoulders.*

la honrilla — *concern for one's reputation*
por la negra honrilla — *for fear of what people may say.*
Lo hago por la negra honrilla. *I'm doing it for fear of what people may say.*

la hora — *hour*
a altas horas — *very late.*

Llegó a casa a altas horas de la noche. *He got home very late at night.*

¡A buenas horas! — *It's about time!*

a estas horas — *now.*
A estas horas no puedo. *I can't now.*

a hora(s) fija(s) — *at a set (fixed) time; right on time.*
No le gustaba comer a horas fijas. *He didn't like to eat at a set (fixed) time.*
Apareció a hora fija. *He arrived right on time.*

a la hora — *on time.*
Llegó a la hora. *He arrived on time.*

a la hora de la hora — *when the time (actually) comes.*
Ya verás como a la hora de la hora ellos sabrán defenderse. *You'll see, when the time (actually) comes, they'll know how to defend themselves.*

a la hora de la verdad — *when it comes right down to it; at the moment of truth.*
A la hora de la verdad, le faltó valor para decírselo. *When it came right down to it (At the moment of truth), he lacked the courage to tell him.*

a primera hora — *early.*
Salieron a primera hora de la tarde. *They left early in the afternoon.*

a última hora — *at the last minute.*
A última hora decidió ir. *At the last minute he decided to go.*

a última hora — *late.*
Pasa el lechero a última hora de la mañana. *The milkman goes by late in the morning.*

de (la) última hora — *last-minute.*
Escuchaban las noticias de (la) última hora. *They were listening to the last-minute news.*

en hora buena — *luckily.*
En hora buena encontré el camino. *Luckily I found the road.*

estar de última hora — *to be the (latest) trend.*
Está de última hora. *It's the (latest) trend.*

horas libres — *free time.*
Leía en sus horas libres. *She would read in her spare time.*

la hora de comer — *mealtime.*
No miramos la televisión a la hora de comer. *We don't watch television at mealtime.*

llegarle la hora — *to have one's hour come.*
Ya le llegó la hora. *His hour has come.*

marcar la hora — *to keep time.*
Mi reloj marca bien la hora. *My watch keeps good time.*

no ver la hora — *not to be able to wait.*
No veo la hora de salir de aquí. *I can't wait to get out of here.*

ser hora de — *to be time to.*
Es hora de estudiar. *It's time to study.*

la horma — *(shoe) form, mold, last*
  hallar la horma del zapato — *to meet one's match; to find just what one wanted.*
  Ha hallado la horma de su zapato. *He's met his match. He's found just what he wanted.*

hoy — *today*
  de hoy a mañana — *(just about) any time now.*
  De hoy a mañana se van a casar. *They're going to get married (just about) any time now.*

  de hoy en adelante — *from now on; henceforth.*
  De hoy en adelante compraremos menos. *From now on (henceforth) we'll buy less.*

  hoy (en) día — *nowadays.*
  Se usan mucho hoy (en) día. *They're worn a lot nowadays.*

  hoy mismo — *this very day.*
  Se lo mandaré hoy mismo. *I'll send it to you this very day.*

  hoy por hoy — *under the present circumstances (as of right now).*
  Hoy por hoy, no me conviene comprar una casa nueva. *Under the present circumstances (As of right now), it's not advisable for me to buy a new house.*

la huelga — *strike*

  declararse en huelga — *to go (out) on strike.*
  Se declararon en huelga. *They went (out) on strike.*

la huella — *track, trace, (foot)print.*

  dejar huella — *to make an impression.*
  Es un hombre que deja huella. *He's a man that makes an impression.*

  seguir las huellas de . . . — *to follow in . . .'s footsteps.*
  Sigue las huellas de su padre. *He's following in his father's footsteps.*

el hueso — *bone*

  estar (quedar) en los huesos — *to be nothing but skin and bones.*
  Está (Quedó) en los huesos. *He's nothing but skin and bones.*

  Está (Quedó) en los huesos. *He's nothing but skin and bones.*

  estar mojado (calado) hasta los huesos — *to be soaked (drenched) to the skin.*
  Está mojado (calado) hasta los huesos. *He is soaked (drenched) to the skin.*

  partírsele los huesos de frío — *to be freezing to death.*
  Los huesos se me parten de frío. *I'm freezing to death.*

  ser un hueso duro de roer — *to be a tough nut to crack.*
  Es un hueso duro de roer. *He's a tough nut to crack.*

  soltar la sin hueso — *to let one's tongue wag; to talk too much.*

Soltó la sin hueso. *He let his tongue wag (talked too much).*

tener los huesos molidos — *to be exhausted.*

Después de correr tanto tengo los huesos molidos. *After running so much I am exhausted.*

---

el huevo — *egg*

poner un huevo — *to lay an egg.*

La gallina puso un huevo. *The hen laid an egg.*

---

el humo — *smoke*

a humo de pajas — *lightly; without good reason.*

No dice eso a humo de pajas. *He's not saying that lightly (without good reason).*

bajarle los humos — *to take someone down a notch (a peg).*

Voy a bajarle los humos. *I'm going to take him down a notch (a peg).*

darse (tener) humos — *to put on airs.*

Se da (Tiene) tantos humos que ya casi no tiene amigos. *She puts on so many airs that she hardly has any friends left.*

irse en humo — *to go up in smoke.*

Todo se fue en humo. *It all went up in smoke.*

¡La (ida) del humo! *Good riddance!*

---

el humor — *humor*

de buen (mal) humor — *in a good (bad) humor (mood).*

Está de buen (mal) humor. *He's in a good (bad) humor (mood).*

---

hurtadillas

a hurtadillas — *on the sly; stealthily.*

Sale a hurtadillas. *He goes out on the sly (stealthily).*

---

la ida — *going*
 un billete (boleto) de ida y vuelta — *a round-trip ticket.*
 Compró un billete (boleto) de ida y vuelta. *He bought a round-trip ticket.*

la idea — *idea*
 cambiar de idea — *to change one's mind.*
 Cambié de idea. *I changed my mind.*

igual — *equal*
 (al) igual que — *like.*
 José, (al) igual que su hermano, no quiso estudiar. *Joe, like his brother,*
 refused to study.

 por igual — *equally.*
 Debemos tratarlos por igual. *We should treat them equally.*

 ser igual — *not to matter; to be all the same.*
 (A mí me) es igual. *It doesn't matter (It's all the same) (to me).*

 sin igual — *matchless; unequaled.*
 Sus pinturas son de una belleza sin igual. *His paintings are of a matchless*
 (unequaled) beauty.

la ijada — *flank*
 tener su ijada — *to have its weak side (point).*
 Tiene su ijada. *It has its weak side (point).*

la ilusión — *illusion*
 forjarse (hacerse) ilusiones — *to build castles in the air.*
 Pasó la vida forjándose (haciéndose) ilusiones. *She spent her life building*
 castles in the air.

imponer — *to dominate*
 imponerse a — *to dominate.*

141

Desde el primer momento se impuso a la situación. *From the first moment, he dominated the situation.*

la importancia — *importance*
darse importancia — *to act important.*
Le gusta darse importancia. *He likes to act important.*

importar — *to matter, be important*
importarle a uno — *to care.*
A mí no me importa. *I don't care.*

imposible — *impossible*
hacer lo(s) imposible(s) — *to do everything possible.*
Hizo lo(s) imposible(s) para ayudarnos. *He did everything he possibly could (everything possible) to help us.*

improviso — *unforeseen*
de improviso — *offhand.*
Así de improviso no sé qué decirle. *Just offhand I don't know what to tell you.*

de (al) improviso — *unexpectedly.*
Salió de (al) improviso. *He left unexpectedly.*

el inconveniente — *obstacle, drawback*
no ver ningún inconveniente — *to see no objection.*
Si quiere comprarlo, no veo ningún inconveniente. *If he wants to buy it, I see no objection.*

tener inconveniente — *to mind; to object to.*
No tenemos inconveniente en que vaya. *We don't mind (object to) his going.*

incorporar — *to incorporate*
incorporarse — *to sit up.*
Apenas puede incorporarse. *He can hardly sit up.*

la indirecta — *hint*

    echar indirectas — *to make insinuations.*

    Al ver la falda corta, echó indirectas. *On seeing the short skirt, he made insinuations.*

---

informar — *to inform*

    informarse de — *to get information about (find out about).*

    Yo fui a la estación para informarme de las salidas de los trenes. *I went to the station to get information about (find out about) the departures of the trains.*

---

ingeniar — *to conceive*

    ingeniárselas para — *to find a way; to manage.*

    Se las ingenió para quedarse en París. *He found a way (He managed) to stay in Paris.*

---

el ingenio — *cleverness, talent*

    aguzar (afilar) el ingenio — *to sharpen one's wits.*

    Vamos a aguzar (afilar) el ingenio. *Let's sharpen our wits.*

---

inmediato — *immediate*

    de inmediato — *immediately.*

    Lo supo de inmediato. *He found it out immediately.*

---

instalar — *to install*

    instalarse en — *to move into.*

    Nos instalamos en una residencia (de estudiantes). *We moved into a dormitory.*

---

la instancia — *(earnest) request*

    a instancias de . . . — *at . . . 's request.*

    A instancias del padre hicieron al viaje. *At the father's request they took the trip.*

---

el instante — *instant*

    a cada instante — *at any moment.*

A cada instante cree que se va a venir abajo el techo. *He thinks that at any moment the roof is going to collapse.*

al instante — *immediately; instantly.*
Tráigamelo al instante. *Bring it to me immediately (instantly).*

la inteligencia — *intelligence*
llegar a una inteligencia — *to reach (to come to) an understanding.*
Han llegado a una inteligencia. *They have reached (come to) an understanding.*

la intención — *intention*
con intención — *deliberately.*
Lo hizo con intención. *He did it deliberately.*

obrar con segunda intención — *to have an ax to grind; to have ulterior motives.*
Obraba con segunda intención. *He had an ax to grind (had ulterior motives).*

tener la intención de — *to intend to.*
Tienen la intención de faltar a la clase. *They intend to miss the class.*

el intento — *intent, purpose*
de intento — *on purpose.*
Lo hizo de intento. *He did it on purpose.*

el interés — *interest*
tener mucho interés en que — *to be eager for.*
Tengo mucho interés en que lo vea. *I am eager for you to see it.*

interesar — *to interest*
interesarse por — *to take an interest in.*
Se interesa por el bienestar de su familia. *He takes an interest in the welfare of his family.*

la inversa — *opposite*
a la inversa — *the other way around.*

Sus deseos no fueron realizados; todo resultó a la inversa. *His wishes were not realized; everything turned out the other way around.*

---

ir — *to go*

¿Cómo le va? — *How are you?*

en lo que va de — *so far.*
En lo que va de verano hemos nadado todos los días. *So far this summer we have gone swimming every day.*

irle a uno bien (mal) — *to turn out well (badly).*
No me fue bien. *It did not turn out well for me.*

irle a uno bien (mal) — *to be becoming (unbecoming) to.*
Ese vestido le va bien. *That dress is becoming to you.*

ir por — *to go after; to go to get.*
¿Cuándo va por el pan? *When is he going after (going to get) the bread?*

ir tirando — *to get by.*
Vamos tirando. *We're getting by.*

no le va ni viene nada — *not to concern one in the least.*
A mí no me va ni viene nada en eso. *That doesn't concern me in the least.*

¡Qué va! — *What nonsense!*

sin ir más lejos — *for example.*
Lo cree mi primo, sin ir más lejos. *My cousin believes it, for example.*

¡Vaya una sugerencia! — *What a suggestion!*

ya ir para — *to have gone on for nearly.*
La lluvia ya iba para una semana. *It had been raining for nearly a week.*

---

izquierdo — *left*

a la izquierda — *on (to) the left.*
Está a la izquierda. *It's on (to) the left.*

---

el jabón — *soap*

darle jabón — *to softsoap someone; to butter someone up.*
Le daban jabón. *They were softsoaping him (buttering him up).*

darle un jabón — *to give someone a dressing-down; to rake someone over the coals.*
Le daban un jabón. *They were giving him a dressing-down (were raking him over the coals).*

el jarabe — *syrup*

jarabe de pico — *empty talk.*
Sus promesas no son más que jarabe de pico. *His promises are just empty talk.*

la jarra — *pitcher*

ponerse en (de) jarras — *to put one's hand on one's hips.*
Se puso en (de) jarras. *She put her hands on her hips.*

Jauja — *Cockaigne (land of plenty)*

¿Estamos aquí o en Jauja? — *Where do you think you are? Come down to earth.*

ser Jauja — *to be the land of milk and honey.*
¡Eso es Jauja! *That's the land of milk and honey.*

Jesús — *Jesus*

en un decir Jesús — *in an instant (a flash).*
Lo abrió en un decir Jesús. *He opened it in an instant (a flash).*

la jeta — *snout*

tener jeta — *to have a nerve.*
¡Qué jeta tiene! *What a nerve he's got!*

la jota — *(the letter) j; jot, iota*
  no saber ni jota de — *not to know a thing about.*
  De eso no sé ni jota. *I don't know a thing about that.*

el juego — *game*
  conocerle (verle) el juego — *to be on to someone; to see through someone.*
  Le conozco (Le veo) el juego. *I'm on to him (see through him).*

  Desgraciado en el juego, afortunado en amores. — *Unlucky at cards, lucky in love.*

  hacer juego — *to match; to go well with.*
  Las sillas hacen juego con la mesa. *The chairs match (go well with) the table.*

  no ser cosa de juego — *to be no laughing matter.*
  No es cosa de juego. *It's no laughing matter.*

  prestarse al juego — *to go along with the game.*
  Se prestó al juego. *She went along with the game.*

la juerga — *spree*
  ir de juerga — *to be out on a spree.*
  Iban de juerga. *They were out on a spree.*

el jueves — *Thursday*
  no ser cosa del otro jueves — *to be nothing out of the ordinary.*
  No es cosa del otro jueves. *It's nothing out of the ordinary.*

jugar — *to play*
  jugar(se) el todo por el todo — *to bet (risk; gamble) everything.*
  Me jugué el todo por el todo. *I bet (risked; gambled) everything.*

  jugar limpio — *to play fair.*
  No juega limpio. *He doesn't play fair.*

el jugo — *juice*
  sacarle jugo a — *to get a lot out of.*

Lea este libro. Estoy seguro de que le sacará mucho jugo. *Read this book. I'm sure you'll get a lot out of it.*

junto — *close, near*

junto a — *next to.*

Está junto a la farmacia. *It's next to the drugstore.*

juzgar — *to judge*

a juzgar por — *judging (to judge) by.*

A juzgar por las apariencias, tienen mucho dinero. *Judging (To judge) by appearances, they have a lot of money.*

el labio — *lip*

cerrar los labios — *to keep quiet.*

Decidí cerrar los labios. *I decided to keep quiet.*

estar pendiente de sus labios — *to be hanging on(to) one's words.*

Estaba pendiente de mis labios. *He was hanging on(to) my words.*

morderse los labios — *to bite one's tongue.*

Me mordí los labios. *I bit my tongue.*

no despegar los labios — *not to utter a word.*

No despegó los labios. *She didn't utter a word.*

la ladilla — *crab louse*

pegársele como una ladilla — *to stick to someone like a leech.*

Se nos pega como una ladilla. *He sticks to us like a leech.*

el lado — *side*

a un lado — *aside.*

Se hizo a un lado. *He stepped aside.*

al lado — *next door.*

Se compran al lado. *You can buy them next door.*

al lado — *on the side.*

Sírvame huevos revueltos con jamón al lado. *Serve me scrambled eggs with ham on the side.*

al otro lado — *on the other side.*

Al otro lado del río hay un pueblo. *On the other side of the river there is a town.*

de lado — *sideways.*

Hay que entrarlo de lado. *You have to bring it in sideways.*

de un lado a otro — *from one side to the other.*

Iban de un lado a otro. *They were going from one side to the other.*

de (por) un lado; de (por) otro — *on the one hand; on the other.*

De (Por) un lado, le gusta el vestido; de (por) otro, le parece caro. *On the one hand, she likes the dress; on the other, she thinks it's expensive.*

lado flaco — *weak spot.*

Hay que buscarle el lado flaco. *You have to find his weak spot.*

levantarse del lado izquierdo — *to get up on the wrong side of the bed.*

Parece que te levantaste del lado izquierdo esta mañana. *It seems that you got up on the wrong side of the bed this morning.*

poner a un lado (de lado) — *to put aside.*

Tuvo que poner a un lado (de lado) sus prejuicios. *She had to put her prejudices aside.*

por ningún lado — *nowhere (not . . . anywhere)*

No se encontraba por ningún lado. *It couldn't be found anywhere.*

por todos lados — *all over.*

Se veían por todos lados. *They were seen all over.*

la lágrima — *tear*

deshacerse en lágrimas — *to weep bitterly.*

Se deshizo en lágrimas. *She wept bitterly.*

lágrimas de cocodrilo — *crocodile tears.*

Son lágrimas de cocodrilo. *They're crocodile tears.*

Son lágrimas de
  cocodrilo.
*They're crocodile
  tears.*

llorar a lágrima viva — *to shed bitter tears; to weep bitterly.*
Lloró a lágrima viva. *She shed bitter tears (wept bitterly).*

saltársele las lágrimas — *to have tears come to one's eyes.*
Se me saltaban las lágrimas. *Tears came to my eyes.*

la lana — *wool*
  ir por lana y volver esquilado (trasquilado) — *(lit.) to go for wool and
  come home shorn; i.e., to have the tables turned on one; the shoe is on
  the other foot.*

largo — *long*
  a la larga — *in the long run.*
  A la larga será mejor ir despacio. *In the long run it will be better to go
  slowly.*

  a lo largo — *along.*
  Buscaban a lo largo del río. *They were searching along the river.*

  a lo largo y a lo ancho — *throughout (the length and the breadth of).*
  Hubo disturbios a lo largo y a lo ancho del país. *There were disturbances
  throughout (the length and the breadth of) the country.*

  ¡Largo (de aquí)! — *Get out (of here)!*

  pasar de largo — *to pass (on) by (without stopping).*
  Pasó de largo. *He passed (on) by (without stopping).*

a lástima — *pity*

dar lástima — *to sadden.*

Me da lástima ver a este enfermo. *It saddens me to see this sick man.*

estar hecho una lástima — *to be a sorry sight (in a sad state).*

Está hecho una lástima. *He's a sorry sight (in a sad state).*

ser (una) lástima — *to be too bad (a pity).*

Es (una) lástima. *It's too bad (a pity).*

---

a lata — *tinplate, tin can*

dar la lata — *to make a nuisance of oneself.*

Hablando tanto, no hace más que dar la lata. *By talking so much, he does nothing but make a nuisance of himself.*

---

l laurel — *laurel*

dormir sobre los laureles — *to rest on one's laurels.*

¡No se duerma sobre los laureles! *Don't rest on your laurels!*

---

l lazo — *loop, bow*

tender un lazo — *to set a trap.*

Me tendieron un lazo. *They set a trap for me.*

---

a leche — *milk*

buscar pelos en la leche — *to find fault.*

Siempre busca pelos en la leche. *He's always finding fault.*

dar una leche — *to hit; to beat up.*

¡Si vuelves a hacer eso, te doy una leche que te enteras! *If you do that again, I'll smack you so hard you won't forget it!*

estar de mala leche — *to be in a foul mood.*

No le hables hoy, está de mala leche. *Don't talk to him today, he's in a foul mood.*

mamar en (con) la leche — *to learn at one's mother's knee.*

Lo mamé en (con) la leche. *I learned it at my mother's knee.*

tener mala leche — *to have a spiteful, vindictive disposition.*

El tiene mucha mala leche — no te fíes de él. *He's really spiteful — don't trust him.*

el lecho — *bed*

un lecho de rosas — *a bed of roses.*

Trabajar en esa fábrica no es un lecho de rosas. *Working in that factory is not a bed of roses.*

la lechuga — *lettuce*

estar más fresco que una lechuga — *to be very sharp (in good form).*

Está más fresco que una lechuga hoy. *He's really sharp (in good form) today.*

la legaña — *rheum*

tener legaña — *to have rheumy eyes (look sleepy).*

A estas horas siempre tiene legaña. *At this hour he's always still looking sleepy.*

la legua — *league*

a la legua — *a mile off (away).*

A la legua se conoce que no es de oro. *You can tell a mile off (away) that it isn't made of gold.*

lejos — *far*

a lo lejos — *in the distance.*

A lo lejos se veía el avión. *In the distance the plane could be seen.*

de (desde) lejos — *from far away.*

Vienen de (desde) lejos. *They come from far away.*

la lengua — *tongue*

la lengua materna — *mother (native) tongue.*

El alemán es su lengua materna. *German is his mother (native) tongue.*

las malas lenguas — *the gossips.*

Según las malas lenguas, su hija está loca. *According to the gossips, her daughter is insane.*

morderse la lengua — *to hold (control) one's tongue.*

En vez de disputar se mordió la lengua. *Rather than argue, he held his tongue.*

sacar la lengua — *to stick out one's tongue.*
Me sacó la lengua. *He stuck out his tongue at me.*

tener la lengua larga — *to be a blabbermouth.*
No se lo diga al secretario; tiene la lengua larga. *Don't tell the secretary; he's a blabbermouth.*

tener lengua de víbora — *to have a poisonous tongue.*
No crea nada que cuente ese señora. Tiene lengua de víbora. *Don't believe anything that woman tells. She has a poisonous tongue.*

tirarle de la lengua — *to draw someone out.*
Nos tiraba de la lengua. *He was drawing us out.*

trabársele la lengua — *to get tongue-tied.*
Se le trabó la lengua. *He got tongue-tied.*

---

la leña — *(fire)wood*
echar leña al fuego — *to add fuel to the flames.*
Así no hace más que echar leña al fuego. *That way he's just adding fuel to the flames.*

llevar leña al monte — *to carry coals to Newcastle.*
Eso sería llevar leña al monte. *That would be carrying coals to Newcastle.*

---

la letra — *letter (of the alphabet)*
a la letra — *to the letter.*
Hay que seguir las instrucciones a la letra. *You must follow the instructions to the letter.*

cuatro letras — *a few lines.*
Voy a escribirle cuatro letras. *I'm going to write him a few lines.*

La letra con sangre entra. — *There's no royal road to learning.*

---

la liebre — *hare*
correr como una liebre — *to run like a deer.*
Ese chico va a ganar el premio. Corre como una liebre. *That boy is going to win the prize. He runs like a deer.*

---

ligero — *light*
a la ligera — *hurriedly; without due care.*

Siempre hace las cosas a la ligera. *She always does things hurriedly (without due care).*

---

limitar — *to limit*

limitar con — *to be bordered by.*

El Canadá limita al sur con los Estados Unidos. *Canada is bordered on the south by the United States.*

---

el límite — *limit*

rebasar los límites de la paciencia — *to exceed the limits of one's patience.*

Habían rebasado los límites de mi paciencia. *They had exceeded the limits of my patience.*

---

limpio — *clean*

en limpio — *clearly.*

Declaró en limpio sus intenciones. *He stated his intentions clearly.*

---

lindo — *pretty, nice*

de lo lindo — *really; very much; greatly.*

¡Me enojé de lo lindo! *I really got mad!*

Me gustó de lo lindo. *I was very much (greatly) pleased.*

---

la línea — *line*

conservar (guardar) la línea — *to keep one's figure; to keep one's weight down.*

Lo hace por conservar (guardar) la línea. *She does it for the sake of keeping her figure (keeping her weight down).*

leer entre líneas — *to read between the lines.*

Hay que leer entre líneas. *You've got to read between the lines.*

ponerle unas líneas (cuatro líneas) — *to drop someone a line.*

Le pondré unas líneas (cuatro líneas) mañana. *I'll drop him a line tomorrow.*

---

el lío — *parcel, bundle; muddle, mess, confusion*

armarse un lío — *to have trouble (a row).*

Se armó un lío entre la policía y los estudiantes. *Trouble (A row) started between the police and the students.*

hacerse un lío — *to get confused; to get in a jam.*
Me hice un lío. *I got confused (got in a jam).*

el lirón — *dormouse*
dormir como un lirón — *to sleep like a log.*
Duerme como un lirón. *He sleeps like a log.*

liso — *smooth, plain*
ser liso y llano — *to be clear and simple.*
Es liso y llano. *It's clear and simple.*

la lista — *list*
pasar lista — *to call (the) roll.*
El profesor pasó lista. *The teacher called (the) roll.*

el lobo — *wolf*
un viejo lobo de mar — *an old salt (sea dog).*
Es un viejo lobo de mar. *He's an old salt (sea dog).*

loco — *insane, crazy*
Cada loco con su tema. — *Everyone does his own thing.*

estar loco de atar — *to be stark raving mad.*
Está loco de atar. *He is stark raving mad.*

estar loco de contento — *to be wild with joy.*
Estaba loco de contento. *He was wild with joy.*

volverse loco — *to go crazy.*
Se volvió loco. *He went crazy.*

el lomo — *back*
a lomo de . . . — *on . . . back.*
Hizo la travesía a lomo de mula. *He made the crossing on mule back.*

la lucha — *fight, struggle*

    una lucha a muerte — *a struggle to the death.*

    Fue una lucha a muerte. *It was a struggle to the death.*

luego — *afterwards, then*

    Desde luego. — *Of course.*

    Hasta luego. — *See you later.*

    luego luego — *right away.*

    Tengo que hacerlo luego luego. *I have to do it right away.*

el lugar — *place*

    dar lugar a — *to give rise to.*

    Da lugar a quejas. *It gives rise to complaints.*

    en lugar de — *in place (instead) of.*

    En lugar de Juan, vino Alberto. *In place (Instead) of John, Albert came.*

    en primer lugar — *in the first place.*

    En primer lugar, hay que tener dieciocho años. *In the first place, you have to be eighteen.*

    tener lugar — *to take place.*

    Tendrá lugar en el teatro. *It will take place in the theater.*

el lujo — *luxury*

    de lujo — *deluxe (luxury).*

    Es un hotel de lujo. *It's a deluxe hotel (luxury hotel).*

la lumbre — *fire*

    darle lumbre — *to give someone a light.*

    Me dio lumbre. *He gave me a light.*

la luna — *moon*

    estar en la luna — *to be daydreaming; to have one's head in the clouds.*

    Está en la luna. *He's daydreaming (has his head in the clouds).*

    Hace (Hay) luna. — *The moon is out (is shining).*

    la luna de miel — *honeymoon.*

    Ya se acabó la luna de miel. *The honeymoon is over.*

el luto — *mourning*
   estar de luto — *to be in mourning.*
   Estaba de luto. *She was in mourning.*

la luz — *light*
   a la luz de la luna — *in the moonlight; by the light of the moon.*
   Me reconoció a la luz de la luna. *He recognized me in the moonlight (by the light of the moon).*

   a todas luces — *evidently; any way you look at it.*
   A todas luces, Rafael es estúpido. *Evidently (Any way you look at it), Rafael is stupid.*

   dar a luz — *to produce.*
   El artista dio a luz una bellísima obra de arte. *The artist produced a most beautiful work of art.*

   dar a luz (a) — *to give birth (to).*
   Dio a luz a un niño de ojos azules. *She gave birth to a blue-eyed baby.*

   entre dos luces — *in the twilight.*
   Así entre dos luces es difícil manejar (conducir). *In the twilight like this it is hard to drive.*

   sacar a luz — *to publish.*
   Casona sacó a luz esa comedia en 1940. *Casona published that play in 1940.*

   ver la luz — *to be born; to first see the light of day.*
   Vio la luz en Caracas. *He was born (first saw the light of day) in Caracas.*

la llama — *flame*
   echar llamas — *to flash.*
   Sus ojos echaban llamas. *Her eyes were flashing.*
   Salir de (las) llamas y caer en (las) brasas. — *Out of the frying pan into the fire.*

llamar — *to call*
    llamarse — *to be called (named).*
    Se llama Juan. *His name is John.*

la llave — *key*
    bajo (debajo de) llave — *under lock and key.*
    Lo tengo bajo (debajo de) llave. *I have it under lock and key.*

    echar la llave (cerrar con llave) — *to lock.*
    No deje de echar la llave (cerrar la puerta con llave). *Don't fail to lock the
        door.*

    encerrar con llave — *to lock in.*
    La encerró con llave. *He locked her in.*

llegar — *to arrive*
    llegar a ser — *to become.*
    Llegó a ser médico. *He became a doctor.*

    llegar tarde — *to be late.*
    Llegué tarde al concierto. *I was late to the concert.*

lleno — *full*
    de lleno — *fully.*
    No participó de lleno en el plan. *She didn't fully take part in the plan.*

llevar — *to carry*
    llevar + gerund — *[to spend time doing something].*
    Llevo cinco años estudiando ruso. *I've been studying Russian for five
        years.*

    llevar adelante — *to go ahead with.*
    Lleva adelante su trabajo. *He goes ahead with his work.*

    llevar aparte — *to take aside.*
    Lo llevaron aparte. *They took him aside.*

    llevar encima — *to have on one.*
    No llevo dinero encima. *I don't have any money on me.*

    llevar la derecha (izquierda) — *to keep to the right (left).*
    Lleve la derecha (izquierda). *Keep to the right (left).*

llevar puesto — *to have on; to be wearing.*
Lleva puesto un abrigo. *He has on (is wearing) an overcoat.*

llevarle a — *to lead one to.*
Me llevó a vender mi casa. *It led me to sell my house.*

llevarse bien (con) — *to get along well (with).*
Se lleva bien con todos. *He gets along well with everyone.*

llover — *to rain*
Mucho ha llovido desde entonces. — *A lot of water has flowed under the bridge since then.*

la madera — *wood*
saber a la madera — *to be a chip off the old block.*
Sabe a la madera. *He's a chip off the old block.*

tener madera para — *to be cut out (made) for.*
No tengo madera para esa vida. *I'm not cut out (made) for that kind of life.*

tocar madera — *to knock on wood.*
Voy a tocar madera por si acaso. *I'm going to knock on wood just in case.*

la madrugada — *early morning*
de madrugada — *early in the morning.*
Salieron de madrugada. *They left early in the morning.*

el mal — *evil, harm, misfortune*
Del mal, el menos. — *The lesser of two evils.*

hacerle mal — *to hurt one.*
Me hizo mal. *It hurt me.*

llevarlo (tomarlo) a mal — *to take it the wrong way (to take it amiss).*
No lo lleve (tome) a mal. *Don't take it the wrong way (take it amiss).*

No hay mal que cien años dure. — *It can't last forever.*

No hay mal que por bien no venga. — *Every cloud has a silver lining; It's an ill wind that blows nobody good.*

---

mal — *badly, poorly*

    de mal en peor — *from bad to worse.*

    Las cosas van de mal en peor. *Things are going from bad to worse.*

    mal que bien — *one way or another.*

    Mal que bien, se casan mañana. *One way or another, they're getting married tomorrow.*

    menos mal — *it's a good thing.*

    Menos mal que no vino. *It's a good thing he didn't come.*

    ¿No vino? Menos mal. *He didn't come? It's a good thing.*

---

la maleta — *suitcase*

    hacer la maleta — *to pack a suitcase.*

    Hagamos las maletas. *Let's pack our suitcases.*

---

malo — *bad*

    andar (estar) de malas — *to have a run of bad luck.*

    En estos días anda (está) de malas. *These days he's having a run of bad luck.*

---

el mamporro — *blow, thump*

    liarse a mamporros — *to come to blows.*

    Se liaron a mamporros. *They came to blows.*

---

el mando — *command*

    estar al mando — *to be in command.*

    En aquella familia, es ella que está al mando. *In that family, it is she who is in command.*

---

la manera — *manner, way*

    a su manera — *(in) one's (own) way.*

    Lo haré a mi manera. *I'll do it (in) my (own) way.*

    de esta manera — *this way; in this manner.*

manga

Se hace de esta manera. *You do it (It's done) this way (in this manner).*

de manera que — *so.*
¿De manera que fueron al cine? *So they went to the movies?*

de manera que — *so (that).*
Hable de manera que lo oigan. *Speak so they can hear you.*

de ninguna manera — *in no way.*
De ninguna manera lo acepto yo. *In no way will I accept it.*

de otra manera — *otherwise.*
De otra manera no llegaremos a tiempo. *Otherwise we won't arrive on time.*

de todas maneras — *at any rate.*
De todas maneras, esperaremos hasta que venga. *At any rate, we'll wait until he comes.*

---

la manga — *sleeve*
en mangas de camisa — *in shirtsleeves.*
Estaba en mangas de camisa. *He was in his shirtsleeves.*

---

manifiesto — *manifest*
poner de manifiesto — *to make clear (evident).*
Lo puso de manifiesto. *He made it clear (evident).*

---

la mano — *hand*
a mano — *at hand; within reach.*
Lo tengo a mano. *I have it at hand (within reach).*

a mano — *by hand.*
Lo hizo a mano. *He made it by hand.*

a manos llenas — *by the handful.*
Daban dinero a manos llenas a la Cruz Roja. *They used to give money by the handful to the Red Cross.*

caer en manos de — *to fall into the hands of.*
Cayó en manos de sus enemigos. *He fell into the hands of his enemies.*

cargar la mano — *to lay it on thick.*
Cargó la mano. *He laid it on thick.*

cargar la mano — *to overcharge.*
Suele cargar la mano. *He usually overcharges.*

coger con las manos en la masa — *to catch in the act; to catch red-handed.*
Lo cogimos con las manos en la masa. *We caught him in the act (red-handed).*

dar una mano a — *to lend (give) a hand to.*
Nadie quería darle una mano. *No one wanted to lend (give) him a hand.*

darse la mano — *to shake hands (with each other).*
Se dieron la mano. *They shook hands (with each other).*

de mano en mano — *from hand to hand.*
Lo pasaron de mano en mano. *They passed it from hand to hand.*

de segunda mano — *secondhand.*
Lo compré de segunda mano. *I bought it secondhand.*

dejado de la mano de Dios — *God-forsaken.*
Viven en no sé qué pueblo dejado de la mano de Dios. *They live in some God-forsaken village or other.*

echarle mano a — *to seize; to grab.*
Le echó mano al niño. *He seized (grabbed) the child.*

echar(le) una mano — *to lend someone a hand.*
Echeme una mano. *Lend me a hand.*

estrecharle la mano — *to shake hands with.*
Le estreché la mano. *I shook hands with him.*

flotar de la mano — *to be readily available.*
En mi casa el dinero no flota de la mano. *Money doesn't exactly grow on trees at my house.*

hecho a mano — *handmade.*
Me regaló un mantel hecho a mano. *She gave me a handmade tablecloth.*

írsele la mano — *to overdo it; to get carried away.*
Se me fue la mano. *I overdid it (got carried away).*

mano sobre mano — *(sitting or standing around) doing nothing.*
La próxima vez que la veas mano sobre mano, me avisas. *The next time you see her (sitting around) doing nothing, let me know.*

¡Manos a la obra! — *Let's get to work!*

pasársele a uno la mano — *to overdo.*
Se te pasó la mano. *You overdid it.*

poner la(s) mano(s) encima — *to lay a hand on.*
No se atrevió a ponerle la(s) mano(s) encima. *He didn't dare lay a hand on her.*

ser mano de santo — *to work wonders.*
El medicamento fue mano de santo. *The medicine worked wonders.*

tener atadas las manos — *to have one's hands tied.*
Tengo atadas las manos. *My hands are tied.*

tener mucha mano — *to have a lot of influence.*
Hay que tener mucha mano para tener éxito en ese país. *You've got to have a lot of pull to be successful in that country.*

venir (llegar) a las manos — *to come to blows.*
Vinieron (llegaron) a las manos. *They came to blows.*

---

la manta — *blanket*
tirar de la manta — *to let the cat out of the bag.*
No tardaron en tirar de la manta. *They soon let the cat out of the bag.*

---

la maña — *skill*
darse maña — *to manage; to contrive.*
Se dio maña para conseguir el dinero. *He managed (contrived) to get the money.*

---

la mañana — *morning*
de la mañana — *in the morning.*
Llegó a las once de la mañana. *She arrived at eleven in the morning.*

(muy) de mañana — *(very) early in the morning.*
Siempre salen (muy) de mañana. *They always go out (very) early in the morning.*

por (en) la mañana — *in the morning.*
Estudia por (en) la mañana. *He studies in the morning.*

163

mañana — *tomorrow*
   Hasta mañana. — *See you tomorrow.*

   mañana mismo — *no later than tomorrow; tomorrow without fail.*
   Los vamos a devolver mañana mismo. *We are going to return them no later than tomorrow (tomorrow without fail).*

la máquina — *machine*
   a toda máquina — *at full speed.*
   El tren iba a toda máquina. *The train was traveling at full speed.*

   escribir a máquina — *to type.*
   Sabe escribir a máquina. *She knows how to type.*

el (la) mar — *sea*
   El que no se arriesga no pasa la mar. — *Nothing ventured, nothing gained.*

   en alta mar — *on the high seas.*
   (Me) enfermé en alta mar. *I got sick on the high seas.*

   hacerse a la mar — *to put out to sea.*
   El barco se hizo a la mar. *The ship put out to sea.*

   la mar de — *no end of.*
   Hay la mar de cosas que hacer. *There is no end of things to do.*

   la mar de — *extremely.*
   Salió la mar de bien. *It turned out extremely well.*

la maravilla — *marvel, wonder*
   a (las mil) maravilla(s) — *marvelously.*
   Los dos bailan a (las mil) maravilla(s). *They both dance marvelously.*

   la octava maravilla — *the eighth wonder of the world.*
   Es la octava maravilla. *It's the eighth wonder of the world.*

la marcha — *march*
   apresurar la marcha — *to speed up.*
   Tuvieron que apresurar la marcha para llegar a tiempo. *They had to speed up to arrive on time.*

dar marcha atrás — *to back up.*
El coche no quiere dar marcha atrás. *The car won't back up.*

poner en marcha — *to start.*
Puso en marcha el motor. *He started the motor.*

ponerse en marcha — *to get under way.*
El desfile se puso en marcha. *The parade got under way.*

la margarita — *daisy; pearl*
No hay que echar margaritas a los puercos. — *You mustn't cast your pearls before swine.*

más — *more, most*

a más (de) — *besides.*
A más, no me gusta la paella. *Besides, I don't like paella.*
A más de ser bonita, es inteligente. *Besides being pretty, she's intelligent.*

a lo más — *at the most.*
Tenemos cinco pesos a lo más. *We have five pesos at the most.*

como el que más — *as well as anybody else (as the next man).*
Hace el trabajo como el que más. *He does the work as well as anybody else (as the next man).*

es más — *not only that; and furthermore.*
Es más, su esposa también es de allí. *Not only that (And furthermore), his wife is from there too.*

estar de más — *to be superfluous.*
Estos están de más. *These are superfluous.*

los más — *most.*
Los más hombres creen eso. *Most men believe that.*

más bien — *rather.*
Es más bien peligroso. *It's rather dangerous.*

más bien — *rather; instead.*
Más bien deseo uno que cueste poco. *Rather (Instead), I want one that doesn't cost much.*

no estar de más. — *not to be out of place.*
No estaría de más decírselo. *It wouldn't be out of place to tell him.*

no . . . más que — *only.*

No compré más que tres. *I bought only three.*

¿qué más da? — *what's the difference?*

Si se lo damos a él o a ella, ¿qué más da? *If we give it to him or to her, what's the difference?*

sin más ni más — *without further ado (just like that).*

Sin más ni más se marchó. *Without further ado (Just like that) he left.*

la masa — *dough*

con las manos en la masa — *red-handed (in the act).*

Cogieron al ladrón con las manos en la masa. *They caught the thief red-handed (in the act).*

la materia — *matter, material*

en materia de — *on the subject of; with regard to.*

Es perito en materia de gatos. *He's an expert on the subject of (with regard to) cats.*

entrar en materia — *to get into the subject; to get to the point.*

Ya vamos entrando en materia. *Now we're getting into the subject (getting to the point).*

mayor — *greater, older*

al por mayor — *wholesale; in large quantity.*

Aquí se vende solamente al por mayor. *Here they sell only wholesale (in large quantity).*

mediado — *half full*

a mediados — *about (around) the middle.*

Se casaron a mediados de junio. *They got married about (around) the middle of June.*

la medianoche — *midnight*

a (la) medianoche — *at midnight.*

Salimos a (la) medianoche. *We left at midnight.*

el médico — *doctor*

médico de cabecera — *family doctor.*

Es nuestro médico de cabecera. *He's our family doctor.*

la medida — *measure*

a la medida — *to order; to measure.*

Lo hicieron a la medida. *They made it to order (to measure).*

a la medida de — *according to.*

Todo se realizó a la medida de sus deseos. *Everything worked out according to his wishes.*

a medida que — *as; at the same time as.*

Yo secaré los platos a medida que usted me los pase. *I'll dry the plates (at the same time) as you hand them to me.*

sin medidas — *boundless.*

Sentía por su padre un amor sin medidas. *She felt a boundless love for her father.*

medio — *half*

a medio . . . — *half . . . .*

Dejó la puerta a medio cerrar. *He left the door half closed.*

de en medio — *out of the way.*

La quitó de en medio. *He got her out of the way.*

en medio de — *in the middle of.*

Se cayó en medio de la calle. *He fell (down) in the middle of the street.*

(hacer) a medias — *(to do) halfway.*

Hizo su trabajo a medias. *He did his work halfway.*

ir a medias — *to go fifty-fifty.*

Vamos a medias en este negocio. *Let's go fifty-fifty on this deal.*

el mediodía — *noon*

a(l) mediodía — *at noon.*

Se reúnen a(l) mediodía. *They get together at noon.*

mejor — *better, best*

a lo mejor — *as likely as not; I wouldn't be surprised if.*

A lo mejor llegarán mañana. *As likely as not they'll (I wouldn't be surprised if they) get here tomorrow.*

Mejor que mejor. — *Excellent (All the better).*
Tanto mejor. — *So much the better.*

la memoria — *memory*
de memoria — *by heart.*
Lo aprendió de memoria. *She learned it by heart.*

refrescarle la memoria — *to refresh someone's memory.*
Quiero refrescarle la memoria. *I want to refresh your memory.*

salirle de la memoria — *to slip one's mind.*
Me salió de la memoria. *It slipped my mind.*

la mención — *mention*
hacer mención de — *to mention; to make mention of.*
Hicieron mención del suceso. *They mentioned (made mention of) the event.*

menor — *less(er), younger*
al por menor — *retail.*
No se vende al por menor aquí. *They don't sell retail here.*

menos — *less, least*
a menos que — *unless.*
A menos que vaya conmigo, me quedo. *Unless you go with me, I'm staying.*

al (a lo, por lo) menos — *at least.*
Se quedó en el jardín al (a lo, por lo) menos tres horas. *She stayed in the garden at least three hours.*

de menos — *too little.*
Le pagué un peso de menos. *I paid him one peso too little.*

echar de menos — *to miss.*
La echo de menos. *I miss her.*

lo de menos — *the least of it; of little importance; insignificant.*

Es lo de menos. *That's the least of it.*

ni mucho menos — *far from it; or anything like it.*
No es mi mejor amigo ni mucho menos. *He's far from being my best friend.*

venir a menos — *to come down in the world.*
Su familia ha venido a menos. *Her family has come down in the world.*

---

la mente — *mind*
quitárselo de la mente — *to get (put) something out of one's mind.*
Se lo quitó de la mente. *He got (put) it out of his mind.*

---

mentir — *to lie*
¡Miento! — *I'm mistaken (My mistake)!*

---

la mentira — *lie*
coger (pescar) en (una) mentira — *to catch in a lie.*
Lo cogí (pesqué) en (una) mentira. *I caught him in a lie.*

parecer mentira — *to seem incredible; to be hard to believe.*
Parece mentira. *It seems incredible (It's hard to believe).*

---

menudo — *small, minute*
a menudo — *often; frequently.*
Nos viene a ver muy a menudo. *She comes to see us very often (frequently).*

---

merced — *mercy, favor, grace*
a (la) merced de — *at the mercy of.*
Lo dejó a (la) merced de su tío. *She left him at the mercy of his uncle.*

merced a — *thanks to.*
Merced a los esfuerzos de Carlos, el niño no murió. *Thanks to Charles's efforts the child did not die.*

---

merecido — *deserved*

  llevar su merecido — *to get what is coming to one.*
  El criminal llevó su merecido. *The criminal got what was coming to him.*

el mérito — *merit*

  hacer méritos — *to deserve.*
  Para que le aumenten el sueldo tiene que hacer méritos. *In order for them to increase his salary, he has to deserve it.*

la mesa — *table*

  levantar (quitar) la mesa (los manteles) — *to clear the table.*
  Levantó (Quitó) la mesa (los manteles). *She cleared the table.*

  levantarse de la mesa — *to get up from the table.*
  Nos levantamos de la mesa. *We got up from the table.*

  poner la mesa — *to set the table.*
  Puso la mesa. *She set the table.*

  servir (a) la mesa — *to wait on tables.*
  Servían (a) la mesa. *They waited on tables.*

el metal — *metal*

  el vil metal — *filthy lucre; dirty money.*
  No puede comprar mi lealtad con su vil metal. *You can't buy my loyalty with your filthy lucre (dirty money).*

meter — *to put*

  meterse con — *to provoke; to pick a quarrel with.*
  Más vale no meterse con él. *It's better not to provoke (pick a quarrel with) him.*

  meterse de (a) — *to become; to choose (a profession).*
  Se metió de (a) monja. *She became a nun.*

  meterse donde no le llaman — *to meddle in things that are none of one's business.*
  No quiere meterse donde no le llaman. *He doesn't want to meddle in things that are none of his business.*

meterse en lo ajeno — *to meddle in other people's business.*

Siempre se mete en lo ajeno. *He's always meddling in other people's business.*

meterse en lo que no le importa — *to butt in.*

¿Por qué te metes en lo que no te importa? *Why do you butt in?*

estar muy metido en — *to be deeply involved in.*

Está muy metido en ese escándalo. *He is deeply involved in that scandal.*

no saber dónde meterse — *not to know where to turn.*

El pobre no sabe dónde meterse. *The poor fellow doesn't know where to turn.*

---

el miedo — *fear*

darle miedo — *to frighten one.*

Me da miedo. *It frightens me.*

de miedo — *terrific, marvelous.*

La casa está de miedo ahora, después de las reformas. *The house looks terrific now, after the remodeling.*

meterle miedo — *to frighten (to inspire fear in) someone.*

Querían meternos miedo. *They wanted to frighten (inspire fear in) us.*

tener miedo — *to be afraid.*

Les tengo miedo. *I'm afraid of them.*

---

las mientes — *thought processes*

parar mientes en — *to reflect on; to consider.*

Paramos mientes en nuestra situación. *We reflected on (considered) our situation.*

venirse a las mientes — *to come to mind; to occur to.*

Se me vino a las mientes que no habíamos sido justos. *It came to my mind (occurred to me) that we had been unfair.*

---

la miga — *crumb*

hacer buenas migas — *to get along (to hit it off) well.*

Hacen buenas migas. *They get along (hit it off) well.*

el milagro — *miracle*
colgarle el milagro — *to pin it on.*
Ricardo robó el dinero, pero trató de colgarle el milagro a Andrés.
  Ricardo stole the money, but he tried to pin it on Andrés.

escapar de milagro — *to have a narrow (miraculous) escape.*
Escapó de milagro. *He had a narrow (miraculous) escape.*

por milagro — *incredibly.*
Por milagro llegaron a tiempo. *Incredibly, they arrived on time.*

mínimo — *minimum*
en lo más mínimo — *in the least.*
No me gustó la charla en lo más mínimo. *I didn't like the talk in the least.*

el minuto — *minute*
al minuto — *right away.*
Cuando le pedimos ayuda vino al minuto. *When we asked him for help he*
  came right away.

mío — *mine*
de mío — *by (of) my own nature.*
De mío no soy así. *By (Of) my own nature I'm not that way.*

la mira — *sight (of a gun).*
estar a la mira — *to be on the lookout.*
Siempre está a la mira para conseguir algo. *He is always on the lookout to*
  get something.

poner la mira en — *to set one's sights on; to have designs on.*

Ha puesto la mira en ese contrato. *He has set his sights on (has designs on) that contract.*

tener la mira puesta en — *to be aiming at; to set one's sights on.*

El senador tiene la mira puesta en la presidencia. *The senator is aiming at (has set his sights on) the presidency.*

la mirada — *look, glance*

  dirigir una mirada (fijar una mirada en) — *to glance at.*

  Le dirigí (Fijé en ella) una mirada. *I glanced at her.*

  huirle la mirada — *to avoid someone's glance.*

  Le huyeron la mirada. *They avoided her glance.*

mirar — *to look at*

  bien mirado — *after careful consideration; taking everything into consideration.*

  Bien mirado, me parece que no es así. *After careful consideration (Taking everything into consideration), I think it's not that way.*

  mirar por — *to look out for; to take care of.*

  Tengo que mirar por mis intereses. *I have to look out for (to take care of) my interests.*

  ser bien mirado — *to be well regarded (well thought of).*

  Es bien mirado. *He's well regarded (well thought of).*

la misa — *Mass*

  ayudar a misa — *to serve at Mass.*

  Ayudaba a misa. *He used to serve at Mass.*

  la misa del gallo — *midnight Mass.*

  Fuimos a la misa del gallo. *We went to midnight Mass.*

  no saber de la misa la media — *not to know what it's all about; not to know a thing.*

  No sabe de la misa la media. *He doesn't know what it's all about (doesn't know a thing).*

  oír misa — *to hear (to attend) Mass.*

  Oye misa todos los días. *He hears (attends) Mass every day.*

mismo — *same; (one)self*
   ayer mismo — *just yesterday.*
   Vino ayer mismo. *He came just yesterday.*

   darle a uno lo mismo — *to be all the same to one.*
   A mí me da lo mismo. *It's all the same to me.*

   eso mismo — *that very thing.*
   Es eso mismo lo que no le gusta. *It's that very thing that she doesn't like.*

   lo mismo que — *just like.*
   Soy profesor lo mismo que Juan. *I'm a professor just like John.*

   lo mismo . . . que . . . — *both . . . and . . . .*
   Lo mismo él que ella lo saben. *Both he and she know it.*

   . . . mismo — *. . . self.*
   Me lo dijo él mismo. *He told me so himself.*

   por lo mismo — *for that very reason.*
   Por lo mismo decidí no comprarlo. *For that very reason I decided not to buy it.*

   ser lo mismo — *to be all the same.*
   Para mí es lo mismo. *It's all the same to me.*

---

la mitad — *half*
   a mitad de — *halfway through.*
   Me lo dijo a mitad de la comida. *He told (it to) me halfway through dinner.*

   en (la) mitad de — *in the middle of.*
   Pusieron el obstáculo en (la) mitad de la calle. *They put the obstacle in the middle of the road.*

   por la mitad — *in two; in half.*
   Lo cortó por la mitad. *He cut it in two (in half).*

---

la moda — *fashion, style*
   estar de (a la) moda — *to be in style.*
   Está de (a la) moda. *It's in style.*

   pasarse de moda — *to go out of style.*
   Se está pasando (Está pasado) de moda. *It's going (gone) out of style.*

poner de moda — *to make fashionable.*
Pusieron de moda la minifalda. *They made the miniskirt fashionable.*

ponerse de moda — *to become fashionable; to come into style.*
Se está poniendo de moda. *It's becoming fashionable (coming into style).*

el modo — *manner, way*

a su modo — *after a fashion.*
Lo explicó a su modo. *He explained it after a fashion.*

a su (modo de) ver — *to one's way of thinking; in one's opinion.*
A mi modo de ver, la solución va a ser difícil. *To my way of thinking (In my opinion) the solution is going to be difficult.*

de algún modo (de un modo u otro) — *one way or another.*
Lo importante es hacerlo de algún modo (de un modo u otro). *The important thing is to do it one way or another.*

de este modo — *this way; in this manner.*
De este modo terminaremos pronto. *This way (In this manner) we'll finish soon.*

de modo que — *so.*
¡De modo que quiere Vd. ser médico! *So you want to be a doctor!*

de ningún modo — *by no means; not at all.*
¿Quieres ir también? — ¡De ningún modo! *Do you want to go too? — By no means (not at all)!*

de todos modos — *at any rate.*
De todos modos, es así. *At any rate, that's the way it is.*

molestar — *to bother, annoy*

molestarse en — *to bother to.*
No se molesta en saludarnos. *He doesn't bother to speak to us.*

el momento — *moment*

al momento — *in a minute.*
Contesto al momento. *I'll answer in a minute.*

así de momento — *right (just) offhand.*
Así de momento no sé. *Right (just) offhand I don't know.*

de (por el) momento — *for the moment.*

De (Por el) momento no hay más. *For the moment there isn't any more.*

de un momento a otro — *any time (now).*

Debe llegar de un momento a otro. *She should arrive any time (now).*

en aquel momento — *at that time.*

En aquel momento trabajaba en una fábrica. *At that time she was working in a factory.*

en el momento actual — *at present.*

En el momento actual la universidad está cerrada. *At present the university is closed.*

---

la mona — *(female) monkey; drunk(enness)*

Aunque la mona se vista de seda, mona se queda. — *Fine feathers don't make fine birds.*

dormir la mona — *to sleep it off.*

Está durmiendo la mona. *He's sleeping it off.*

---

la moneda — *coin*

pagarle en la misma moneda — *to pay someone back in his own coin.*

Le pagué en la misma moneda. *I paid him back in his own coin.*

---

el moño — *bun (of hair)*

estar hasta el moño — *to have had it up to here; to be fed up.*

¡Estoy hasta el moño con mi jefe! *I've had it up to here with my boss!*

---

el monte — *mountain; woods*

No todo el monte es orégano. — *You've got to take the rough with the smooth (Things aren't always the way we'd like them to be).*

---

el montón — *heap, pile*

a montones — *in abundance.*

Los producimos a montones. *We produce them in abundance.*

ser del montón — *to be very ordinary; a dime a dozen.*

Es del montón. *It's very ordinary (a dime a dozen).*

---

morir — *to die*

  morirse (estarse muriendo) por — *to be dying to.*

  Se mueren (Se están muriendo) por verla. *They're dying to see her.*

---

el moro — *Moor*

  Hay moros en la costa. — *The coast isn't clear.*

---

el morro — *snout*

  tener un morro que se lo pisa — *to have a lot of nerve.*

  Ese tiene un morro que se lo pisa. *That guy's got an incredible nerve.*

---

la mosca — *fly*

  cazar moscas — *to do useless things.*

  Rogelio pasa demasiado tiempo cazando moscas. *Roger spends too much time doing useless things.*

  Más moscas se cazan con miel que con vinagre. — *You can catch more flies with honey than with vinegar.*

  No se oía ni una mosca. — *You could hear a pin drop.*

  por si las moscas — *just in case.*

  Tráigame tres, por si las moscas. *Bring me three, just in case.*

  ¿Qué mosca te ha picado? — *What's eating (bugging) you?*

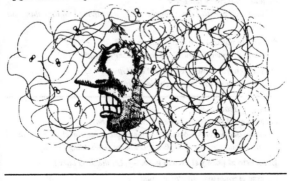

---

el motivo — *reason*

  con motivo de — *on the occasion of.*

  Se celebró un banquete con motivo del fin de cursos. *They held a banquet on the occasion of the end of school.*

  por motivo de — *on account of.*

  Se quedó dos semanas por motivo de la feria. *He stayed two weeks on account of the fair.*

  por ningún motivo — *under no circumstances.*

  No haré ese viaje por ningún motivo. *I won't take that trip under any circumstances.*

la moza — *girl*

  ser buena moza — *to be a good-looking girl.*

  Es muy buena moza. *She's a very good-looking girl.*

mucho — *much*

  ni con mucho — *not by a good deal; not by a long shot.*

  No lo terminamos ni con mucho. *We didn't finish it by a good deal (by a long shot).*

la muerte — *death*

  de mala muerte — *third-rate.*

  Vivían en un pueblo de mala muerte. *They were living in a little third-rate town.*

  de muerte natural — *a natural death.*

  Se murió de muerte natural. *She died a natural death.*

  emborracharse a muerte — *to get dead drunk.*

  Se emborrachó a muerte. *He got dead drunk.*

muerto — *dead*

  cargar con el muerto — *to be left holding the bag.*

  Hagan lo que hagan los demás, Pedro siempre carga con el muerto. *No matter what the others do, Pedro is always left holding the bag.*

  El muerto al pozo y el vivo al gozo. — *Let the dead bury the dead.*

  hacerse el muerto — *to play possum.*

Se hacía el muerto. *He was playing possum.*

no tener donde caerse muerto — *not to have a penny to one's name; to be as poor as a church mouse.*

No tiene donde caerse muerto. *He hasn't got a penny to his name (He's as poor as a church mouse).*

tocar a muerto — *to toll the bell.*

Tocaban a muerto. *They were tolling the bell.*

la muestra — *sample*

dar muestras de — *to show signs of.*

Daba muestras de impaciencia. *He was showing signs of impatience.*

Para muestra, basta un botón. — *It only takes a small sample.*

la mujer — *woman*

ser muy mujer — *to be all woman.*

Es muy mujer. *She's all woman.*

la multa — *fine*

imponerle una multa — *to fine someone.*

Le impusieron una multa. *They fined him.*

el mundo — *world*

desde que el mundo es mundo — *since the world began.*

Es así desde que el mundo es mundo. *It's been that way since the world began.*

medio mundo — *a lot of people.*

Medio mundo lo estaba mirando. *A lot of people were watching him.*

tener mucho mundo — *to be very sophisticated.*

Tiene mucho mundo. *She's very sophisticated.*

todo el mundo — *everybody.*

Todo el mundo debe leerlo. *Everybody should read it.*

ver mundo — *to see the world.*

Tiene muchas ganas de viajar y ver mundo. *He's eager to travel and see the world.*

la muñeca — *doll*

  jugar a las muñecas — *to play dolls.*

  Jugaban a las muñecas. *They were playing dolls.*

la musaraña — *shrew; spot before the eyes*

  pensar en las musarañas — *to be daydreaming (woolgathering).*

  Pensaba en las musarañas. *He was daydreaming (woolgathering).*

el nacimiento — *birth*

  de nacimiento — *from birth.*

  Era ciego de nacimiento. *He was blind from birth.*

nada — *nothing*

  así nada más — *just like that.*

  La abandonó así nada más. *He left her just like that.*

  como si nada — *as if there were nothing to it.*

  Lo hizo como si nada. *He did it as if there were nothing to it.*

  De nada. — *You're welcome (Don't mention it).*

  en nada — *very nearly; within an inch of.*

  En nada estuvo que se ahogara. *He very nearly drowned (came within an inch of drowning).*

  nada más — *just.*

  Nada más estoy esperando. *I'm just waiting.*

  nada más — *the minute.*

  Nada más entrar, vimos a mi hermana. *The minute we entered, we saw my sister.*

  no . . . (para) nada — *not . . . at all.*

  No nos ayudó (para) nada. *He didn't help us at all.*

  Peor es nada. — *It's better than nothing.*

la naranja — *orange*

  media naranja — *better half.*

  Quiero presentarte a mi media naranja. *I want to present you to my better half.*

---

la nariz — *nose*

  hablar por las narices — *to talk through one's nose.*

  Habla por las narices. *He talks through his nose.*

  delante de las narices — *right under one's nose.*

  Lo tenía delante de las narices. *It was right under his nose.*

  meter las narices en todo — *to poke (to stick) one's nose into everything.*

  Mete las narices en todo. *He pokes (sticks) his nose into everything.*

  no ver más allá de sus narices — *not to be able to see past the end of one's nose.*

  No ve más allá de sus narices. *He can't see past the end of his nose.*

---

la nave — *ship*

  quemar las naves — *to burn one's bridges (behind one); to burn one's boats.*

  Han quemado las naves. *They have burnt their bridges (behind them) (burnt their boats).*

181

la necesidad — *necessity*

   hacer de la necesidad virtud — *to make a virtue of necessity.*
   Hizo de la necesidad virtud. *He made a virtue of necessity.*

   La necesidad carece de ley. — *Necessity knows no law.*

   por necesidad — *(out) of necessity.*
   Lo vendió por necesidad. *He sold it (out) of necessity.*

   verse en la necesidad de — *to find it necessary to*
   Me vi en la necesidad de despedir a mi secretario. *I found it necessary to fire my secretary.*

negar — *to deny*

   negarse a — *to refuse to.*
   Se negó a aceptarlo. *He refused to accept it.*

   negarse a sí mismo — *to practice self-denial; to deny oneself.*
   Se niega a sí mismo. *He practices self-denial (denies himself).*

el nervio — *nerve*

   tener los nervios de punta — *to have one's nerves on edge; to be (feel) edgy.*
   Tengo los nervios de punta. *My nerves are on edge (I am [feel] edgy).*

ni — *neither, nor*

   ni. . . ni. . . — *neither. . . nor. . . .*
   Ni Juan ni Carlos pudieron contestar. *Neither John nor Charles could answer.*

   ni que — *as if.*
   ¡Ni que tuvieran tanto dinero! *As if they had that much money!*

   ni siquiera — *not even.*
   Ni siquiera su hermana asistió a la boda. *Not even her sister attended the wedding.*

la niña — *pupil (of the eye)*

   la niña de sus ojos — *the apple of one's eye.*
   Es la niña de sus ojos. *He's the apple of her eye.*

el niño — *child*

desde niño — *since one was a child; from childhood on.*
Vivía en París desde niño. *He had lived in Paris since he was a child (from childhood on).*

no — *not*

no bien — *no sooner.*
No bien salió, empezó a llover. *No sooner had he left than it started to rain.*

no ya — *not only.*
Los vemos a menudo, no ya en el campo sino en la ciudad también. *We see them often, not only in the country but in the city also.*

la noche — *night*

cerrar la noche — *for night to fall.*
Ya había cerrado la noche. *Night had already fallen.*

dar las buenas noches — *to say good night.*
Nos dio las buenas noches. *He said good night to us.*

de la noche a la mañana — *overnight; all at once.*
De la noche a la mañana perdió todo su dinero. *Overnight (All at once) he lost all his money.*

de noche — *at night.*
Asiste a la universidad de noche. *He attends the university at night.*

De noche todos los gatos son pardos. — *At night all cats are gray.*

esta noche — *tonight.*
Van al cine esta noche. *They're going to the movies tonight.*

hacerse de noche — *to get dark.*
Se hace de noche a las ocho. *It gets dark at eight.*

muy (de) noche — *late at night.*
Volvieron muy (de) noche. *They returned late at night.*

el nombre — *name*

a (en) nombre de . . . — *in . . . 's name.*
Nos habló a (en) nombre del gobernador. *He spoke to us in the governor's name.*

no tener nombre — *to be unspeakable.*
Lo que hizo no tiene nombre. *What he did is unspeakable.*

la nota — *note*
    dar la nota discordante — *to be the disturbing element.*
    Un borracho dio la nota discordante. *A drunk was the disturbing element.*

    tomar nota de — *to make a note of.*
    Tomó nota del número. *He made a note of the number.*

las noticias — *news*
    atrasado de noticias — *behind the times.*
    Están atrasados de noticias. *They are behind the times.*

la novedad — *news*
    sin novedad — *as usual.*
    Todos están sin novedad. *They are all as usual.*

el novillo — *young bull*
    hacer novillos — *to play hooky.*
    Hace novillos casi todos los días. *He plays hooky almost every day.*

la nube — *cloud*
    estar en las nubes — *to be daydreaming.*
    Está en las nubes en vez de estudiar. *She's daydreaming instead of studying.*

    poner en (sobre; por) las nubes — *to praise to the skies.*
    La puso en (sobre; por) las nubes. *He praised her to the skies.*

    por las nubes — *sky high.*
    Los precios (se) están (poniendo) por las nubes. *Prices are (going) sky high.*

el nudo — *knot*
    sentir un nudo en la garganta — *to get a lump in one's throat.*
    Sintió un nudo en la garganta. *He got a lump in his throat.*

nuevo — *new*

   de nuevo — *again.*

   Mañana le escribo de nuevo. *Tomorrow I'll write you again.*

   ¿Qué hay de nuevo? — *What's new?*

el número — *number*

   mirar por el número uno — *to look out for number one (oneself).*

   Hay que mirar por el número uno. *You've got to look out for number one (for yourself).*

   sin número — *countless.*

   Tiene amigos sin número. *He has countless friends.*

o — *either, or*

   o. . . o. . . — *either . . . or . . . .*

   Tome o el rojo o el verde. *Take either the red one or the green one.*

obedecer — *to obey*

   obedecer a — *to arise from (to be based on).*

   Su enojo obedece a un malentendido. *Her anger arises from (is based on) a misunderstanding.*

la objeción — *objection*

   hacer objeciones a — *to raise objections to.*

   Hizo objeciones al plan. *He raised objections to the plan.*

el objeto — *object*

   con objeto de — *(in order) to.*

   Pasaron con objeto de despedirse. *They came by (in order) to say good-bye.*

la obra — *work*

   de palabra y de obra — *in word and deed.*

Mostró su hostilidad de palabra y de obra. *He showed his hostility in word and deed.*

en obra de — *in a matter of.*
Volverán en obra de tres semanas. *They'll come back in a matter of three weeks.*

en obras — *under construction.*
Hay muchos edificios en obras. *There are many buildings under construction.*

Obras son amores, que no buenas razones. — *Actions speak louder than words.*

poner por obra — *to put into execution.*
Puso por obra sus planes. *He put his plans into execution.*

ponerse a la obra — *to go to work.*
Se puso a la obra en seguida. *He went to work immediately.*

---

obscuro — *dark*
    a obscuras — *in the dark.*
    No podemos trabajar a obscuras. *We can't work in the dark.*

    estar (hacer) obscuro — *to be dark.*
    Está (Hace) obscuro. *It's dark.*

---

obsequiar — *to give*
    obsequiar con — *to present with.*
    Me obsequiaron con una copa de plata. *They presented me with a silver cup.*

---

obstante — *standing in the way*
    no obstante — *however; nevertheless.*
    Es de Colombia; no obstante, habla muy bien el inglés. *He is from Colombia; however (nevertheless), he speaks English very well.*

    no obstante — *notwithstanding; in spite of.*
    No obstante su pereza, realiza mucho. *His laziness notwithstanding (In spite of his laziness), he accomplishes a lot.*

---

la ocasión — *occasion*

    A la ocasión la pintan calva. — *Opportunity knocks but once.*

    de ocasión — *second-hand.*

    Vendemos libros de ocasión. *We sell second-hand books.*

    en ocasiones — *at times; on occasion.*

    En ocasiones parece coja. *At times (On occasion) she appears lame.*

    Hay que tomar (coger) la ocasión por los cabellos. — *You've got to seize the opportunity when it comes.*

la ociosidad — *idleness*

    La ociosidad es la madre de todos los vicios. — *An idle brain is the devil's workshop; The devil finds mischief for idle hands.*

ocupar — *to occupy*

    ocuparse de — *to look out for; to look after.*

    Se ocupará de nosotros. *He'll look out for (look after) us.*

la ocurrencia — *occurrence; clever thought*

    tener la ocurrencia de — *to have the bright idea of.*

    Tuvimos la ocurrencia de no comer en casa. *We had the bright idea of eating out.*

ocurrir — *to occur*

    ocurrírsele — *to occur (to one).*

    No se me ocurrió pedírselo. *It didn't occur to me to ask him for it.*

el oído — *ear, hearing*

    aguzar los oídos (el oído) — *to prick up one's ears.*

    Aguzó los oídos (el oído). *He pricked up his ears.*

    corto de oído — *hard of hearing.*

    Es un poco corto de oído. *He's a little hard of hearing.*

    dar oídos — *to listen.*

    No quiso dar oídos a mis quejas. *He refused to listen to my complaints.*

    decirle al oído — *to whisper in one's ear.*

    Me lo dijo al oído. *He whispered it in my ear.*

entrar por un oído y salir por el otro — *to go in one ear and out the other.*

Le entra por un oído y le sale por el otro. *It goes in one ear and out the other.*

llegar a oídos de — *to reach (to come to) the ears of.*

Llegó a oídos de su padre. *It reached (came to) the ears of his father.*

ser todo oídos — *to be all ears.*

Soy todo oídos. *I'm all ears.*

tener buen oído — *to have a good ear (for music).*

Tiene buen oído. *She has a good ear (for music).*

tocar de oído — *to play by ear.*

Eugenia toca la guitarra de oído. *Eugenia plays the guitar by ear.*

---

oír — *to hear*

oír decir — *to hear.*

Oí decir que no iba. *I heard he wasn't going.*

oír hablar de — *to hear of.*

He oído hablar de ellos. *I've heard of them.*

---

la ojeada — *glance*

echar una ojeada a — *to glance at.*

Le echó una ojeada y la saludó. *He glanced at her and greeted her.*

---

el ojo — *eye*

a ojos cerrados — *blindfolded; with one's eyes closed.*

Sabía tejer a ojos cerrados. *She could knit blindfolded (with her eyes closed).*

comerse con los ojos — *to ogle.*

El viejo se comía con los ojos a las chicas en la playa. *The old man was ogling the girls on the beach.*

costar un ojo de la cara — *to cost a fortune (an arm and a leg).*

Me costó un ojo de la cara. *It cost me a fortune (an arm and a leg).*

¡Dichosos los ojos! — *How nice to see you!*

echar el ojo a — *to have one's eye on.*

La niña le echaba el ojo a una preciosa muñeca española. *The little girl had her eye on a lovely Spanish doll.*

el ojo derecho — *the darling.*
Era el ojo derecho de los jóvenes. *She was the darling of the young men.*

en un abrir y cerrar de ojos — *in the twinkling of an eye; in a wink (flash).*
Lo terminaron todo en un abrir y cerrar de ojos. *They finished it all in the twinkling of an eye (in a wink; in a flash).*

Más ven cuatro ojos que dos. — *Two heads are better than one.*

mirar con buenos ojos — *to look favorably on.*
No nos miran con buenos ojos. *They don't look favorably on us.*

no pegar (los) ojo(s) — *not to sleep a wink.*
No pegó (los) ojo(s). *He didn't sleep a wink.*

¡Ojo con lo que dice! — *Watch what you're saying!*

Ojo por ojo, diente por diente. — *An eye for an eye and a tooth for a tooth.*

Ojos que no ven, corazón que no siente. — *Out of sight, out of mind.*

tener buen ojo — *to have a good eye.*
Tiene buen ojo para el tiro a blanco. *He has a good eye for target practice.*

tener (poner) mucho ojo con — *to look out for; to pay (close) attention to.*
Hay que tener (poner) mucho ojo con el tren. *You have to look out for the train.*

---

oler — *to smell*
  oler a — *to smell like.*
  Huele a vino. *It smells like wine.*

---

operar — *to operate*
  operarle — *to operate on one.*
  Me operaron. *They operated on me.*

  operarle de. . . — *to operate on one's. . . .*
  Me operaron del hígado. *They operated on my liver.*

---

la opinión — *opinion*

   cambiar (mudar) de opinión — *to change one's mind.*

   Ha cambiado (mudado) de opinión. *He has changed his mind.*

   variar de (en) opinión — *to change one's mind.*

   Ha variado de (en) opinión. *He has changed his mind.*

---

oponer — *to oppose*

   oponerse a — *to object to; to be opposed to.*

   Se opone a que le escriba. *She objects to (is opposed to) my writing to her.*

---

optar — *to choose, opt*

   optar por — *to decide in favor of; to choose to.*

   Opté por comprar un coche. *I decided in favor of buying (chose to buy) a car.*

---

ora — *now*

   ora . . ., ora . . . — *now . . ., now (then) . . . .*

   Vive ora en Madrid, ora en Roma. *She lives now in Madrid, now (then) in Rome.*

---

el orden — *order*

   de segundo orden — *second-rate.*

   Este hotel es de segundo orden. *This is a second-rate hotel.*

---

la orden — *order, command; (religious) order*

   cumplir una orden — *to carry out an order.*

   Cumplió la orden. *He carried out the order.*

---

ordinario — *ordinary*

   de ordinario — *usually.*

   De ordinario va sola. *Usually she goes alone.*

---

la oreja — *ear*

   aguzar las orejas (parar la oreja) — *to prick up one's ears.*

   Aguzaron las orejas (Pararon la oreja). *They pricked up their ears.*

verle las orejas al lobo — *to be in great danger.*
Le veían las orejas al lobo. *They were in great danger.*

el oro — *gold*
No es oro todo lo que reluce (brilla). — *All that glitters is not gold.*

Vale tanto oro como pesa. — *It's worth its weight in gold.*

otro — *other, another*
el otro . . . — *next. . . .*
El otro martes lo llevo. *Next Tuesday I'll take you.*

¡Otro que tal (Otro que bien baila)! — *(He's, she's, etc.) another one
(another such)!*

otros tantos — *as many (more).*
Había diez hombres y otras tantas mujeres. *There were ten men and as
many (more) women.*

la oveja — *sheep*
la oveja negra de la familia — *the black sheep of the family.*
Era la oveja negra de la familia. *He was the black sheep of the family.*

la paciencia — *patience*
Paciencia y barajar. — *If at first you don't succeed, try, try again.*

probarle la paciencia — *to try one's patience.*
Ese niño me prueba la paciencia. *That child tries my patience.*

el padre — *father*
una pelea de padre y muy señor mío — *a fight to end all fights.*
Fue una pelea de padre y muy señor mío. *It was a fight to end all fights.*

pagar — *to pay*

   estar muy pagado de sí mismo — *to have a high opinion of oneself; to be sold on oneself.*

   Está muy pagado de sí mismo. *He has a high opinion of himself (is sold on himself).*

   pagársela — *to get even with someone; to make someone pay for it.*

   Me la pagarán. *I'll get even with them (make them pay for it).*

el pájaro — *bird*

   Más vale pájaro en mano que ciento volando. — *A bird in the hand is worth two in the bush.*

   matar dos pájaros de (en) un tiro (una pedrada) — *to kill two birds with one stone.*

   Mataron dos pájaros de (en) un tiro (una pedrada). *They killed two birds with one stone.*

   tener pájaros en la cabeza — *to have bats in the belfry.*

   Tiene pájaros en la cabeza. *He has bats in the belfry.*

Tiene pájaros en la cabeza.
He has bats in the belfry.

la palabra — *word*

   A palabras necias, oídos sordos. — *To foolish talk, deaf ears.*

   cumplir la palabra — *to keep one's word.*

   Siempre cumple su palabra. *He always keeps his word.*

   dejarle con la palabra en la boca — *to cut someone off.*

   Me dejó con la palabra en la boca. *He cut me off.*

dirigir la palabra a — *to address.*
Les dirigió la palabra en español. *He addressed them in Spanish.*

en otras palabras — *in other words.*
En otras palabras, no me gusta. *In other words, I don't like it.*

ligero de palabra — *a loose talker; a blabbermouth.*
Es muy ligero de palabra. *He's a very loose talker (a real blabbermouth).*

pesar las palabras — *to weigh one's words.*
Hay que pesar bien las palabras antes de hablar. *You've got to weigh your words before speaking.*

sin cruzar la palabra — *not to say a word to each other; not to speak to each other.*
Llevan cinco meses sin cruzar la palabra. *They haven't said a word to each other (spoken to each other) for five months.*

tener la palabra — *to have the floor.*
Ahora tiene la palabra. *Now you have the floor.*

tomarle la palabra — *to take one at one's word.*
No sabía que ibas a tomarme la palabra. *I didn't know you were going to take me at my word.*

---

la palanca — *lever*
 tener palanca — *to have pull.*
 Sin tener palanca no se llega a ninguna parte. *You can't get anywhere if you don't have pull.*

---

la palmada — *pat, slap*
 dar unas palmadas — *to clap one's hands.*
 Di unas palmadas. *I clapped my hands.*

 darle unas palmadas en la espalda — *to pat someone on the back.*
 Me dio unas palmadas en la espalda. *He patted me on the back.*

---

el palmo — *span*
 palmo a palmo — *inch by inch.*
 Lo exploró palmo a palmo. *He explored it inch by inch.*

---

el palo — *stick*

   De tal palo, tal astilla. — *A chip off the old block; Like father, like son.*

   matar a palos — *to beat to death.*
   Lo mataron a palos. *They beat him to death.*

el pan — *bread*

   Con su pan se lo coma. — *That's his problem; It's his funeral.*

   Contigo, pan y cebolla. — *You and I together, come what may; I'll go through thick and thin with you.*

   llamar al pan pan y al vino vino — *to call a spade a spade.*
   Llama al pan pan y al vino vino. *He calls a spade a spade.*

   ponerle a pan y agua — *to put someone on bread and water.*
   Los puso a pan y agua. *He put them on bread and water.*

   ser un pedazo de pan — *to have a heart of gold.*
   Puedes contar con la ayuda de Paco. Es un pedazo de pan. *You can count on Paco's help. He has a heart of gold.*

el pañal — *diaper*

   estar en pañales — *to be a babe in arms.*
   En cuanto a filosofía todavía estoy en pañales. *As far as philosophy is concerned, I'm still a babe in arms.*

la papa — *potato*

   no entender ni papa — *not to understand a thing.*
   No entendió ni papa. *He didn't understand a thing.*

el papel — *paper; role*

   hacer buen (mal) papel — *to make a good (bad) impression.*
   Hiciste muy buen (mal) papel anoche. *You made a very good (bad) impression last night.*

   hacer (desempeñar) el papel de — *to play the role (part) of.*
   Hace (Desempeña) el papel del abuelo. *He plays the role (part) of the grandfather.*

   representar su papel de — *to play one's role as.*

Representaba bien su papel de marido ejemplar. *He was playing his role as an exemplary husband well.*

---

par — *equal, like*

a la par (al par) que — *at the same time.*

Comía a la par (al par) que miraba la televisión. *He was eating and at the same time watching television.*

abierto de par en par — *wide open.*

Estaba abierto de par en par. *It was wide open.*

sin par — *incomparable.*

Es un profesor sin par. *He's an incomparable teacher.*

---

para — *for*

¿para qué? — *what's the good of; why?*

¿Para qué gastar tanto dinero? *What's the good of spending (Why spend) so much money?*

para sí — *to oneself.*

Lo pensaba para sí. *He was thinking it to himself.*

---

parar — *to stop*

¿Dónde va a parar? — *Where will it all end?*

---

parecer — *to seem, appear*

a su parecer — *in one's opinion.*

A mi parecer, debe comprar la casa. *In my opinion, she ought to buy the house.*

al parecer (a lo que parece) — *apparently.*

Al parecer (A lo que parece) es de alta calidad. *Apparently it's of high quality.*

parecerse a — *to look like.*

Se parece a su madre. *She looks like her mother.*

¿qué le parece? — *what do you think (of something)?*

¿Qué le parece (la novela)? *What do you think (of the novel)?*

---

la pared — *wall*
  Las paredes oyen. — *Walls have ears.*

  vivir pared por medio — *to live next door.*
  Viven pared por medio. *They live next door.*

---

el paréntesis — *parenthesis*
  entre paréntesis — *incidentally; by the way.*
  Entre paréntesis, ¿quién se lo vendió? *Incidentally (By the way), who sold it to you?*

  hacer un paréntesis — *to digress.*
  En vez de hablar de México, hizo un paréntesis y habló de España. *Instead of talking about Mexico, he digressed and talked about Spain.*

---

el paro — *unemployment*
  estar en paro — *to be unemployed.*
  Estuvo en paro durante un año. *He was out of work for a year.*

---

el párrafo — *paragraph*
  echar un párrafo — *to have a little chat.*
  Me detuve a echar un párrafo con Juan. *I stopped to have a little chat with John.*

  párrafo aparte — *not to change the subject.*
  Párrafo aparte, ¿qué piensa hacer esta noche? *Not to change the subject, (but) what are you planning to do tonight?*

---

la parranda — *spree*
  andar de parranda — *to go out on a spree.*
  Anda de parranda todas las noches. *He goes out on a spree every night.*

---

el parte — *dispatch, communiqué*
  dar parte de — *to report; to notify.*
  Dio parte del accidente a la policía. *He reported the accident to the police (notified the police of the accident).*

---

la parte — *part*
  a ninguna parte — *nowhere.*

No van juntos a ninguna parte. *They don't go anywhere together.*

a todas partes — *everywhere.*
El niño le seguía a todas partes. *The child followed him everywhere.*

de parte de . . . — *on . . .'s side.*
Creo que están de nuestra parte (de parte de Juan). *I think they're on our side (on John's side).*

de parte de . . . — *on one's . . .'s side.*
De parte de padre es alemán. *On his father's side he's German.*

de su parte — *for one.*
Salúdela de mi parte. *Say hello to her for me.*

en alguna parte — *somewhere; someplace.*
En alguna parte tiene que estar. *It's got to be somewhere (someplace).*

en gran parte — *to a great (large) extent.*
En gran parte es a causa de las lluvias. *To a great (large) extent it's because of the rains.*

en (por) ninguna parte (en parte alguna) — *not anywhere (at all); nowhere.*
Ya no se compran en ninguna parte (en parte alguna). *You can't buy them anywhere (at all) any more.*

en parte — *in part.*
Me gustó en parte. *I liked it in part.*

en todas partes — *everywhere.*
Se veían en todas partes. *They were seen everywhere.*

En todas partes cuecen habas. — *Things are (about) the same all over.*

formar parte de — *to be a part (member) of.*
No forma parte de este grupo. *He is not a part (member) of this group.*

la mayor parte de — *most of; the majority (of).*
La mayor parte de las chicas no vinieron. *Most of (The majority of) the girls didn't come.*

no ir a ninguna parte — *not to get anywhere.*
Dejemos de discutir. Así no vamos a ninguna parte. *Let's stop arguing. We won't get anywhere that way.*

por otra parte — *on the other hand.*

Por otra parte, le van a indemnizar por sus pérdidas. *On the other hand they are going to indemnify him for his losses.*

por su parte — *as far as one is concerned.*
Yo por mi parte prefiero quedarme aquí. *As far as I'm concerned, I prefer to stay here.*

por todas partes — *on all sides.*
Está rodeado de agua por todas partes. *It's surrounded by water on all sides.*

tomar parte en — *to take part in.*
No tomó parte en el concurso. *He didn't take part in the contest.*

particular — *particular, private*
en particular — *especially; in particular.*
Me gustan las obras de Azuela, y en particular **Los de abajo.** *I like Azuela's works, and especially (in particular) **Los de abajo.***

nada de particular — *nothing unusual.*
No vimos nada de particular. *We did not see anything (We saw nothing) unusual.*

la partida — *game*
echar una partida de dados — *to shoot (throw) dice.*
Echaron una partida de dados. *They shot (threw) dice.*

el partidario — *supporter, follower*
ser partidario de — *to be in favor of (to favor).*
Soy partidario de elecciones democráticas. *I'm in favor of (I favor) democratic elections.*

el partido — *(political) party; advantage, profit; resolve, decision*
sacar partido de — *to derive benefit (advantage) from.*
¿Cómo podemos sacar un poco de partido de lo ocurrido? *How can we derive a little benefit (advantage) from what has happened?*

tomar partido — *to take sides (to take a stand).*
Tarde o temprano tendrán que tomar partido. *Sooner or later they'll have to take sides (take a stand).*

partir — *to depart, start (out)*

  a partir de — *beginning; starting.*

  A partir de mañana, se servirá el desayuno a las siete. *Beginning (Starting) tomorrow, breakfast will be served at seven.*

---

la pasada — *passage, (act of) passing*

  jugarle una mala pasada — *to play a dirty trick on someone.*

  Me jugaron una mala pasada. *They played a dirty trick on me.*

---

pasar — *to pass*

  pasar de — *not to care about.*

  Ella pasa de su trabajo. *She doesn't care about her work.*

  pasarse — *to go too far.*

  No te pases con el café. *Don't put in too much coffee.*

  pasar por alto — *to overlook.*

  Lo pasó por alto. *He overlooked it.*

  pasar(se) sin — *to get along without; to do without.*

  No puedo pasar(me) sin comer. *I can't get along without (do without) eating.*

  pasarlo — *to get along.*

  ¿Cómo lo pasa usted? *How are you getting along?*

  pasarlo bien — *to enjoy oneself.*

  ¡Que lo pase bien! *Enjoy yourself!*

  pasarse de listo — *to be too smart for one's own good.*

  Un día de éstos va a pasarse de listo. *One of these days he's going to get too smart for his own good.*

  pasarse volando el tiempo — *for time to fly (by).*

  El tiempo se ha pasado volando. *Time has flown (by).*

  pasársele — *to forget.*

  Se me pasó llamarla. *I forgot to call her.*

  pasársele con el tiempo — *to get over it in time.*

  Con el tiempo se le pasará. *He'll get over it in time.*

  ¿Qué le pasa? — *What's the matter (What's wrong) with him?*

  Ya pasó. — *It's over now.*

la pascua — *any of various religious holidays, especially Passover, Easter, and Christmas*

  de Pascuas a Ramos — *every once in a while; occasionally.*

  De Pascuas a Ramos me hacen una visita. *Every once in a while (Occasionally) they pay me a visit.*

  estar como unas pascuas — *to be feeling very jolly.*

  Estaba como unas pascuas. *He was feeling very jolly.*

  ¡Felices Pascuas! — *Merry Christmas!*

  Santas pascuas. — *Well, so be it; It can't be helped.*

el paseo — *stroll, walk; (pleasure) drive, ride*

  dar un paseo — *to take (to go for) a walk.*

  Dimos un paseo. *We took (went for) a walk.*

  dar un paseo en coche — *to take (to go for) a drive.*

  Dimos un paseo en coche. *We took (went for) a drive.*

  mandar a paseo — *to send packing; to send about one's business.*

  Lo mandaron a paseo. *They sent him packing (sent him about his business).*

el paso — *step; passing, passage*

  a buen paso — *at a good pace.*

  Se acercaba a buen paso. *He was approaching at a good pace.*

  a cada paso — *at every turn.*

  A cada paso se veía algo nuevo. *Something new could be seen at every turn.*

  a cada paso — *every little while; every so often.*

  Lava su coche a cada paso. *He washes his car every little while (every so often).*

  a dos pasos — *very near; just a stone's throw from.*

  Está a dos pasos de aquí. *It's very near (just a stone's throw from) here.*

  a este paso — *at this rate.*

  A este paso nunca terminaré. *At this rate I'll never finish.*

  a paso de tortuga — *at a snail's pace.*

  Caminaban a paso de tortuga. *They were traveling at a snail's pace.*

a su paso — *as one passes.*
Aplaudieron a su paso. *They applauded as he passed.*

a un paso — *(just) a step away.*
Estaba a un paso de la victoria. *He was (just) a step away from victory.*

abrir paso — *to make way.*
Abrieron paso y él entró. *They made way and he went in.*

abrirse paso — *to make one's way.*
Se abrió paso por la multitud. *He made his way through the crowd.*

apretar el paso — *to speed up.*
Tuvieron que apretar el paso para llegar a tiempo. *They had to speed up to arrive on time.*

cerrar (impedir) el paso — *to block the way.*
Le cerraron (impidieron) el paso. *They blocked his way.*

dar pasos — *to take steps.*
Dio dos pasos. *He took two steps.*

de paso — *at the same time; on the way.*
Iré al correo y de paso compraré un periódico. *I'll go to the post office and at the same time (on the way) I'll buy a newspaper.*

de paso por — *while passing through.*
La visitamos de paso por la ciudad. *We visited her while passing through the city.*

dicho sea de paso — *incidentally.*
Mi padre, dicho sea de paso, no sabe español. *My father, incidentally, doesn't know Spanish.*

paso por (a) paso — *step by step.*
Nos guió por la selva paso por paso. *He guided us through the jungle step by step.*

salir del paso — *to get out of the jam (difficulty); to get by; to manage.*
Con la ayuda de Pablo salió del paso. *With Paul's help he got out of the jam (difficulty) (he got by).*

volver sobre sus pasos — *to retrace one's steps.*
Volvimos sobre nuestros pasos. *We retraced our steps.*

la pasta — *paste, dough*

   ser de buena pasta — *to be a good guy; to have a nice disposition.*
   Es de buena pasta. *He's a good guy (has a nice disposition).*

   ser de la pasta de su . . . — *to take after one's. . . .*
   Es de la pasta de su madre. *She takes after her mother.*

---

la pata — *paw, foot, leg (of an animal)*

   andar a cuatro patas — *to be down on all fours.*
   Andaban a cuatro patas. *They were down on all fours.*

   estirar la pata — *to kick the bucket.*
   Estiró la pata el mes pasado. *He kicked the bucket last month.*

   meter la pata — *to put one's foot in one's mouth.*
   Metí la pata. *I put my foot in my mouth.*

   patas arriba — *topsy turvy.*
   Está todo patas arriba y no puedo encontrar nada. *Everything is topsy-
      turvy and I can't find anything.*

   ponerle de patitas en la calle — *to throw someone out.*
   La pusieron de patitas en la calle. *They threw her out.*

   tener mala pata — *to be unlucky (have bad luck).*
   No sé por qué siempre tenemos tan mala pata. *I don't know why we are
      always so unlucky (have such bad luck).*

---

el pato — *duck*

   pagar el pato — *to be the (scape) goat (fall-guy; patsy); to take the
      blame (for someone else).*
   Yo tuve que pagar el pato. *I had to be the scapegoat (the fall-guy; the
      patsy) (I had to take the blame).*

---

el patrón — *patron; pattern*

   cortado por (con) el mismo patrón — *of the same stamp; cut to (from)
      the same pattern.*
   Parecen todos cortados por (con) el mismo patrón. *They all seem to be of
      the same stamp (cut to (from) the same pattern).*

---

el pavo — *turkey*

    subírsele el pavo — *to get red in the face.*

    Se le subió el pavo. *He got red in the face.*

---

la paz — *peace*

    dejarle en paz — *to let someone alone.*

    ¡Déjenos en paz! *Let us alone!*

    estar (quedar) en paz — *to be even.*

    Ahora estamos (quedamos) en paz. *Now we are even.*

    hacer las paces — *to make peace.*

    Hicieron las paces. *They made peace.*

    Que en paz descanse. — *May he (she) rest in peace.*

    quedar en paz — *to be left in peace.*

    Todo el mundo quedó en paz. *Everyone was left in peace.*

---

la pe — *(the letter) p*

    de pe a pa — *from A to Z; from beginning to end.*

    Lo ha aprendido de pe a pa. *She has learned it from A to Z (from beginning to end).*

---

el pecho — *breast, chest*

    A lo hecho, pecho. — *There's no use crying over spilt milk.*

    darle el pecho — *to nurse.*

    Le daba el pecho al niño. *She was nursing the child.*

    sacar el pecho — *to throw out one's chest.*

    Sacó el pecho. *He threw out his chest.*

    tomar a pecho(s) — *to take to heart.*

    Lo tomó a pecho(s). *She took it to heart.*

---

el pedazo — *piece*

    a pedazos — *in pieces; dismantled.*

    Se llevaron el piano a pedazos. *They took the piano away in pieces (dismantled).*

hacer pedazos — *to break (to pieces).*
Hizo pedazos la jarra. *He broke the pitcher (to pieces).*

vender (comprar) por un pedazo de pan — *to sell (buy) for a song.*
Vendieron (compraron) la casa por un pedazo de pan. *They sold (bought) the house for a song.*

Pedro — *Peter*
como Pedro por su casa — *as if he owned the place.*
Se pasea por aquí como Pedro por su casa. *He walks around here as if he owned the place.*

pegar — *to stick, attach*
pegársela a — *to deceive.*
Se la pegó a su mujer. *He deceived his wife.*

el peligro — *danger*
correr peligro — *to be in danger.*
No corremos peligro. *We're not in (any) danger.*

estar fuera de peligro — *to be out of danger.*
Ya está fuera de peligro. *He's out of danger now.*

Quien ama el peligro en él perece. — *He who loves danger perishes in it.*

el pelo — *hair*
con todos sus pelos y señales — *in greatest detail; in all the gory details.*
Me lo explicó con todos sus pelos y señales. *He explained it to me in greatest detail (in all the gory details).*

montar en pelo — *to ride bareback.*
Le gusta montar en pelo. *She likes to ride bareback.*

no tener pelo de tonto — *to be nobody's fool.*
No tiene pelo de tonto. *He's nobody's fool.*

ponérsele los pelos de punta — *to have one's hair stand on end.*
Se me pusieron los pelos de punta. *My hair stood on end.*

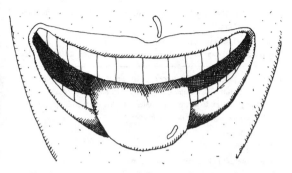

no tener pelos en la lengua — *to be very outspoken; not to mince words.*
No tiene pelos en la lengua. *He's very outspoken (doesn't mince words).*

por los pelos — *by the skin of one's teeth.*
Se escapó por los pelos. *He escaped by the skin of his teeth.*

tirarle del pelo — *to pull someone's hair.*
Me tiró del pelo. *She pulled my hair.*

tomarle el pelo — *to pull someone's leg.*
Les está tomando el pelo. *He's pulling their leg.*

traído por los pelos — *far-fetched.*
Me parece un poco traído por los pelos. *I think it's a little far-fetched.*

un hombre de (con) pelo en pecho — *a real he-man.*
Es un hombre de (con) pelo en pecho. *He's a real he-man.*

---

la pelota — *ball*
    hacerle la pelota — *to suck up to.*
    Le hace la pelota al jefe siempre que puede. *He sucks up to the boss whenever he can.*

---

el pellejo — *skin, hide*
    arriesgarse el pellejo — *to risk one's neck (life).*
    Se arriesgó el pellejo. *He risked his neck (life).*

    estar (hallarse) en el pellejo de — *to be in one's shoes.*

Si estuviera (Si me hallara) en su pellejo, no iría. *If I were in his shoes, I wouldn't go.*

salvarse el pellejo — *to save one's skin (hide).*
Huyó para salvarse el pellejo. *He fled in order to save his skin (hide).*

la pena — *penalty, punishment; pain, grief; hardship, trouble*
  a duras penas — *with utmost difficulty; just barely.*
  A duras penas pudo llegar a la frontera. *With utmost difficulty he (He just barely) managed to reach the border.*

  dar(le) pena — *to grieve one.*
  Me da pena. *It grieves me.*

  valer (merecer) la pena — *to be worthwhile; to be worth the trouble.*
  Esa comedia no vale (merece) la pena. *That play isn't worthwhile (worth the trouble).*

pendiente — *hanging, dangling*
  estar pendiente de — *to be waiting for.*
  Estoy pendiente de su decisión. *I'm waiting for his decision.*

pensar — *to think*
  cuando menos se piensa — *when one least expects it.*
  Cuando menos se piensa, dice cosas graciosas. *When you least expect it he says funny things.*

  ¡Eso ni pensarlo! — *That's out of the question!*

  ser mal pensado — *to be evil-minded.*
  No sea mal pensado. *Don't be evil-minded.*

peor — *worse, worst*
  ¡Peor que peor! — *Worse and worse; It couldn't be worse!*

  Tanto peor. — *So much the worse.*

el pepino — *cucumber*
  importarle un pepino — *not to be able to care less.*

Mañana es su cumpleaños, pero a mí me importa un pepino. *Tomorrow is his birthday, but I couldn't care less.*

---

la pequeñez — *littleness, pettiness*
por pequeñeces — *over trifles.*
Ha sufrido mucho por pequeñeces. *He's suffered a lot over trifles.*

---

la pera — *pear*
pedir peras al olmo — *to expect the impossible.*
No hay que pedir peras al olmo. *You mustn't expect the impossible.*

---

el perejil — *parsley*
Huyendo del perejil, dio en el berenjenal. — *Out of the frying pan into the fire.*

---

la perfección — *perfection*
a la perfección — *to perfection; perfectly.*
Lo copió a la perfección. *He copied it to perfection (perfectly).*

---

la perilla — *pear-shaped ornament*
venir de perillas — *to be just the thing (just right).*
Viene de perillas. *It's just the thing (just right).*

---

la perla — *pearl*
venir de perlas — *to be just the thing (just right).*
Viene de perlas. *It's just the thing (just right).*

ser una perla — *to be a treasure (a jewel).*
Esta cocinera es una perla. *This cook is a treasure (jewel).*

---

el permiso — *permission*
Con permiso. — *Excuse me.*

con su permiso — *if it's all right with you.*
Con su permiso, Juan me acompañará. *If it's all right with you, John will go with me.*

pero — *but*

> **¡No hay pero que valga!** — *no buts about it.*
> ¡Hazlo en seguida! ¡No hay pero que valga! *Do it immediately! No buts about it!*

> **poner peros** — *to raise objections.*
> No le ponga peros. *Don't raise objections to it.*

el perro — *dog*

> **A otro perro con ese hueso.** — *Tell it to the marines.*

> **andar como perros y gatos** — *to fight like cats and dogs.*
> Ese matrimonio anda como perros y gatos. *That couple fights like cats and dogs.*

> **El perro del hortelano, que ni come la berza ni la deja comer.** — *The dog in the manger.*

> **Perro que ladra no muerde.** — *A barking dog never bites.*

> **ser perro viejo** — *to be a wise old owl.*
> Don Luis es perro viejo. Puedes confiar en sus consejos. *Don Luis is a wise old owl. You can have confidence in his advice.*

la persona — *person*

> **en persona** — *in person.*
> Me habló en persona. *He spoke to me in person.*

persuadir — *to persuade*

> **estar persuadido de** — *to be convinced.*
> Estoy persuadido de que es inútil. *I'm convinced it's useless.*

el pesar — *grief, sorrow*

> **a pesar de** — *in spite of.*
> Iremos a pesar de la lluvia. *We'll go in spite of the rain.*

pesar — *to weigh (on), grieve*

> **mal que le pese** — *whether one likes it or not.*
> Yo lo voy a hacer, mal que les pese. *I'm going to do it whether they like it or not.*

pese a — *in spite of.*
Pese a mis protestas, vendieron la casa. *In spite of my protests they sold the house.*

pese a quien pese — *no matter what anybody says.*
Pese a quien pese, van a leerlo. *No matter what anybody says, they're going to read it.*

la pesca — *fishing*
ir de pesca — *to go fishing.*
Vamos de pesca. *We're going fishing.*

el peso — *weight*
caerse de (por) su (propio) peso — *to be self-evident.*
Eso se cae de (por) su (propio) peso. *That is self-evident.*

de peso — *important.*
Asistieron personas de peso. *Important people attended.*

la pestaña — *eyelash*
quemarse las pestañas — *to burn the midnight oil.*
Se quemaba las pestañas. *He was burning the midnight oil.*

pestañear — *to blink*
sin pestañear — *without batting an eye.*
Me lo dijo sin pestañear. *He told me so without batting an eye.*

la peste — *plague, pest*
decir (hablar) pestes de — *to speak ill of; to criticize.*
Decía (hablaba) pestes de su suegra. *She was speaking ill of (criticizing) her mother-in-law.*

echar pestes contra — *to inveigh (to fulminate) against.*
Echaba pestes contra el presidente. *He was inveighing (fulminating) against the president.*

la petición — *request, petition*
a petición de — *at the request of.*

A petición del señor Ayala le mandaremos la revista. *At the request of Mr. Ayala we will send you the magazine.*

---

el pez — *fish*

    estar como el pez en el agua — *to feel right at home (to be as snug as a bug in a rug).*

    Estaba como el pez en el agua. *He felt right at home (was as snug as a bug in a rug).*

    un pez gordo — *a bigwig (big shot).*

    Es un pez gordo. *He's a bigwig (big shot).*

---

la picada — *nose dive*

    caer en picada — *to fall (off) sharply.*

    El mercado ha caído en picada. *The market has fallen off sharply.*

---

el picadillo — *hash; minced pork*

    hacerlo picadillo — *to make mincemeat out of someone.*

    Los hizo picadillo. *He made mincemeat out of them.*

---

picar — *to prick, pierce, sting*

    picar muy alto — *to aim too high.*

    Picaban muy alto. *They were aiming too high.*

---

el pico — *beak*

    ser un pico de oro — *to be very eloquent.*

    Es un pico de oro. *He's very eloquent.*

    . . . y pico — *some . . ., . . .-odd.*

    Vinieron cincuenta y pico invitados. *Some fifty (Fifty-odd) guests came.*

---

el pie — *foot*

    a pie juntillas — *firmly.*

    Lo creen a pie juntillas. *They firmly believe it.*

    al pie de la letra — *word for word.*

    Lo repetí todo al pie de la letra. *I repeated it all word for word.*

    al pie de la página — *at the bottom of the page.*

    Está al pie de la página. *It's at the bottom of the page.*

andar (caminar) con pie(s) de plomo — *to move (proceed) cautiously (with caution).*
Conviene andar (caminar) con pie(s) de plomo en tales asuntos. *It is a good idea to move (proceed) cautiously (with caution) in such matters.*

buscarle tres pies al gato — *to go looking for trouble.*
No le busque tres pies al gato. *Don't go looking for trouble.*

Déle el pie y se tomará la mano. — *Give him an inch and he'll take a mile.*

empezar con buen pie — *to get off to a good start.*
Empecé mi trabajo con buen pie. *I got off to a good start in my job.*

en pie — *in effect.*
El reglamento sigue en pie. *The regulations are still in effect.*

estar de (en) pie — *to be standing.*
Está de (en) pie. *He's standing.*

ir a pie — *to go on foot.*
Más vale ir a pie. *It's better to go on foot.*

nacer de pie — *to be born lucky.*
Ese chico sí que nació de pie. *That kid really was born lucky.*

no tener pies ni cabeza — *not to make any sense at all; to have no rhyme or reason to it.*
No tiene pies ni cabeza. *It doesn't make any sense at all (has no rhyme or reason to it).*

poner pies en polvorosa — *to beat it (take to one's heels).*
Al ver al policía el ladrón puso pies en polvorosa. *When he saw the policeman, the thief beat it (took to his heels).*

ponerse en (de) pie — *to stand up; to get to one's feet.*
Nos pusimos en pie. *We stood up (got to our feet).*

quedarse en pie — *to remain standing.*
Prefiero quedarme en pie. *I prefer to remain standing.*

saber de qué pie cojea — *to know someone's weak points.*
Sé de qué pie cojea. *I know his weak points.*

volver a pie — *to walk back.*
Volvió a pie. *He walked back.*

la piedra — *stone*

    no dejar piedra por (sin) mover — *to leave no stone unturned.*
    No dejó piedra por (sin) mover. *He left no stone unturned.*

    no dejar piedra sobre piedra — *to wipe out.*
    El huracán no dejó piedra sobre piedra en el pueblo. *The hurricane wiped out the town.*

la pierna — *leg*

    a media pierna — *halfway up (one's leg).*
    Tenía los pantalones enrollados a media pierna. *His pants were rolled halfway up.*

    dormir a pierna suelta — *to sleep like a log.*
    Dormí a pierna suelta. *I slept like a log.*

la pieza — *piece*

    ¡Mala pieza! — *You old rascal!*

    quedarse de una pieza — *to be dumbfounded.*
    Me quedé de una pieza. *I was dumbfounded.*

la píldora — *pill*

    dorar la píldora — *to sugar-coat the pill.*
    No tiene que dorar la píldora. *You don't have to sugar-coat the pill.*

    tragarse la píldora — *to be taken in; to swallow a lie.*
    Se tragó la píldora. *He was taken in (He swallowed the lie).*

pino — *steep*

    hacer (sus) pin(it)os — *to take one's first steps.*
    Está haciendo (sus) pin(it)os. *He's taking his first steps.*

pintado — *painted*

    como el más pintado — *with the best of them.*
    Sabe contar chistes como el más pintado. *He can tell jokes with the best of them.*

la pintura — *painting*
  no poder verlo ni en pintura — *not to be able to stand (the sight of)*
    someone.
  Ni en pintura la puedo ver. *I can't stand (the sight of) her.*

el pío — *chirping, peeping*
  no decir ni pío — *not to say a word.*
  No dijeron ni pío. *They didn't say a word.*

pique — *sharp-cut (cliff)*
  echar a pique — *to ruin.*
  Echaron a pique la empresa. *They ruined the firm (company).*

  echar a pique — *to sink.*
  Echaron a pique nuestro barco. *They sank our ship.*

  irse a pique — *to sink.*
  Nuestro barco se fue a pique. *Our ship sank.*

el piso — *floor*
  el piso bajo — *the ground floor.*
  Está en el piso bajo. *It's on the ground floor.*

el pistoletazo — *pistol shot*
  matar a pistoletazos — *to shoot with a pistol.*
  Lo mataron a pistoletazos. *They shot him with a pistol.*

plano — *flat*
  de plano — *plainly.*
  Les habló de plano. *He spoke plainly to them.*

la planta — *plant; floor, story*
  la planta baja — *the ground floor.*
  Está en la planta baja. *It's on the ground floor.*

plantar — *to plant*
  dejar plantado — *to leave in the lurch.*
  Lo dejó plantado. *She left him in the lurch.*

---

el plato — *dish, plate*
  Del plato a la boca se pierde la sopa. — *There's many a slip twixt (the) cup and (the) lip.*

---

el plazo — *term (period of time)*
  a largo plazo — *in the long run.*
  A largo plazo nos resultará más provechoso. *In the long run it will be more profitable for us.*

  a plazos — *in installments.*
  Lo demás se puede pagar a plazos. *The rest can be paid in installments.*

  en breve plazo — *in short order.*
  Debe terminarse en breve plazo. *It should be finished in short order.*

---

el pleito — *lawsuit*
  poner pleito — *to sue.*
  Le aconsejé que pusiera pleito a la compañía. *I advised him to sue the company.*

---

pleno — *full*
  en (a) pleno día — *in broad daylight.*

Lo robaron en (a) pleno día. *They stole it in broad daylight.*

en pleno verano — *(right) in the middle of the summer.*
Crecen en pleno verano. *They grow (right) in the middle of the summer.*

---

pobre — *poor*
¡Pobre de mí! — *Poor me!*

---

poco — *little*
a poco — *shortly afterwards, presently.*
A poco llegó Juan. *Shortly afterwards (Presently) John arrived.*

a poco de — *shortly after.*
A poco de comprar el coche tuvo un choque. *Shortly after he bought the
car he had an accident (collision).*

dentro de poco — *in a little while.*
Nos veremos dentro de poco. *We'll see each other in a little while.*

poco — *not very.*
Su conferencia fue poco importante. *His lecture was not very important.*

poco a poco — *little by little.*
Poco a poco se está mejorando. *Little by little he's getting better.*

poco antes (después) — *shortly before (afterwards).*
Habían salido poco antes (después). *They had left shortly before
(afterwards).*

poco más o menos — *give or take a few.*
Tiene veinticuatro primos, poco más o menos. *He has twenty-four
cousins, give or take a few.*

por poco — *almost.*
Por poco se rompe la cabeza. *He almost broke his neck.*

tener (estimar) en poco — *not to think much of; to hold in low esteem.*
Lo tienen (estiman) en poco. *They don't think much of him (hold him in
low esteem).*

un poco de — *a little.*
Tráigame un poco de agua. *Bring me a little water.*

y por si eso fuera poco — *and as if that weren't enough.*

215

Y por si eso fuera poco, también me robaron el reloj. *And as if that weren't enough, they also stole my watch.*

---

el poder — *power*

   estar en su poder — *to be in one's hands.*

   La decisión estaba en su poder. *The decision was in his hands.*

   por poder — *by proxy.*

   Votamos por poder. *We voted by proxy.*

---

poder — *can, to be able*

   hasta (a) más no poder — *for all one is worth; to the limit.*

   Se esforzó hasta (a) más no poder. *He exerted himself for all he was worth (to the limit).*

   no poder con — *not to be able to do anything with; to be too much for.*

   No puedo con él. *I can't do anything with him (He's too much for me).*

   no poder con — *not to be able to stand.*

   No puedo con esa mujer. *I can't stand that woman.*

   no poder más — *not to be able to go on; to be all in.*

   No puede más. *He can't go on (He's all in).*

   no poder menos de — *not to be able to help.*

   No puede menos de llorar. *She can't help crying.*

   no poder verlo — *not to be able to stand (the sight of).*

   No la puedo ver. *I can't stand (the sight of) her.*

   obrar en poder de — *to be in the hands of.*

   La carta obra en poder del abogado. *The letter is in the hands of the lawyer.*

   poder más que — *to win out over.*

   La curiosidad pudo más que el temor. *Curiosity won out over fear.*

   puede que — *maybe.*

   Puede que terminen esta noche. *They may finish tonight.*

   Puede que no. — *Maybe not.*

   Puede que sí. — *Maybe so.*

   ¿Se puede? — *May I come in?*

---

el polvo — *dust*
  hacer polvo — *to grind to dust.*
  Lo hizo polvo. *He ground it to dust.*

  sacudirle el polvo a uno — *to beat up.*
  Un día de estos le voy a sacudirle el polvo. *One of these days I'm going to beat him up.*

---

la pólvora — *(gun)powder*
  no haber inventado la pólvora — *to be no genius.*
  No ha inventado la pólvora. *He's no genius.*

---

poner — *to put*
  No se ponga así. — *Don't get that way.*

  ponerse — *to put on.*
  Se puso el abrigo. *He put on his (over)coat.*

  ponerse — *to turn.*
  Se puso pálida. *She turned pale.*

  ponerse a — *to begin to.*
  Se pusieron a bailar. *They began to dance.*

---

por — *by, through, for*
  por (más) — *however.*
  Por (más) inteligente que sea, saca malas notas. *However intelligent she may be, she gets bad grades.*

---

pos
  salir en pos de — *to set out after (in pursuit of).*
  Salió en pos de su hermano. *He set out after (in pursuit of) his brother.*

---

la posesión — *possession*
  tomar posesión de — *to take possession of.*
  Tomó posesión de su herencia. *He took possession of his inheritance.*

---

posible — *possible*
  en lo posible (en cuanto sea posible) — *insofar as possible.*

Obedeceré en lo posible (en cuanto sea posible). *I will obey insofar as possible.*

todo lo posible — *everything possible.*
Está haciendo todo lo posible. *He's doing everything possible.*

postre — *last, final*
  a la (al) postre — *finally; in the long run.*
  A la (Al) postre cedieron. *Finally (In the long run) they yielded.*

preciar — *to appraise*
  preciarse de — *to boast of.*
  Raúl se precia de su habilidad. *Raoul boasts of his ability.*

el precio — *price*
  no tener precio — *to be priceless.*
  Esta pintura no tiene precio. *This painting is priceless.*

la pregunta — *question*
  hacer una pregunta — *to ask a question.*
  Hizo una pregunta. *He asked a question.*

preguntar — *to ask*
  preguntar por — *to inquire (to ask) about.*
  Preguntaré por él. *I'll inquire (ask) about him.*

el premio — *prize*
  sacar el premio gordo — *to win the grand prize (jackpot).*
  Sacó el premio gordo. *He won the grand prize (jackpot).*

la prenda — *pledge, pawn, token*
  no dolerle prendas — *not to be concealing anything; to have nothing to hide.*
  No me duelen prendas. *I'm not concealing anything (I have nothing to hide).*

prendar — *to captivate*
  quedarse prendado de — *to be captivated by; to take a fancy to.*
  Se quedó prendado de París. *He fell in love with Paris.*

---

la prensa — *press*
  tener buena (mala) prensa — *to have a good (bad) press.*
  Tuvo buena (mala) prensa. *He had a good (bad) press.*

---

preocupar — *to preoccupy, concern, worry*
  preocuparse de (por) — *to take up; to concern oneself with.*
  Se ha preocupado del (por el) robo. *He has taken up (concerned himself with) the matter of the theft.*

---

presente — *present*
  hacer presente — *to notify.*
  Nos hizo presente que no iría a la reunión. *He notified us that he would not go to the meeting.*

  mejorando lo presente — *present company excepted.*
  Mejorando lo presente, son unos ladrones. *Present company excepted, they're a bunch of thieves.*

  tener presente — *to bear (keep) in mind.*
  Tenga presente que la clase empieza a las ocho. *Bear (Keep) in mind that the class starts at eight.*

---

prestar — *to lend*
  pedir prestado — *to borrow.*
  Nos pidieron prestado el coche. *They borrowed our car.*

---

presumir — *to presume*
  presumir de — *to consider oneself.*
  Presume de sabio. *He considers himself a sage.*

---

pretender — *to try*
  pretender decir — *to be driving at (be getting at).*
  Yo no sé que pretende decir. *I don't know what he's driving at.*

el pretexto — *pretext*

> **tomar a pretexto** — *to use as an excuse (pretext).*
> Lo tomó a pretexto para quedarse. *She used it as an excuse (pretext) for staying.*

prevenir — *to prepare*

> **prevenirse contra** — *to take precautions against.*
> Ella nunca se previene contra las enfermedades. *She never takes precautions against illness.*

primero — *first*

> **de primera** — *first rate.*
> Este hotel es de primera. *This hotel is first-rate.*

> **ser lo primero** — *to come first.*
> Mi familia es lo primero. *My family comes first.*

el principio — *beginning; principle*

> **a principios de** — *early in; around the beginning of.*
> Se murió a principios de mayo. *She died early in (around the beginning of) May.*

> **al (en un) principio** — *at first.*
> Al (En un) principio me gustó. *At first I liked it.*

> **dar principio a** — *to open.*
> Se dio principio al congreso con el himno nacional. *The conference was opened with the national anthem.*

> **desde un (el) principio** — *all along; right from the start.*
> Lo sabía desde un (el) principio. *I knew it all along (right from the start).*

> **en principio** — *in principle.*
> En principio es verdad. *In principle it's true.*

la prisa — *haste*

> **a (de) prisa** — *fast.*
> Siempre va muy a (de) prisa. *He always goes very fast.*

> **a toda prisa** — *in great haste.*
> Abandonó la tienda a toda prisa. *She left the shop in great haste.*

andar de prisa — *to be in a rush.*
Siempre andan de prisa. *They are always in a rush.*

¡Dése prisa! — *Hurry up!*

No corre prisa. — *There's no hurry; It's not urgent.*

tener (estar de; estar con) prisa — *to be in a hurry.*
Tengo (Estoy de; Estoy con) prisa. *I'm in a hurry.*

el pro — *profit*
  en pro de — *for the benefit of.*
  Es una colecta en pro de las víctimas del terremoto. *It is a collection for the benefit of the victims of the earthquake.*

el progre[sista] — *leftish, politically progressive person*
  ir de progre — *to pretend to be progressive (hip).*
  Ellos van de progres, pero ella es médico y él conduce un Mercedes. *They act like they're hip, but she's a doctor, and he drives a Mercedes.*

pronto — *soon*
  al pronto — *at first.*
  Al pronto la rechazó. *At first he rejected her.*

  de pronto — *suddenly.*
  De pronto lo vi acercarse. *Suddenly I saw him approaching.*

  lo más pronto posible — *as soon as possible.*
  Regrese lo más pronto posible. *Return as soon as possible.*

  por lo (el) pronto (por de pronto) — *for the time being.*
  Por lo (el) pronto (Por de pronto) no necesito más. *For the time being I don't need any more.*

la propina — *tip*
  de propina — *into the bargain.*
  Nos invitó a comer y de propina nos llevó al cine. *He invited us to dinner and took us to the movies into the bargain.*

el propósito — *purpose*
  a propósito — *by the way.*

A propósito, ¿me puede prestar su coche? *By the way, can you lend me your car?*

de propósito — *on purpose.*
Lo hizo de propósito. *He did it on purpose.*

fuera de propósito — *irrelevant; out of place.*
Su comentario fue totalmente fuera de propósito. *His comment was entirely irrelevant (out of place).*

---

el provecho — *profit, benefit*
¡Buen provecho! — *Good appetite!; Enjoy your meal!*

de provecho — *respectable.*
Son hombres de provecho. *They are respectable men.*

sacar provecho de — *to profit from.*
Sacó mucho provecho de la conferencia. *He profited a lot from the lecture.*

---

próximo — *next, close*
estar próximo a — *to be about to.*
Están próximo a comprar una casa. *They are about to buy a house.*

---

la prueba — *proof; test, trial*
a prueba de agua (de sonido, etc.) — *waterproof (soundproof, etc.).*
Es a prueba de agua (de sonido, etc.). *It's waterproof (soundproof, etc.).*

poner a prueba — *to put to the test.*
Vamos a ponerlo a prueba. *Let's put it to the test.*

---

la puerta — *door*
a puerta cerrada — *behind closed doors.*
Lo discutieron a puerta cerrada. *They discussed it behind closed doors.*

cerrarle todas las puertas — *to close all avenues to someone.*
Se le cerraron todas las puertas. *All avenues were closed to him.*

darle con (cerrarle) la puerta en las narices — *to slam the door in someone's face.*
Me dio con (Me cerró) la puerta en las narices. *He slammed the door in my face.*

estar a las puertas de la muerte — *to be at death's door.*

Está a las puertas de la muerte. *She's at death's door.*

llamar a la puerta — *to knock at the door.*
Llamó a la puerta. *He knocked at the door.*

---

pues — *then, well; since*
pues bien — *well then.*
Pues bien, ¿qué hacemos? *Well then, what shall we do?*

---

la pulga — *flea*
tener malas pulgas — *to be short-tempered.*
Tiene muy malas pulgas. *He's very short-tempered.*

---

el pulso — *pulse*
con pulso firme — *with a steady hand.*
Apuntó con pulso firme. *He aimed with a steady hand.*

---

la punta — *point*
de punta en blanco — *all dressed up; in full regalia.*
Vinieron vestidos de punta en blanco. *They came all dressed up (in full regalia).*

de puntillas — *on tiptoe.*
Entró de puntillas. *She went in on tiptoe.*

sacar punta a — *to sharpen.*
Sacó punta al lápiz. *He sharpened the pencil.*

tener en la punta de la lengua — *to have on the tip of one's tongue.*
Lo tengo en la punta de la lengua. *It's (I have it) on the tip of my tongue.*

---

el punto — *point*
a punto de — *on the point of; about to.*
Está a punto de comprarlo. *He's on the point of buying it (about to buy it).*

a punto fijo — *exactly; definitely.*
Quiero saber esto a punto fijo. *I want to know this exactly (definitely).*

a tal punto (hasta el punto) — *to such an extent; so much.*
Llovió a tal punto (hasta el punto) que no salimos. *It rained to such an extent (so much) that we didn't go out.*

al punto — *at once.*

Me devolvió el dinero al punto. *He returned the money to me at once.*

en punto — *sharp; on the dot.*

Me levanto a las siete en punto. *I get up at seven (o'clock) sharp (on the dot).*

estar en su punto — *to be just right.*

Las verduras estaban en su punto. *The vegetables were (cooked) just right.*

hasta cierto punto — *in a way; to some extent; up to a point.*

Hasta cierto punto lo que dice es verdad. *In a way (To some extent, Up to a point) what you say is true.*

llegar a su punto cumbre — *to reach its peak.*

Todavía no ha llegado a su punto cumbre. *It hasn't reached its peak yet.*

poner los puntos sobre las íes — *to be very meticulous.*

No te preocupes, Juan siempre pone los puntos sobre las íes. *Don't worry, John is always very meticulous.*

punto de vista — *point of view.*

No lo habían considerado desde ese punto de vista. *They hadn't considered it from that point of view.*

punto menos que — *very nearly.*

Lo encuentro punto menos que insoportable. *I find it very nearly unbearable.*

punto por punto — *in detail.*

Explicó el procedimiento punto por punto. *He explained the procedure in detail.*

---

el puñado — *handful*

a puñados — *in abundance; by the handful.*

Los distribuyó a puñados. *He distributed them in abundance (by the handful).*

---

la puñalada — *stab (with a dagger)*

darle una puñalada — *to stab someone.*

Le di una puñalada. *I stabbed him.*

darle una puñalada trapera — *to stab in the back.*

Le dio una puñalada trapera su mejor amigo. *His best friend stabbed him in the back.*

matar a puñaladas — *to stab to death.*
Lo mataron a puñaladas. *They stabbed him to death.*

ser una puñalada por la espalda — *to be a stab in the back.*
Fue una puñalada por la espalda. *It was a stab in the back.*

el puño — *fist*

de su puño y letra — *in one's own handwriting.*
Esta carta es de su puño y letra. *This letter is in his own handwriting.*

por (sus) puños — *on one's own.*
Llegó a ser presidente por (sus) puños. *He got to be president on his own.*

tener en un puño — *to have under one's thumb.*
Lo tiene en un puño. *She has him under her thumb.*

qué — *what*
¿A qué discutirlo? — *Why argue (What's the good of arguing) about it?*

¿En qué quedamos? — *What do you say?; What about it?*

qué — *what a.*
¡Qué hombre! *What a man!*

¿Qué quiere? — *What can you expect?*

¿y qué? — *so what?*
No saliste bien en el examen. ¿Y qué? *You didn't pass the exam. So what?*

que — *that*
a que — *I'll bet (you).*
A que no llega antes que yo. *I'll bet (you) you won't arrive before I do.*

el que más y el que menos — *everybody.*

El que más y el que menos estaban de acuerdo. *Everybody was in agreement.*

---

quedar — *to remain, stay, be left*

hacer quedar en ridículo — *to make look ridiculous.*
Me hizo quedar en ridículo. *He made me look ridiculous.*

quedar bien con — *to get along with.*
Lo que quiere él es quedar bien con los vecinos. *What he wants is to get along with the neighbors.*

quedar ciego — *to be blinded.*
Quedó ciego por toda la vida. *He was blinded for life.*

quedar en — *to agree to.*
Han quedado en verse en la plaza. *They have agreed to meet in the square.*

quedar en nada — *for nothing to come of; to come to naught.*
Sus planes quedaron en nada. *Nothing came of their plans (Their plans came to naught).*

quedar entendido — *to be understood.*
Queda entendido que nos pagarán cada dos semanas. *It is understood that we will be paid every two weeks.*

quedar mal con — *to be in one's bad books.*
No quiero quedar mal con ellos. *I don't want to be in their bad books.*

quedarle — *to have left.*
Me quedan sólo tres. *I only have three left.*

quedarle grande (estrecho) — *to be too big (tight) for (on) one.*
Le queda grande (estrecho). *It's too big (tight) for (on) him.*

---

quedarse con — *to keep.*
Se quedó con el coche — *She kept the car.*

---

quemarropa — *point blank*
a quemarropa — *at close range.*
Le disparó a quemarropa. *He fired at him at close range.*

---

querer — *to want*
querer decir — *to mean.*

No sé qué quiere decir. *I don't know what it means.*

sin querer — *unintentionally; by accident.*
Lo hice sin querer. *I did it unintentionally (by accident).*

---

el quicio — *door jamb, eye of a door hinge*
sacarle de quicio — *to drive someone to distraction; to drive wild; to unhinge.*
Me saca de quicio. *It drives me to distraction (drives me wild; unhinges me).*

---

quién — *who*
Dime con quién andas y te diré quién eres. — *Show me your friends and I'll tell you what you are. A man is known by the company he keeps. Birds of a feather flock together.*

Haz bien y no mires a quién. — *Cast your bread upon the waters.*

¡Mira quién habla! — *Look who's talking!*

---

quien — *(he) who*
como quien no dice nada — *as if it were quite unimportant.*
Nos vino con esta noticia como quien no dice nada. *He came to us with this news as if it were quite unimportant.*

Como quien oye llover. — *In one ear and out the other; Like water off a duck's back.*

Quintín — *Quentin*
armarse la de San Quintín — *for there to be a terrible row.*
Se armó la de San Quintín. *There was a terrible row.*

---

quitar — *to remove*
quitarse de en medio — *to get out of the way.*
Le pedí que se quitara de en medio. *I asked him to get out of the way.*

ser de quita y pon — *to be detachable (removable).*
Es de quita y pon. *It's detachable (removable).*

---

el rábano — *radish*

  tomar el rábano por las hojas — *to put the cart before the horse.*

  Muchas veces fracasaba porque tomaba el rábano por las hojas. *He often failed because he put the cart before the horse.*

la rabia — *rage*

  darle rabia — *to make one mad.*

  Me da (mucha) rabia. *It (really) makes me mad.*

  tener rabia a — *to have a grudge against.*

  No sé por qué me tiene tanta rabia. *I don't know why he has such a grudge against me.*

el rabillo — *(little) tail*

  con el rabillo del ojo — *out of the corner of one's eye.*

  Me miró con el rabillo del ojo. *He looked at me out of the corner of his eye.*

el rabo — *tail*

  con el rabo entre las piernas — *with one's tail between one's legs.*

  Se fue con el rabo entre las piernas. *He went off with his tail between his legs.*

la racha — *gust of wind*
  tener una mala racha — *to have a run (streak) of bad luck.*
  El pobre acaba de tener una mala racha. *The poor man has just had a run (streak) of bad luck.*

---

la raíz — *root*
  cortar de raíz — *to nip in the bud.*
  Cortaron de raíz el rumor. *They nipped the rumor in the bud.*

  echar raíces — *to take root.*
  La planta echó raíces. *The plant took root.*

  echar raíces — *to put down roots; to settle down.*
  Quiero echar raíces aquí. *I want to put down roots (settle down) here.*

---

la rama — *branch*
  andarse por las ramas — *to beat around the bush.*
  No pueden hablar del asunto sin andarse por las ramas. *They can't talk about the matter without beating around the bush.*

---

el rape — *quick haircut or shave.*
  cortado al rape — *cut very short.*
  Tenía el pelo cortado al rape. *He had his hair cut very short.*

---

el rasgo — *stroke, flourish; trait, characteristic*
  a grandes rasgos — *in broad strokes; in outline.*
  Describió la escena a grandes rasgos. *He described the scene in broad strokes (in outline).*

---

raso — *level, even, smooth*
  al raso — *out in the open.*
  Pasaron la noche al raso. *They spent the night out in the open.*

---

la rastra — *track, trail (of something dragged)*
  ir a rastras — *to crawl.*
  Apenas podían ir a rastras. *They could scarcely crawl.*

  llevarse a rastras (a la rastra) — *to drag off.*
  Se lo llevaron a rastras (a la rastra). *They dragged him off.*

229

el rastro — *track, trail*

  seguirle el rastro — *to track down.*

  Le siguieron el rastro con dificultad. *They had a hard time tracking him down.*

---

la rata — *rat*

  ser más pobre que una rata — *to be as poor as a church mouse.*

  Es más pobre que una rata. *He's as poor as a church mouse.*

---

el rato — *while, short time*

  a cada rato — *every little while; every so often*

  A cada rato se oía un grito. *Every little while (Every so often) you could hear a shout.*

  a(l) poco rato — *shortly afterwards; in a little while.*

  A(l) poco rato me llamó. *Shortly afterwards (In a little while) she called me.*

  a ratos perdidos — *in one's spare time.*

  Mi hermana lee novelas a ratos perdidos. *My sister reads novels in her spare time.*

  de rato en rato (a ratos) — *from time to time.*

  De rato en rato (A ratos) se asoma a la ventana. *From time to time she looks out the window.*

  pasar (un) buen rato — *to have a good time.*

  Pasamos (un) buen rato en su casa. *We had a good time at your house.*

  pasar el rato — *to kill time; to pass the time.*

  Leía una revista para pasar el rato. *I was reading a magazine to kill time (pass the time).*

---

el ratón — *mouse*

  un ratón de biblioteca — *a bookworm.*

  Es un ratón de biblioteca. *He's a bookworm.*

---

la raya — *stripe, line*

  pasarse de (la) raya — *to go too far; to overstep the mark.*

  Ya se pasaron de la raya. *Now they've gone too far (overstepped the mark).*

tener a raya — *to keep in line.*
Es muy difícil tenerla a raya. *It's very hard to keep her in line.*

la razón — *reason*
  a razón de — *at the rate of.*
  Andaba a razón de ochenta kilómetros la hora. *He was traveling at the rate of eighty kilometers an hour.*

  asistirle la razón — *to be in the right.*
  Le asiste la razón. *He is in the right.*

  con razón — *rightly so.*
  Se lo quitó y con razón. *He took it away from her, and rightly so.*

  dar razón de — *to give information about.*
  Era el único que podía darles razón de su hijo. *He was the only one that could give them information about their son.*

  darle la razón a — *to side with.*
  Siempre le daba la razón a mi hermano. *He always used to side with my brother.*

  ponerse en (la) razón — *to be reasonable; to listen to reason.*
  Hay que ponerse en (la) razón. *You've got to be reasonable (listen to reason).*

  tener la razón de su parte — *to be in the right.*
  Tiene la razón de su parte. *He's in the right.*

  tener razón — *to be right.*
  No tiene razón. *She's not right.*

la realidad — *reality*
  en realidad — *as a matter of fact.*
  En realidad es mentira. *As a matter of fact it's not true.*

rebajar — *to reduce, lower*
  rebajarse a — *to condescend to; to stoop to.*
  No quiere rebajarse a comer con nosotros. *He won't condescend to eat (stoop to eating) with us.*

rebajarse ante — *to humble oneself to.*
No se rebaje ante nadie. *Don't humble yourself to anybody.*

rebosar — *to overflow*
rebosar de — *to be brimming with.*
Rebosa de salud. *He is brimming with health.*

recaer — *to fall again*
recaer sobre — *to fall upon.*
Todas las tareas recaen sobre ese pobre. *All the tasks fall upon that poor man.*

recapacitar — *to run over in one's mind*
recapacitar sobre — *to think over.*
Tenemos que recapacitar sobre lo que dijo. *We have to think over what he said.*

el recibo — *receipt*
acusar recibo de — *to acknowledge receipt of.*
Acusamos recibo de su atenta. . . . *We acknowledge receipt of your letter . . . .*

el recuerdo — *remembrance*
muchos recuerdos — *kindest regards.*
Muchos recuerdos a Elena. *Kindest regards to Helen.*

reducir — *to reduce*
reducirse a — *to amount to (come down to).*
Todo se reduce a una cuestión de dinero. *It all amounts to (comes down to) a question of money.*

referir — *to refer, relate*
en lo que se refiere a . . . — *as far as . . . is concerned.*
En lo que se refiere a su futuro, sin duda se casará. *As far as her future is concerned, she will no doubt get married.*

el regalo — *gift, present*
  hacerle un regalo — *to present someone with a gift.*
  Me hizo un regalo. *He presented me with a gift.*

regañadientes
  a regañadientes — *reluctantly; grudgingly.*
  Fue convencida, aunque a regañadientes. *She was convinced, although reluctantly (grudgingly).*

el régimen — *regimen; régime*
  ponerse a régimen — *to go on a diet.*
  Se puso a régimen. *She went on a diet.*

la regla — *rule*
  en regla — *in order.*
  Todo estaba en regla. *Everything was in order.*

  por regla general — *as a (general) rule.*
  Por regla general nos acostamos a las once. *As a (general) rule we go to bed at eleven.*

el regreso — *return*
  de regreso — *upon returning.*
  De regreso a casa se acostó. *When she got home she went to bed.*

  estar de regreso — *to be back.*
  Todavía no están de regreso. *They aren't back yet.*

  venir de regreso — *to come back.*
  Venía de regreso de la guerra. *He was coming back from the war.*

regular — *regular*
  por lo regular — *as a rule.*
  Por lo regular no aceptamos cheques personales. *As a rule we don't accept personal checks.*

reír — *to laugh*
  El que ríe al último ríe mejor. — *He who laughs last laughs best.*
  reírse de — *to laugh at.*

233

Se ríe de nosotros. *He's laughing at us.*

ser para reírse — *to be enough to make one laugh.*
Es para reírse. *It's enough to make you laugh.*

la relación — *relation*

con relación a — *regarding.*
Con relación a lo que me dijo ayer . . . *Regarding what you told me yesterday . . . .*

el relieve — *relief*

poner de relieve — *to point out.*
Puso de relieve las ventajas del programa. *He pointed out the advantages of the program.*

el remate — *end*

estar loco de remate — *to be stark raving mad; to be hopelessly insane.*
Está loco de remate. *He's stark raving mad (hopelessly insane).*

por remate — *finally.*
Nos sirvió jerez, cerveza y por remate coñac. *He served us sherry, beer, and finally cognac.*

el remedio — *remedy*

ni para remedio — *(not) for love nor money.*
No pude comprar pan ni para remedio. *I was unable to buy bread for love nor money.*

No hay (No tiene) (más) remedio. — *It can't be helped; It's beyond repair.*

no hay más remedio que — *there's nothing to do but.*
No hay más remedio que aceptar el veredicto. *There's nothing to do but accept the verdict.*

el rencor — *rancor*

guardarle rencor — *to hold a grudge against someone.*
Todavía me guarda rencor. *He still holds a grudge against me.*

rendido — *tired*
  estar rendido — *to be exhausted.*
  Estamos rendidos. *We are exhausted.*

el renglón — *line*
  leer entre renglones — *to read between the lines.*
  Hay que leer entre renglones. *You've got to read between the lines.*

reojo — *to look out of the corner of one's eye*
  mirar de reojo — *to look askance.*
  La miró de reojo. *He looked askance at her.*

reparar — *to repair*
  reparar en — *to consider.*
  No reparamos en lo que iba a pasar. *We did not consider what was going to happen.*

  reparar en — *to notice.*
  No reparó en que Adriana se había ido. *He did not notice that Adrienne had left.*

el reparo — *objection*
  poner reparo a — *to raise objections.*
  Puso reparo a lo que dijo el presidente. *He raised objections to what the president said.*

el repente — *sudden movement*
  de repente — *suddenly.*
  De repente se desmayó. *Suddenly she fainted.*

la representación — *representation*
  en representación de — *as a representative of.*
  Habló en representación de los obreros. *He spoke as a representative of the workers.*

reprochar — *to reproach*
    reprocharle — *to reproach one for.*
    Me reprochó mi conducta. *He reproached me for my conduct.*

el reproche — *reproach*
    hacer un reproche — *to reproach.*
    Le hizo un reproche injusto. *He reproached her unjustly.*

la reserva — *reserve*
    con (bajo) la mayor reserva — *in the strictest confidence.*
    Me lo dijo con (bajo) la mayor reserva. *He told (it to) me in the strictest confidence.*

    guardar reserva — *to be discreet.*
    Siempre guarda reserva con sus clientes. *He is always discreet with his customers.*

    sin reserva — *freely; openly*
    Me lo dijo sin reserva. *He told (it to) me freely (openly).*

la resistencia — *resistance*
    oponer resistencia — *to resist.*
    Todos opusieron resistencia a los invasores. *They all resisted the invaders.*

resistir — *to resist*
    resistirse a — *to refuse.*
    Se resistía a envejecer. *She refused to grow old.*

respectar — *to concern*
    por lo que respecta (toca) a — *as far as . . . is concerned.*
    Por lo que respecta (toca) a su plan, estoy muy contento. *As far as your plan is concerned, I'm very happy.*

el respecto — *respect*
    al respecto — *about this matter.*
    No me ha dicho nada al respecto. *He has said nothing to me about the matter.*

(con) respecto a — *with respect to.*

Nos habló (con) respecto a su problema. *He spoke to us with respect to his problem.*

---

el respeto — *respect*

faltarle al respeto — *to be disrespectful to.*

Le faltaron al respeto. *They were disrespectful to her.*

---

restar — *to deduct, subtract; to remain*

restarle — *to have left.*

Me resta un año de estudios. *I have a year of studies left.*

restarle el tiempo — *to take up one's time.*

Siempre me resta el tiempo cuando estoy ocupado. *He's always taking up my time when I'm busy.*

---

la resulta — *result*

de (por) resultas de — *as a result of.*

Cojea de (por) resultas del accidente. *He limps as a result of the accident.*

---

el resumen — *summary, résumé*

en resumen — *in short.*

En resumen, se les perdió todo. *In short, they lost everything.*

---

el retraso — *delay*

llegar con . . . de retraso — *to arrive . . . late.*

El tren llega con dos horas de retraso. *The train is arriving two hours late.*

---

reunir — *to unite, join*

reunirse con — *to join.*

Se reunirán con nosotros. *They'll join us.*

---

el reverso — *reverse*

el reverso de la medalla — *just the opposite.*

Pepe es buenísimo pero su hijo es el reverso de la medalla. *Pepe is very good but his son is just the opposite.*

---

el revés — *reverse*

   al revés — *the other way around; the opposite.*
   No es así, es al revés. *It's not like that, it's the other way around.*

la revista — *review; magazine*

   pasar revista a — *to review.*
   Pasaron revista a las tropas. *They reviewed the troops.*

ridículo — *ridiculous*

   hacer el ridículo — *to make a fool of oneself.*
   Está haciendo el ridículo. *He's making a fool of himself.*

   poner en ridículo — *to make look ridiculous.*
   Nos puso en ridículo. *He made us look ridiculous.*

la rienda — *rein*

   a rienda suelta — *without restraint.*
   Habló a rienda suelta toda la tarde. *He spoke without restraint all
      afternoon.*

   aflojar las riendas — *to ease up.*
   Aflojó un poco las riendas. *He eased up a little.*

   dar rienda suelta (a) — *to give free rein (to).*
   Dio rienda suelta a su imaginación. *He gave free rein to his imagination.*

el riesgo — *risk*

   correr el riesgo de — *to run the risk of.*
   No quiero correr el riesgo de perder mi propiedad. *I don't want to run the
      risk of losing my property.*

el rigor — *rigor*

   de rigor — *de rigueur; absolutely essential.*
   Para esta fiesta, un smoking es de rigor. *For this party, a dinner jacket is
      de rigueur (absolutely essential).*

   en rigor — *strictly speaking.*
   En rigor no es el jefe. *Strictly speaking he's not the boss.*

el riñón — *kidney*

forrarse el riñón — *to feather one's nest.*
Trabaja mucho para forrarse el riñón. *He's working hard to feather his nest.*

pegarse al riñón — *to stick to one's ribs.*
Es un alimento que se pega al riñón. *It's a food that sticks to your ribs.*

tener el riñón bien cubierto — *to be well-heeled.*
Tiene el riñón bien cubierto. *He's well-heeled.*

---

el río — *river*

A río revuelto, ganancia de pescadores. — *There's good fishing in troubled waters.*

Cuando suena el río, agua lleva. — *Where there's smoke there's fire.*

---

la risa — *laughter*

llorar de risa — *to laugh till one cries.*
Lloró de risa. *She laughed till she cried.*

morirse (ahogarse) de risa — *to die laughing.*
Se murió (Se ahogó) de risa. *He died laughing.*

tomar a risa — *to take lightly.*
No hay que tomar las cosas a risa. *You mustn't take things lightly.*

---

el roble — *oak*

fuerte como un roble — *(as) strong as an ox.*
Ahora que levanta pesas, se está poniendo fuerte como un roble. *Now that he is lifting weights he's getting (as) strong as an ox.*

---

el rodeo — *detour, roundabout way*

andar con rodeos — *to beat around (about) the bush.*
Siempre anda con rodeos. *He always beats around (about) the bush.*

dar rodeos — *to make detours.*
Tuvimos que dar varios rodeos. *We had to make several detours.*

dejarse de rodeos — *to stop beating around (about) the bush.*
¡Déjate de rodeos! *Stop beating around (about) the bush!*

hablar sin rodeos — *not to mince words.*
Siempre hablan sin rodeos. *They never mince words.*

---

la rodilla — *knee*
  caminar de rodillas — *to walk on one's knees.*
  Caminaban de rodillas. *They were walking on their knees.*

  estar de rodillas — *to be kneeling; to be on one's knees.*
  Está de rodillas. *She is kneeling (is on her knees).*

  ponerse (hincarse) de rodillas — *to kneel; to get down on one's knees.*
  Se puso (Se hincó) de rodillas. *He knelt (got down on his knees).*

---

rojo — *red*
  al rojo (vivo) (al rojo blanco) — *red-hot (white-hot).*
  Se usó un hierro al rojo (vivo) (al rojo blanco). *A red-hot (white-hot) iron was used.*

---

el rollo — *roll*
  contar un rollo — *to make up a big story.*
  No me cuentes ese rollo otra vez. *Don't tell me that story again.*

---

romance — *Romance*
  decir en buen romance — *to tell in plain language.*
  Díganoslo en buen romance. *Tell (it to) us in plain language.*

  hablar en romance — *to speak plainly (clearly).*
  Hable en romance. *Speak plainly (clearly).*

---

romper — *to break*
  romper a reír (llorar) — *to burst out laughing (crying).*
  Rompió a reír (llorar). *He burst out laughing (crying).*

  romper con — *to break off with; to have a falling-out with.*
  Rompió con sus amigos. *He broke off with (had a falling-out with) his friends.*

---

rondar — *to patrol, prowl about*
  rondar — *to be around.*
  Ronda ya los treinta años. *He's around thirty.*

el rosario — *rosary*

terminar como el rosario de la aurora — *to end badly.*

Eso va a terminar como el rosario de la aurora. *That's going to end badly.*

---

la rueda — *wheel*

ir sobre ruedas — *to run smoothly.*

Todo va sobre ruedas. *Everything is running smoothly.*

---

el ruido — *noise*

meter ruido — *to be noisy.*

Esos chicos siempre están metiendo ruido. *Those kids are always noisy.*

Mucho ruido y pocas nueces. — *Much ado about nothing.*

sin hacer ruido — *without causing a stir.*

Llegó a la ciudad sin hacer ruido. *He arrived in the city without causing a stir.*

---

el rumor — *rumor*

correr el rumor — *to be rumored.*

Corrió el rumor de que se iba. *It was rumored that he was leaving.*

---

la sábana — *bed sheet*

pegársele las sábanas — *to be bad about getting up; to act sleepy in the morning.*

Se le pegan las sábanas por la mañana. *He has a hard time getting up in the morning.*

---

saber — *to know*

a saber — *namely.*

Leyeron una novela muy famosa, a saber, *Don Quijote. They read a very famous novel, namely,* Don Quixote.

no saber en lo que se mete — *not to know what one is getting into.*

Ten cuidado, no sabes en lo que te metes. *Be careful, you don't know what you're getting into.*

no sé qué — *some . . . or other.*

Está leyendo no sé qué libro sobre España. *She's reading some book or other about Spain.*

¿Qué sé yo? — *How do I know?*

que yo sepa — *as (so) far as I know.*

Que yo sepa, no. *Not as (so) far as I know.*

saber a — *to taste like.*

Esto sabe a mostaza. *This tastes like mustard.*

un no sé qué — *(a certain) something.*

Tiene un no sé qué simpático. *There's something likable about him.*

Vaya usted a saber. — *Who knows?*

---

sabiendas

a sabiendas — *knowingly.*

Lo hizo a sabiendas. *He did it knowingly.*

---

sacar — *to take out*

sacar a relucir — *to bring up.*

Lo sacó a relucir. *He brought it up.*

sacar en limpio — *to deduce.*

¿Qué sacaste en limpio de lo que nos contó? *What did you deduce from what he told us?*

sacar las entradas (los boletos) — *to buy the tickets.*

Sacó las entradas (los boletos). *She bought the tickets.*

---

el saco — *bag, sack*

echar en saco roto — *to forget.*

No eché en saco roto sus consejos. *I didn't forget his advice.*

---

salir — *to go out, come out, leave*

salir — *to turn out to be.*

Salió conservador. *He turned out to be a conservative.*

salir adelante — *to win out; to come out on top.*
Salió adelante. *He won out (came out on top).*

salir bien — *to come out well; to pass.*
Salió bien en su examen. *He came out well in (passed) his exam.*

salir ganando — *to come out ahead.*
Seguí sus consejos y salí ganando. *I followed his advice and came out ahead.*

salir muy caro — *to cost a lot*
Me salió muy caro. *It cost me a lot.*

salirse con la suya — *to get one's own way.*
Cada vez se sale con la suya. *Each time he gets his own way.*

la saliva — *saliva*
    gastar saliva en balde — *to waste one's breath; to talk in vain.*
    Gastan saliva en balde. *They're wasting their breath (talking in vain).*

    tragar saliva — *to grin and bear it.*
    Lo trataron muy mal, pero tuvo que tragar saliva. *They treated him very badly, but he had to grin and bear it.*

la salsa — *sauce*
    dejar. . . cocerse en su propia salsa — *to let. . . stew in one's own juice.*
    Lo mejor será dejarlos cocerse en su propia salsa. *The best thing will be to just let them stew in their own juice.*

salto — *jump, leap*
    dar saltos de alegría — *to jump for joy.*
    Dábamos saltos de alegría. *We were jumping for joy.*

    dar un salto — *to jump.*
    El perro dio un salto. *The dog jumped.*

    de un salto — *in a flash.*
    De un salto se encontró al otro lado. *In a flash he was on the other side.*

la salud — *health*
    beber por (a) la salud de . . . — *to drink (to) . . . 's health.*
    Bebieron por (a) la salud de su padre. *They drank (to) their father's health.*

tener salud de piedra — *to have an iron constitution; to be as strong as an ox.*

Tenía salud de piedra. *He had an iron constitution (was as strong as an ox).*

salvar — *to save*

¡Sálvese el que pueda! — *Every man for himself!*

salvo — *safe*

estar a salvo — *to be safe.*

Los soldados están a salvo. *The soldiers are safe.*

poner a salvo — *to save; to bring to safety.*

Logró ponerla a salvo. *He succeeded in saving her (bringing her to safety).*

salvo — *except (for).*

Todos fueron salvo Juan. *They all went except (for) John.*

la sangre — *blood*

a sangre fría — *in cold blood.*

Los asesinó a sangre fría. *He murdered them in cold blood.*

bajársele la sangre a los talones — *to be scared stiff (to death).*

Al ver el fantasma se me bajó la sangre a los talones. *When I saw the ghost I was scared stiff (to death).*

no tener sangre en las venas — *to be a cool customer.*

No tiene sangre en las venas. *He's a cool customer.*

sano — *healthy, sound*

cortar por lo sano — *to take drastic measures; to use desperate remedies.*

Tuve que cortar por lo sano. *I had to take drastic measures (use desperate remedies).*

sano y salvo — *safe and sound.*

Llegó sano y salvo. *He arrived safe and sound.*

el santiamén — *jiffy, instant*

en un santiamén — *in the twinkling of an eye.*

Me los quitó en un santiamén. *He took them away from me in the twinkling of an eye.*

santo — *saintly, holy*

a santo de qué — *why; for what reason.*

¿A santo de qué me dice eso? *Why (For what reason) are you telling me that?*

alzarse con el santo y la limosna — *to make off with the whole thing; to make a clean sweep.*

Se alzó con el santo y la limosna. *He made off with the whole thing (made a clean sweep).*

desnudar a un santo para vestir a otro — *to rob Peter to pay Paul.*

Desnudan a un santo para vestir a otro. *They're robbing Peter to pay Paul.*

hacerse el santo — *to act saintly (innocent).*

No se haga el santo. *Don't act so saintly (innocent).*

írsele el santo al cielo — *to forget what one is doing*

Se le fue el santo al cielo. *He forgot what he was doing.*

no ser santo de su devoción — *to be no favorite of one's; not to be especially fond of someone.*

No es santo de mi devoción. *He's no favorite of mine (I'm not especially fond of him).*

santo y seña — *password.*

No supo dar el santo y seña, y no lo dejaron entrar. *He couldn't give the password, and they wouldn't let him in.*

el sapo — *toad*

echar sapos y culebras — *to swear (curse; cuss) a blue streak.*

Echaba sapos y culebras. *He was swearing (cursing, cussing) a blue streak.*

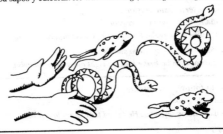

satisfacer — *to satisfy*
   darse por satisfecho — *to accept; to declare oneself satisfied.*
   Se dio por satisfecho con mi explicación. *He accepted (declared himself satisfied with) my explanation.*

---

la sazón — *time, season*
   a la sazón — *at the time.*
   A la sazón no funcionaba. *At the time it wasn't working.*

---

seco — *dry*
   a secas — *just plain.*
   La llamaba María a secas. *He called her just plain María.*

   dejar en seco — *to leave high and dry.*
   Nos dejó en seco. *He left us high and dry.*

---

el secreto — *the secret*
   estar en el secreto — *to be in on the secret.*
   No tienes que callarte delante de Rogelio. El está en el secreto. *You don't have to keep quiet in front of Roger. He's in on the secret.*

---

la sed — *thirst*
   darle sed — *to make one thirsty.*
   Me da sed. *It makes me thirsty.*

   tener sed — *to be thirsty.*
   Tengo sed. *I'm thirsty.*

---

la seguida — *series, succession*
   de seguida — *in a row; in succession.*
   Llovió tres días de seguida. *It rained three days in a row (in succession).*

   en seguida — *right away; immediately.*
   Tráigamelo en seguida. *Bring it to me right away (immediately).*

---

seguir — *to follow; to continue*
   seguidos — *in a row.*
   Habló cuatro horas seguidas. *He talked four hours in a row.*

seguir — *to go on; to keep on; to continue.*
Siguen jugando. *They go on (keep on, continue) playing.*

---

según — *according to*
Según y conforme. — *That (It all) depends.*

---

el segundo — *second*
por breves segundos — *for a few seconds.*
Se había quedado dormido por breves segundos. *He had fallen asleep for a few seconds.*

---

la seguridad — *security, safety*
tener la seguridad de — *to rest assured.*
Tenga la seguridad de que lo visitaremos. *Rest assured that we will visit you.*

---

seguro — *sure*
de seguro — *surely; for sure.*
El año que viene iremos de seguro. *Next year we'll surely go (we'll go for sure).*

---

la semana — *week*
entre semana — *during the week.*
Vienen los domingos y entre semana también. *They come on Sunday and also during the week.*

---

sentar — *to seat; to suit, fit*
dar por sentado — *to take for granted; to regard as settled.*
Dio por sentado que irían. *He took it for granted (regarded it as settled) that they would go.*

sentarle bien — *to do one good; to agree with one.*
El sol me ha sentado bien. *The sun has done me good (agreed with me).*

---

el sentido — *sense*
de un solo sentido — *one-way.*
Esta calle es de un solo sentido. *This is a one-way street.*

en sentido contrario — *just the opposite.*
Fue interpretado en sentido contrario. *It was interpreted just the opposite.*

perder el sentido — *to lose consciousness; to faint.*
Perdió el sentido. *She lost consciousness (fainted).*

sentido común — *common sense.*
Lo que les hace falta es un poco de sentido común. *What they need is a little common sense.*

tener sentido — *to make sense.*
Eso no tiene sentido. *That doesn't make sense.*

---

sentido — *sensitive, touchy*
darse por sentido — *to take offense; to show resentment.*
Se dio por sentido. *He took offense (showed resentment).*

estar (muy) sentido — *to be (to have one's feelings) hurt.*
Estuve muy sentido por causa de su indiferencia. *I was (My feelings were) hurt because of her indifference.*

---

sentir — *to feel; to regret*
dar que sentir — *to give cause for regret.*
Sus acciones darán que sentir. *His actions will give cause for regret.*

---

la seña — *sign*
hacerle señas — *to motion to someone.*
Le hizo señas. *She motioned to him.*

por más señas — *to be more exact.*
Es francés y por más señas parisiense. *He's a Frenchman and to be more exact a Parisian.*

---

la señal — *sign*
dar señales de vida — *to show signs of life.*
La víctima da señales de vida. *The victim shows signs of life.*

---

ser — *to be*
a no ser que — *unless.*
Iremos a no ser que llueva. *We'll go unless it rains.*

(ello) es que — *the fact is (the thing is) that.*

(Ello) es que no quiso ir. *The fact is (The thing is) that he refused to go.*

lo que es . . . — *as for . . . .*

Lo que es yo, prefiero no comprarlo. *As for me, I prefer not to buy it.*

o sea — *that is; in other words.*

Lo presentaron a la señorita Pérez, o sea a mi prima. *They introduced him to Miss Pérez, that is (in other words), to my cousin.*

sea lo que sea — *whatever it may be.*

Sea lo que sea, no me va a gustar. *Whatever it may be, I'm not going to like it.*

ser de — *to become of.*

¿Qué será de nosotros? *What will become of us?*

ser de lamentar — *to be too bad.*

Es de lamentar que no haya venido. *It's too bad that he has not come.*

ser de llorar — *to be something to cry about.*

No es de llorar. *It's nothing to cry about.*

serle a uno indiferente — *to be all the same to.*

Me es indiferente. *It's all the same to me.*

si no fuera por — *if it weren't for.*

Si no fuera por mi hijo, no sé qué haría. *If it weren't for my son, I don't know what I'd do.*

un sí es no es — *a trifle; a little bit.*

Es un sí es no es irrespetuoso. *He's just a trifle (a little bit) disrespectful.*

---

el sereno — *night dew, night air*

al sereno — *in the open.*

Lo dejó al sereno toda la noche. *She left it out in the open all night long.*

---

la serie — *series*

fuera de serie — *really outstanding.*

Fue una presentación fuera de serie. *It was a really outstanding presentation.*

---

serio — *serious*

  en serio — *seriously.*
  Me habló en serio. *He spoke to me seriously.*

  tomar en serio — *to take seriously.*
  Toma en serio sus estudios. *He takes his studies seriously.*

---

el servicio — *service*

  hacerle a uno un flaco servicio — *to play a dirty trick on one.*
  Se enfadó porque le hizo un flaco servicio. *She got mad because he played a dirty trick on her.*

  hacer servicio a domicilio — *to deliver.*
  No hacen servicio a domicilio. *They don't deliver.*

---

el servidor — *servant*
  ¡Servidor de usted! — *At your service!*

---

servir — *to serve*

  no sirve — *it's no good.*
  No sirve para eso. *It's no good for that.*

  Para servirle (a usted). — *At your service.*

  servirle de — *to be of use to one.*
  No me sirve de nada. *It's of no use to me.*

  servirse de — *to make use of.*
  Se sirve del libro. *He makes use of the book.*

  sírvase — *please.*
  Sírvase leer las instrucciones. *Please read the instructions.*

---

el seso — *brain*

  devanarse los sesos — *to rack one's brains.*
  Me devanaba los sesos. *I was racking my brains.*

  perder el seso — *to lose one's mind.*
  Está perdiendo el seso. *He's losing his mind.*

---

sí — *yes*

porque sí — *just because.*

¿Por qué lo hizo? Porque sí. *Why did you do it? Just because.*

sí — *do (emphatic).*

No habla francés, pero sí habla español. *He doesn't speak French but he does speak Spanish.*

El no asistió, pero yo sí. *He didn't attend, but I did.*

uno sí y otro no — *every other.*

Visitaba el médico una semana sí y otra no. *He visited the doctor every other week.*

---

sí — *(one)self*

de por sí — *in itself.*

La cuestión de por sí no es muy importante. *The question is not very important in itself.*

---

si — *if*

si — *why.*

¡Si nunca dice la verdad! *Why, he never tells the truth!*

---

siempre — *always*

de siempre — *the same old.*

Nos sirvieron la comida de siempre. *They served us the same old food.*

para siempre — *forever.*

Adiós para siempre. *Good-bye forever.*

siempre que — *as long as.*

Irán siempre que vaya Juan. *They'll go as long as John goes.*

siempre que — *whenever.*

Siempre que podía, iba al cine. *Whenever he could, he went to the movies.*

---

la siesta — *(afternoon) nap*

dormir la siesta (echar una siesta) — *to take one's afternoon nap.*

Están durmiendo la siesta (echando una siesta). *They're taking their afternoon nap.*

---

siete — *seven*
  hablar más que siete — *to talk a lot (too much).*
  Habla más que siete. *He talks a lot (too much).*

el siglo — *century*
  por los siglos de los siglos — *forever and ever.*
  Siempre habrá políticos, por los siglos de los siglos. *There will always be politicians, forever and ever.*

siguiente — *following*
  al (el) día siguiente — *(on) the following day.*
  Me lo devolvió al (el) día siguiente. *She returned it to me (on) the following day.*

el silencio — *silence*
  en silencio — *in silence.*
  Sufría en silencio. *He suffered in silence.*

  guardar silencio — *to remain silent.*
  Guardó silencio. *He remained silent.*

sin — *without*
  sin explicar — *unexplained.*
  Lo dejaron sin explicar. *They left it unexplained.*

siquiera — *at least*
  ni siquiera — *not even; not so much as.*
  Ni siquiera nos saludó. *He didn't even (so much as) speak to us.*

la sobra — *surplus, excess*
  de sobra — *left over; more than enough.*
  Tenemos comida de sobra. *We have food left over (more than enough food).*

  estar de sobra — *to be in the way.*
  ¡Vamos! Aquí estamos de sobra. *Let's go! We're in the way here.*

  saber de sobra — *to be fully aware of.*
  Lo sabemos de sobra. *We are fully aware of it.*

sobrar — *to be in excess*
  Sobra tiempo. — *There's more than enough time.*

la sobremesa — *sitting at the table after eating*
  estar de sobremesa — *to be chatting at the table (after eating).*
  Están de sobremesa. *They're chatting at the table (after eating).*

la soga — *rope*
  No hay que mentar la soga en la casa del ahorcado. — *Don't talk of
    ropes in the house of a man that was hanged. (There's a time and a
    place for everything.)*
  ¿Para qué echar la soga tras el caldero? — *Why throw good money
    after bad?*

el sol — *sun*
  a pleno sol — *right out in the sun; in full sunshine.*
  Nos sentamos a pleno sol. *We sat right out in the sun (in full sunshine).*

  de sol a sol — *from sun(rise) to sun(set).*
  Trabajaron de sol a sol. *They worked from sun(rise) to sun(set).*

  no dejar ni a sol ni a sombra — *to breathe down someone's neck.*
  Ese joven no me deja ni a sol ni a sombra. *That young man is always
    breathing down my neck.*

  ponerse el sol — *for the sun to go down (to set).*
  Se puso el sol. *The sun went down (set).*

  tomar el sol — *to get out in the sun; to sun oneself.*
  Nos gusta tomar el sol. *We like to get out in the sun (sun ourselves).*

solo — *alone*
  a solas — *(all) alone.*
  La dejó a solas. *He left her (all) alone.*

sólo — *only*
  no sólo — *not only.*
  Toca no sólo el piano sino también el violín. *He plays not only the piano
    but also the violin.*

la sombra — *shadow*

  no ser ni su sombra — *to be just (but) a shadow of one's former self.*

  ¿Has visto a Rogelio? No es ni su sombra. *Have you seen Roger? He's just (but) a shadow of his former self.*

---

el son — *sound*

  a son de qué (a qué son) — *for what reason; under what pretext.*

  ¿A son de qué (A qué son) me dice eso? *For what reason (Under what pretext) are you saying that to me?*

  saber bailar al son que le tocan — *to know how to adjust (adapt) to the circumstances; to know how to roll with the punches.*

  Sabe bailar al son que le tocan. *He knows how to adjust (adapt himself) to the circumstances (He knows how to roll with the punches).*

---

sonado — *famous, sensational*

  hacer una que sea sonada — *to give them something to talk about.*

  Voy a hacer una que sea sonada. *I'm going to give them something to talk about.*

---

sonar — *to sound*

  No me suena. — *It doesn't ring a bell.*

  ser tal como suena — *to be exactly the way it sounds.*

  Es tal como suena. *It's exactly the way it sounds.*

  sonar a — *to sound like.*

  Me suena a música. *It sounds like music to me.*

---

la sonrisa — *smile*

  hacer una sonrisa — *to give a smile.*

  Me hizo una sonrisa de lástima. *He gave me a pitying smile.*

---

soñar — *to dream*

  ni soñar — *wouldn't dream (think) of it.*

  ¿Tú quieres que le ayude? ¡Ni soñar! *You want me to help him? I wouldn't dream (think) of it!*

  soñar con — *to dream about.*

  Soñé con mi familia. *I dreamed about my family.*

la sopa — *soup*

comer la sopa boba — *to live off other people.*

¿No le da vergüenza comer la sopa boba? *Aren't you ashamed to live off other people?*

hecho una sopa — *soaking wet; drenched.*

Llegó a casa hecha una sopa. *She got home soaking wet (drenched).*

---

sordo — *deaf; dull, muffled*

con voz sorda — *in a muffled voice.*

Lo dijo con voz sorda. *She said it in a muffled voice.*

hacerse el sordo — *to turn a deaf ear.*

Se hizo el sordo. *He turned a deaf ear.*

No hay peor sordo que el que no quiere oír. — *None (are) so deaf as those that won't hear.*

---

la sorpresa — *surprise*

coger (pescar) de sorpresa — *to take by surprise.*

Nos cogió (pescó) de sorpresa. *He took us by surprise.*

---

soslayo — *oblique*

mirar de soslayo — *to watch (look at) someone out of the corner of one's eye.*

Me miraba de soslayo. *He was watching (looking at) me out of the corner of his eye.*

---

la subasta — *auction*

sacar a pública subasta — *to sell at auction.*

Lo sacaron a pública subasta. *They sold it at auction.*

---

subir — *to go up*

subir a (un coche, taxi, etc.) — *to get into (a car, taxi, etc.).*

Al subir al coche, se le cayó la bolsa. *As she was getting into the car, she dropped her purse.*

subir a (un tren, autobús, etc.) — *to get on (a train, bus, etc.).*

Se despidió de su mamá y subió al autobús. *She said goodbye to her mother and got on the bus.*

súbito — *sudden*
  de súbito — *suddenly.*
  De súbito se oyó un tiro. *Suddenly a shot was heard.*

sucesivo — *successive*
  en lo sucesivo — *in the future; hereafter.*
  En lo sucesivo lo haremos de la manera que usted ha sugerido. *In the future (Hereafter) we will do it the way you have suggested.*

sueco — *Swedish*
  hacerse el sueco — *to pretend not to understand.*
  Se hizo el sueco. *He pretended not to understand.*

el sueño — *sleep, sleepiness; dream*
  conciliar el sueño — *to fall asleep; to get to sleep.*
  No pudo conciliar el sueño. *He couldn't fall asleep (get to sleep).*

  ni en sueños — *by no means.*
  No es amigo mío, ni en sueños. *He is by no means a friend of mine.*

  un sueño hecho realidad — *a dream come true.*
  Es un sueño hecho realidad. *It's a dream come true.*

la suerte — *luck, fortune*
  abandonar a su suerte — *to leave to one's fate.*
  Lo abandoné a su suerte. *I left him to his fate.*

  caerle en suerte — *to fall to one's lot.*
  Le cayó en suerte ir a España. *It fell to his lot to go to Spain.*

  de esta suerte — *this way.*
  De esta suerte sabré lo que pasa. *This way I'll know what's going on.*

  tener suerte — *to be lucky.*
  Tenemos suerte. *We're lucky.*

la suma — *sum*
  en suma — *in short.*
  En suma, no pudieron cruzar. *In short, they couldn't cross.*

sumo — *highest, greatest*

a lo sumo — *at (the) most.*

Estuvo enferma dos meses a lo sumo. *She was sick two months at (the) most.*

---

supuesto — *supposed, assumed*

por supuesto — *of course.*

Por supuesto no es necesario. *Of course it isn't necessary.*

---

el suspiro — *sigh*

exhalar el último suspiro — *to breathe one's last; to draw one's last breath.*

Exhaló el último suspiro. *She breathed her last (drew her last breath).*

soltar un suspiro de alivio — *to heave (to give) a sigh of relief.*

Soltó un suspiro de alivio. *He heaved (gave) a sigh of relief.*

---

el susto — *fright, scare*

estar muerto de susto — *to be frightened (scared) to death.*

Estaba muerta de susto. *She was frightened (scared) to death.*

---

el susurro — *whisper, murmur*

hablar en susurros — *to talk in whispers.*

Hablaban en susurros. *They were talking in whispers.*

---

suyo — *his, hers, its, theirs, yours, one's*

caerse de suyo — *to be self-evident.*

Se cae de suyo. *It's self-evident.*

hacer de las suyas — *to pull one of one's pranks; to be up to one's old tricks.*

Siempre está haciendo de las suyas. *He's always pulling one of his pranks (always up to his old tricks).*

salir(se) con la suya — *to get one's (own) way.*

Siempre (se) sale con la suya. *She always gets her (own) way.*

---

la tabla — *board*

  tener muchas tablas — *to have a lot of style and social assurance; to have a lot of experience in a field.*

  Sólo lleva un año como gerente, pero ya tiene muchas tablas. *She's only been manager for a year, but she's already an old hand at it.*

---

tal — *such*

  con tal que — *provided (that).*

  Iré con tal que usted me acompañe. *I'll go provided (that) you go along.*

  ¿Qué tal? — *How are you?*

  ser tal para cual — *to be two of a kind.*

  Son tal para cual. *They're two of a kind.*

  tal como — *just as.*

  Tal como él lo suponía, ella volvió. *Just as he supposed, she returned.*

  tal cual — *an occasional.*

  Sólo se ve en el cielo tal cual avión. *Only an occasional airplane is seen in the sky.*

  un tal — *a certain.*

  Llegó un tal capitán Pérez. *A certain Captain Pérez arrived.*

---

el talante — *mien, countenance*

  estar de buen talante — *to be in a good mood.*

  Está de buen talante. *He's in a good mood.*

---

tanto — *so much, as much*

  de tanto en tanto — *from time to time.*

  Se enjugaba los ojos de tanto en tanto. *She was wiping her eyes from time to time.*

  en (entre) tanto — *meanwhile; in the meantime.*

En (Entre) tanto recibimos un telegrama. *Meanwhile (In the meantime) we received a telegram.*

en tanto que — *whereas.*

A mí me gusta la música clásica, en tanto que a él le gusta la moderna. *I like classical music, whereas he likes modern.*

estar al tanto de — *to be up to date on.*

Está al tanto de la situación. *He's up to date on the situation.*

No es para tanto. — *It isn't as bad as (all) that (isn't all that bad).*

otro tanto — *the same; that much again.*

Yo le di un peso y Juan le dio otro tanto. *I gave him a peso and John gave him the same (that much again).*

por lo tanto — *therefore.*

Por lo tanto nos quedamos en casa. *Therefore we stayed home.*

tanto . . . como . . . — *both . . . and . . . .*

Tanto mis primos como mis padres viven en Lima. *Both my cousins and my parents live in Lima.*

Tanto monta el uno como el otro. — *One has the same importance as the other.*

un (algún) tanto — *a little.*

Llegó a la fiesta un (algún) tanto borracho. *He arrived at the party a little drunk.*

uno de tantos . . .s — *on a certain . . . .*

Uno de tantos miércoles llegó el circo. *On a certain Wednesday the circus arrived.*

y tantos — *some.*

Hemos invitado a veinte y tantas personas. *We've invited some twenty people.*

---

la tapa — *lid, cover*

saltarse la tapa de los sesos — *to blow one's brains out.*

Se saltó la tapa de los sesos. *He blew his brains out.*

---

la tapia — *wall*

ser más sordo que una tapia — *to be (as) deaf as a post.*

Es más sordo que una tapia. *He's (as) deaf as a post.*

la taquilla — *box office*

ser un éxito de taquilla — *to be a box-office success.*

La obra no les gustó a los críticos, pero fue un éxito de taquilla. *The critics didn't like the work, but it was a box-office success.*

---

tardar — *to be long*

a más tardar — *at the latest.*

Nos vemos mañana a más tardar. *We'll get together tomorrow at the latest.*

tardar poco — *not to take long.*

Tardaron muy poco en hacerlo. *It didn't take them very long to do it.*

---

la tarde — *afternoon*

por (en) la tarde — *in the afternoon.*

Van a reunirse por (en) la tarde. *They're going to meet in the afternoon.*

---

tarde — *late*

de tarde en tarde — *from time to time; once in a while.*

De tarde en tarde vamos al cine. *From time to time (Once in a while) we go to the movies.*

hacérsele tarde — *to be late.*

Se me hace tarde. *I'm late.*

tarde o temprano — *sooner or later.*
Tarde o temprano ganaremos. *Sooner or later we'll win.*

la tarea — *task*
darse a la tarea — *to undertake the task.*
Se dio a la tarea de escribir una novela. *He undertook the task of writing a novel.*

la tela — *cloth*
poner en tela de juicio — *to question (call into question).*
Puso en tela de juicio la decisión del presidente. *He questioned (called into question) the president's decision.*

el teléfono — *telephone*
llamar por teléfono — *to (tele)phone; to call up.*
Nos llamó por teléfono. *He (tele)phoned us (called us up).*

el telegrama — *telegram*
poner un telegrama — *to send a telegram.*
Me pusieron un telegrama. *They sent me a telegram.*

el tema — *theme*
concretarse al tema — *to stick to the subject.*
Usted debiera concretarse al tema. *You should stick to the subject.*

temblar — *to tremble*
temblar de miedo — *to tremble with fear.*
Temblaba de miedo. *He was trembling with fear.*

la tempestad — *storm*
una tempestad en un vaso de agua — *a tempest in a teapot.*
Todo eso es una tempestad en un vaso de agua. *All that's just a tempest in a teapot.*

tener — *to have*
aquí tiene usted — *here is.*

Aquí tiene usted su diccionario. *Here's your dictionary.*

no tener nada de particular — *for there to be nothing unusual about it.*
No tiene nada de particular. *There's nothing unusual about it.*

qué tiene — *what's the matter with; what's wrong with.*
¿Qué tiene Felipe? *What's the matter with (What's wrong with) Philip?*

tener a bien — *to see fit to.*
Tuvo a bien comprar un yate. *He saw fit to buy a yacht.*

tener a menos — *to think (feel) it beneath one.*
El profesor no tiene a menos ayudar a sus alumnos. *The professor doesn't think (feel) it beneath him to help his students.*

tener algo de — *for there to be something . . . about it.*
Tiene algo de aburrido. *There's something boring about it.*

tener como (por) — *to consider (to be).*
Se les tenía como (por) importantes. *They were considered (to be) important.*

tener con qué — *to have the wherewithal; to have what it takes.*
No tengo con qué vivir bien. *I don't have the wherewithal (what it takes) to live well.*

tener . . . de — *to have . . . (for).*
Tenía dos años de casada. *She had been married (for) two years.*

tener de (por) qué — *to have reason to.*
No tiene de (por) qué quejarse. *You have no reason to complain (nothing to complain about).*

tener puesto — *to have on.*
Tiene puestos los zapatos. *He has his shoes on.*

tener que — *to have to.*
Tiene que escribir una carta. *He has to write a letter.*

tener . . . que — *to have . . . to.*
Tiene una carta que escribir. *He has a letter to write.*

tener que ver con — *to have to do with.*
No tiene nada que ver con el asunto. *It has nothing to do with the matter.*

la teoría — *theory*

en teoría — *theoretically; in theory.*
En teoría es así. *Theoretically (In theory) that's the way it is.*

---

terminar — *to end, finish*

terminar por — *to end up by.*
Terminó por aceptar la explicación. *He ended up by accepting the explanation.*

---

el término — *end; term*

al término de — *at the end of.*
Al término de la primera semana volvió a casa. *At the end of the first week she returned home.*

en primer término — *in the foreground.*
En primer término se ven dos árboles. *In the foreground are (seen) two trees.*

poner término a — *to put a stop (an end) to.*
Puso término a los chismes. *He put a stop (an end) to the gossip.*

por término medio — *on the (an) average.*
Por término medio asiste dos veces a la semana. *On the (an) average he attends twice a week.*

---

el terreno — *land, ground*

ganar (perder) terreno — *to gain (lose) ground.*
Estamos ganando (perdiendo) terreno en la lucha. *We are gaining (losing) ground in the struggle.*

---

el tiempo — *time; weather*

a su tiempo — *in due time.*
Recibirá el dinero a su tiempo. *He'll receive the money in due time.*

al mismo tiempo — *at the same time.*
Compré un traje y un sombrero al mismo tiempo. *I bought a suit and a hat at the same time.*

andando el tiempo — *in the course of time; eventually.*

263

Andando el tiempo, se va a dar cuenta. *In the course of time (Eventually) he's going to realize it.*

costar tiempo — *to take time.*

Costó tiempo acostumbrarse. *It took time to get used to it.*

cuánto tiempo — *how long.*

¿Cuánto tiempo lleva aquí? *How long have you been here?*

darle tiempo — *to have time.*

No nos dio tiempo. *We didn't have time.*

de tiempo en tiempo — *from time to time.*

Nos escriben de tiempo en tiempo. *They write to us from time to time.*

en algún tiempo — *at one time.*

En algún tiempo me gustaban. *At one time I used to like them.*

en (por) aquel tiempo — *at (around) that time.*

En (Por) aquel tiempo se usaba la falda larga. *At (Around) that time long skirts were being worn.*

en los últimos tiempos — *in recent times (lately).*

En los últimos tiempos ha empezado a ir a misa. *In recent times (Lately) she has started going to Mass.*

en otro tiempo — *formerly.*

En otro tiempo se producía mucho trigo aquí. *Formerly they grew a lot of wheat here.*

en tiempos de Maricastaña — *long, long ago; in days of yore; in olden days (times).*

Así era en tiempos de Maricastaña. *That's the way it was long, long ago (in days of yore; in olden days).*

en todo tiempo — *always; at all times.*

En todo tiempo pensaba en él. *She was always thinking (At all times she was thinking) of him.*

en (a) un tiempo — *at the same time.*

Los dos entraron en (a) un tiempo. *The two entered at the same time.*

ganar tiempo — *to save time.*

Vamos por aquí para ganar tiempo. *Let's go this way to save time.*

Hace buen (mal) tiempo. — *The weather is nice (bad).*

llegar a tiempo — *to be (to arrive) on time.*
Es necesario llegar a tiempo. *It is necessary to be (to arrive) on time.*

llevar (exigir) su tiempo — *to take time.*
Aprender un idioma extranjero lleva (exige) su tiempo. *Learning a foreign language takes time.*

matar el (hacer) tiempo — *to kill time.*
Estábamos leyendo para matar el (hacer) tiempo. *We were reading to kill time.*

mucho tiempo — *a long time.*
Se quedó mucho tiempo. *He stayed a long time.*

pasar el tiempo — *to spend one's time.*
Pasa el tiempo trabajando. *He spends his time working.*

perder (el) tiempo — *to waste time.*
Estamos perdiendo (el) tiempo. *We're wasting time.*

poco tiempo — *a short time; not long.*
Se quedó poco tiempo. *She stayed a short time (didn't stay long).*

ponerle al mal tiempo buena cara — *to make the best of things.*
Si no hay más remedio, trataremos de ponerle al mal tiempo buena cara. *If there's nothing to be done, we'll just try to make the best of things.*

quitarle el tiempo — *to take (up) one's time.*
No quiero quitarle el tiempo. *I don't want to take (up) your time.*

tiempo atrás — *some time back; earlier.*
Tiempo atrás dijo que no quería ir. *Some time back (Earlier) he said he didn't want to go.*

---

a tienta — *sounding rod; shrewdness*
ir a tientas — *to feel one's way along.*
Hay que ir a tientas en la obscuridad. *You have to feel your way along in the dark.*

---

el tiento — *touch; caution, care*
con tiento — *cautiously.*
Lo abrió con mucho tiento. *He opened it very cautiously.*

---

la tierra — *earth, land*

   echar por tierra — *to upset; to spoil.*

   La lluvia echó por tierra nuestros planes. *The rain upset (spoiled) our plans.*

   echar tierra a — *to hush up.*

   Echaron tierra al asunto. *They hushed the matter up.*

   En tierra de ciegos, el tuerto es rey. — *In the land of the blind, the one-eyed man is king. Everything is relative.*

   tierra adentro — *inland.*

   Se marcharon tierra adentro. *They set off inland.*

---

el tintero — *inkwell*

   quedarse en el tintero — *to overlook; to omit.*

   Se le quedó en el tintero. *He overlooked (omitted) it.*

---

el tiro — *shot*

   dar (pegar) un tiro — *to shoot.*

   Le dio (pegó) un tiro. *He shot her.*

   errar el tiro — *to miss the mark.*

   A pesar de ser inteligente, erró el tiro. *In spite of being intelligent, he missed the mark.*

   matar a tiros — *to shoot dead (to death).*

   Lo mataron a tiros. *They shot him dead (to death).*

   ni a tiros — *not for love or money.*

   No compraré ese coche ni a tiros. *I won't buy that car for love or money.*

   salir el tiro por la culata — *to backfire.*

   El tiro salió por la culata. *It backfired.*

---

el tirón — *jerk, pull*

   de un tirón — *all at once; all in one stretch.*

   Vamos a hacer el trabajo de un tirón. *Let's do the work all at once (all in one stretch).*

---

tocante — *touching*

   tocante a — *regarding.*

Tocante al puesto que me ofreciste, lo acepto. *Regarding the position you offered me, I accept it.*

---

tocar — *to touch; to play (music)*

por lo que a mí me toca — *as far as I'm concerned.*

Por lo que a mí me toca, es igual. *As far as I'm concerned, it's all the same.*

tocarle (a uno) — *to be one's turn.*

A mí me toca trabajar mañana. *It's my turn to work tomorrow.*

tocarle — *to be time for.*

Al niño le toca la medicina. *It's time for the child's medicine.*

---

todavía — *still, yet*

todavía no — *not yet.*

Todavía no ha llamado. *He hasn't called yet.*

---

todo — *all*

ante todo — *above all; first of all.*

Ante todo, hay que ser sincero. *Above all (First of all), one must be sincere.*

con todo (así y todo) — *even so.*

Con todo (Así y todo) es el mejor que tenemos. *Even so it's the best one we have.*

con todo y — *in spite of.*

Con todo y ser yo su madre, a veces no me explico por qué se porta así. *In spite of being her mother, I sometimes can't understand why she behaves that way.*

de todo — *a little of everything.*

Aquí hay de todo. *Here there's a little of everything.*

del todo — *entirely; completely.*

No es del todo imposible. *It's not entirely (completely) impossible.*

después de todo — *after all.*

Después de todo no estoy convencido. *After all, I'm not convinced.*

estar en todo — *to be involved in everything.*

Está en todo. *She's involved in everything.*

jugar el todo por el todo — *to gamble (risk) everything.*

Jugué el todo por el todo. *I gambled (risked) everything.*

sobre todo — *especially; above all.*
Hace mucho frío, sobre todo en invierno. *It's very cold, especially (above all) in winter.*

todos los — *every.*
Voy a mi clase todos los días. *I go to my class every day.*

---

tomar — *to take*
  tomar a mal — *to take amiss.*
  Lo tomó a mal. *She took it amiss.*

  tomar por — *to go down.*
  Tome por esa calle. *Go down that street.*

  tomar por — *to take for.*
  Me tomó por extranjero. *He took me for a foreigner.*

  tomar sobre sí — *to take upon oneself.*
  Lo tomó sobre sí. *He took it upon himself.*

  tomarse el trabajo de — *to take the trouble to; to go to the trouble of.*
  No se tomó el trabajo de escribirme. *She didn't take the trouble to write me (go to the trouble of writing me).*

  ¡Tome! — *Here!*

---

el ton — *motive*
  sin ton ni son — *without rhyme or reason.*
  Me despidió sin ton ni son. *He fired me without rhyme or reason.*

---

el tono — *tone*
  darse tono — *to put on airs.*
  Se da mucho tono. *She puts on a lot of airs.*

---

tonto — *foolish, stupid*
  hablar a tontas y a locas — *to prattle away; to say the first thing that comes into one's head.*
  Habla a tontas y a locas. *She prattles away (says the first thing that comes into her head).*

  hacer el tonto — *to make a fool of oneself; to act like a fool.*

¡Deje ya de hacer el tonto! *Stop making a fool of yourself (acting like a fool)!*

hacerse el tonto — *to play dumb.*
Se hizo el tonto. *He played dumb.*

el tope — *top, maximum*
a tope — *as much as possible.*
Tendremos que trabajar a tope si queremos terminar hoy. *We'll have to work all out if we want to finish today.*

el torneo — *tournament*
hacer un torneo — *to hold a tournament.*
Hicieron un torneo de tenis. *They held a tennis tournament.*

el tornillo — *screw*
faltarle un tornillo — *to have a screw loose.*
Le falta un tornillo. *He has a screw loose.*

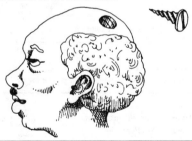

el torno — *turn*
girar en torno a — *to revolve around.*
Su vida giraba en torno a su padre. *Her life revolved around her father.*

la torta — *cake*
ser tortas y pan pintado — *to be child's play; to be as easy as pie.*

Estos trabajos son tortas y pan pintado. *These jobs are child's play (as easy as pie).*

---

la torre — *tower*
    una torre de marfil — *an ivory tower.*
    Algunos creen que todos los intelectuales viven en una torre de marfil. *Some people think that all intellectuals live in an ivory tower.*

---

total — *total*
    en total — *in short.*
    No jugaron bien anoche. En total, fue un desastre. *They did not play well last night. In short, it was a disaster.*

---

el trabajo — *work*
    costarle trabajo — *to be hard for one.*
    Me cuesta trabajo entenderlo. *It's hard for me to understand it.*

---

tragar — *to swallow*
    no poder tragar — *not to be able to stomach.*
    No puedo tragar a ese tipo. *I can't stomach that guy.*

---

el trago — *swallow*
    echar un trago — *to have a drink.*
    ¿Qué le parece que echemos un trago? *What do you say we have a drink?*

---

la trampa — *trap, snare; trick, deceit*
    caer en la trampa — *to fall into the trap.*
    Cayó en la trampa. *He fell into the trap.*

    hacer trampas — *to cheat.*
    Siempre hace trampas. *He always cheats.*

    llevar a la trampa — *to lead into the trap.*
    Una mujer lo llevó a la trampa. *A woman led him into the trap.*

---

el trance — *difficult moment*
    a todo trance — *at all cost; at any risk.*
    Lo conseguiré a todo trance. *I'll get it at all costs (at any risk).*

estar en el mismo trance — *to be in the same boat.*
No te quejes. Todos estamos en el mismo trance. *Don't complain. We're all in the same boat.*

el trapo — *rag*
poner como un trapo — *to rake over the coals; to give a dressing-down.*
Lo pusieron como un trapo. *They raked him over the coals (gave him a dressing-down).*

soltar el trapo — *to burst out crying (laughing).*
Soltó el trapo. *She burst out crying (laughing).*

tener lengua de trapo — *not to pronounce well; to speak incorrectly; to stammer.*
Ese cantante tiene una lengua de trapo cuando le entrevistan. *That singer speaks very poorly when they interview him.*

el traste — *bottom*
irse al traste — *to fail.*
Esas empresas se han ido al traste. *Those companies have gone bust.*

tratar — *to treat, handle, deal with*
tratar con — *to have dealings with.*
No trato con los ricos. *I have no dealings with the rich.*

tratar de — *to be about; to deal with.*
La novela trata de los indios. *The novel is about (deals with) the Indians.*

tratarlo (hablarle) de — *to address someone as.*
Lo trato (Le hablo) de Vuestra Majestad. *I address him as Your Majesty.*

tratarse — *to associate with each other.*
No se tratan. *They don't associate with each other.*

tratarse de — *to be a question of; to be a matter of; to involve.*
Se trata de un malentendido (una equivocación). *It's a question of (It's a matter of, It involves) a misunderstanding.*

el trato — *treatment; deal*
¡Trato hecho! — *It's a deal!*

el través — *inclination, bias, misfortune*
  a través de — *through(out)*.
  A través de los años se ha hecho famoso. *Through(out) the years he has become famous.*

  a través de — *through*.
  Nos hablaba a través de un biombo. *He was talking to us through a screen.*

---

la traza — *design*
  tener trazas de — *to show signs of*.
  Esta conferencia no tiene trazas de acabar. *This lecture shows no signs of ending.*

---

trece — *thirteen*
  estarse en sus trece — *to stick to one's guns*.
  Se estuvo en sus trece. *He stuck to his guns.*

---

el trecho — *stretch*
  de trecho en trecho — *from time to time*.
  Me escribe de trecho en trecho. *He writes me from time to time.*

---

la tregua — *truce*
  sin tregua — *without letting up*.
  Trabajó todo el día sin tregua. *He worked all day long without letting up.*

---

la tripa — *intestine*
  hacer de tripas corazón — *to pluck up one's courage*.
  Hizo de tripas corazón. *He plucked up his courage.*

  ¿Qué tripa se le habrá roto a ése? — *What's his problem (What's the matter with him)?*

---

el tris — *slight sound (of something breaking); hair's breadth*
  estar en un tris de — *to be within an inch (to come within an ace) of*.
  Estaba en un tris de caerse. *He was within an inch (came within an ace) of falling.*

---

el triunfo — *triumph*
  costar un triunfo — *to take all one's efforts.*
  Me costó un triunfo domar ese caballo. *It took all my efforts to tame that horse.*

la triza — *shred, fragment*
  hacer trizas — *to smash.*
  Hizo trizas el florero. *He smashed the vase.*

tronar — *to thunder*
  tronar con — *to break (off) with; to quarrel with.*
  Tronó con su familia. *She broke (off) with (quarreled with) her family.*

el tronco — *trunk*
  dormir como un tronco (estar hecho un tronco) — *to sleep like a log; to be sound asleep.*
  Estaba durmiendo como un tronco (Estaba hecho un tronco). *He was sleeping like a log (sound asleep).*

el tropel — *rush, bustle, confusion*
  en tropel — *in a mad rush.*
  Se fueron en tropel. *They left in a mad rush.*

tropezar — *to trip, stumble*
  tropezar con — *to run into.*
  Tropezó con Enrique. *She ran into Henry.*

el tropezón — *stumbling*
  a tropezones — *stumblingly; haltingly.*
  Lee a tropezones. *He reads stumblingly (haltingly).*

el tuétano — *marrow*
  hasta los tuétanos — *through and through (to the core).*
  Es republicano hasta los tuétanos. *He's a republican through and through (to the core).*

273

tuntún

    al (buen) tuntún — *any old way; at random.*

    Contestaba las preguntas al (buen) tuntún. *He was answering the questions any old way (at random).*

el turno — *turn*

    estar de turno — *to be on duty.*

    El doctor López está de turno. *Dr. López is on duty.*

ubicar — *to locate*

    ¡Ubícate! — *Remember where you are!*

    ¡Ubícate! No se puede hablar así en la iglesia. *Remember where you are! You can't talk this way in church.*

último — *last*

    estar en las últimas — *to be at death's door.*

    Está en las últimas. *He's at death's door.*

    por último — *finally.*

    Por último pasaron las bandas. *Finally the bands passed by.*

uno — *one*

    ser uno de tantos — *to be run-of-the-mill.*

    Es uno de tantos escritores. *He's a run-of-the-mill writer.*

    uno que otro — *an occasional; a few.*

    Fuma uno que otro cigarrillo. *He smokes an occasional cigarette (a few cigarettes).*

    uno tras otro — *one after another.*

    Salieron uno tras otro. *They went out one after another.*

    uno y otro — *both of them.*

    Uno y otro nos saludaron. *Both of them spoke to us.*

    unos cuantos — *a few.*

Me trajo unos cuantos libros. *He brought me a few books.*

unos y otros — *all of them.*
Unos y otros se acercaron. *All of them approached.*

---

la uña — *fingernail, toenail*
ser uña y carne — *to be as thick as thieves; to be hand in glove.*
Son uña y carne. *They're thick as thieves (hand in glove).*

---

el uso — *use, usage*
El uso hace maestro. — *Practice makes perfect.*

estar en buen uso — *to be in good condition.*
El coche todavía está en buen uso. *The car is still in good condition.*

---

la vacación — *vacation*
estar de vacaciones — *to be on vacation.*
Están de vacaciones. *They're on vacation.*

---

valer — *to be worth*
más vale (valiera) — *it is (would have been) better to.*
Más vale (valiera) venderlo. *It's (It would have been) better to sell it.*

Más vale tarde que nunca. — *Better late than never.*

valer lo que pesa — *to be worth one's weight in gold.*
Ese joven vale lo que pesa. *That young man is worth his weight in gold.*

valerse de — *to use.*
Hay que valerse de todos los medios posibles. *One has to use all possible means.*

---

el valle — *valley*
valle de lágrimas — *vale of tears.*

Se sufre mucho en este valle de lágrimas — *You suffer a lot in this vale of tears.*

vano — *vain*
  en vano — *in vain.*
  Suplicó en vano. *He pleaded in vain.*

la vara — *twig, stick*
  tener vara alta — *to carry a lot of weight.*
  Tiene vara alta en esa compañía. *He carries a lot of weight in that company.*

Vargas — *(proper name)*
  ¡Averígüelo Vargas! — *Heaven only knows!*

variar — *to vary*
  para variar — *just for a change.*
  Para variar voy a tomar café. *Just for a change I'm going to have coffee.*

el vaso — *glass*
  ahogarse en un vaso de agua — *to get all upset over nothing; to start a tempest in a teapot.*
  Se ahogó en un vaso de agua. *He got all upset over nothing (He started a tempest in a teapot).*

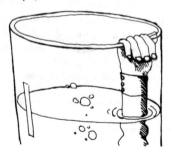

no dar ni un vaso de agua — *to be a real Scrooge.*

Mi abuelo no da ni un vaso de agua. *My grandfather is a real Scrooge.*

---

la vela — *vigil, wakefulness; candle; sail*

a toda vela — *at full speed.*

Las cosas marchan a toda vela en la fábrica. *Things are going at full speed in the factory.*

estar a dos velas — *to be down to nothing; to be out of money or necessary items.*

Estamos a dos velas aquí en la oficina. *We're operating on a shoestring here in the office.*

pasar la noche en vela — *to stay awake (all night); to keep a vigil.*

Pasó la noche en vela por su hijo enfermo. *She stayed awake all night with (kept a vigil over) her sick son.*

¿Quién le ha dado a usted vela en este entierro? *Who asked you to butt in?*

---

velar — *to watch over*

velar por — *to look after.*

Su esposa vela constantemente por él. *His wife constantly looks after him.*

---

el velo — *veil*

correr un velo (sobre) — *to hush up.*

El gobierno corrió un velo sobre el escándalo. *The government hushed up the scandal.*

tomar el velo — *to take the veil.*

Desde joven, siempre era muy pía, y finalmente tomó el velo. *Since her youth she was always very religious, and finally she took the veil.*

---

la velocidad — *velocity*

llevar una velocidad de — *to travel at a speed of.*

Llevaba una velocidad de cien kilómetros la (por) hora. *I was traveling at a speed of one hundred kilometers an hour.*

---

la vena — *vein*

sangrar de las venas — *to bleed white.*

El chantajista le estaba sangrando de las venas. *The blackmailer was bleeding him white.*

vencer — *to conquer, vanquish*
  darse por vencido — *to give up.*
  Se dio por vencido. *He gave up.*

vender — *to sell*
  vender regalado — *to sell for a song (for almost nothing).*
  Me lo vendió regalado. *He sold it to me for a song (for almost nothing).*

venir — *to come*
  . . . que viene — *next. . . .*
  Nos reuniremos el mes (año, etc.) que viene. *We will meet next month (year, etc.).*

  venir a aparecer — *to turn up.*
  Mire donde vino a aparecer. *Look where he turned up.*

  venir a menos — *to come down in the world.*
  Es un aristócrata venido a menos. *He is an aristocrat who has come down in the world.*

  venir a parar — *to turn out.*
  ¿En qué vino a parar la discusión? *How did the discussion turn out?*

  venir mal de — *to have a case of.*
  Venía muy mal de gripe. *I had a bad case of the flu.*

  venirle bien — *to be good for one; to do one good.*
  El sol le vendría bien. *The sun would be good for you (would do you good)*

la venta — *sale*
  ponerse a la venta — *to be put on sale.*
  Se puso a la venta. *It was put on sale.*

la ventaja — *advantage*
  llevar (una) ventaja — *to have (to hold) an advantage; to be ahead; to have a lead.*

Me lleva (una) ventaja. *He has (holds) an advantage (a lead) over me (He is ahead of me).*

sacar ventaja de — *to profit from.*
Sacaron ventaja de su contrato con Pérez y Cía. *They profited from their contract with Pérez and Co.*

---

ver — *to see*

a mi ver — *in my opinion (to my way of thinking).*
A mi ver su sugerencia no vale nada. *In my opinion (to my way of thinking) his suggestion isn't worth anything.*

(Vamos) a ver. — *Let's see.*

aquí donde usted me ve — *believe it or not.*
Aquí donde usted me ve, hablo doce idiomas. *Believe it or not, I speak twelve languages.*

¡Fue de ver! — *You should have seen it!*

¡Habráse visto! — *The very idea!*

por lo visto — *apparently; evidently*
Por lo visto no está. *Apparently (Evidently) he's not in.*

se ve — *it's evident (obvious).*
Se ve que es muy joven. *It's evident (obvious) that she's very young.*

Si te vi, no me acuerdo. — *Favors are soon forgotten.*

tener buen ver — *to be looking good (well).*
Tiene buen ver. *He's looking good (well).*

Ver y creer. — *Seeing is believing.*

verlo venir — *to see what someone is up to.*
Lo veo venir. *I see what he's up to.*

verse con — *to meet.*
Me veré con ella en el café. *I'll meet her at the cafe.*

verse forzado (obligado) a — *to be forced (compelled) to.*
Se vio forzado (obligado) a abandonarlos. *He was forced (compelled) to abandon them.*

---

las veras — *earnestness, sincerity, truth*
   de veras — *really.*
   Es de veras muy simpático. *He's really very nice.*

la verdad — *truth*
   a decir verdad — *to tell the truth.*
   A decir verdad, no sé. *To tell the truth, I don't know.*

   de verdad — *real.*
   Tenía una pistola de verdad. *He had a real pistol.*

   decirle cuatro verdades — *to tell someone a thing ar two.*
   Un día de éstos le voy a decir cuatro verdades. *One of these days I'm
     going to tell him a thing or two.*

   en verdad — *truly.*
   Es en verdad un hombre muy capaz. *He is truly a very capable man.*

   ¿verdad? — *right?, don't you?, isn't he?, won't they?, can't I?, etc.*
   Usted habla inglés, ¿verdad? *You speak English, right? (don't you?)*

la vergüenza — *shame*
   darle vergüenza — *to make one ashamed.*
   Me da vergüenza. *It makes me ashamed.*

   tener vergüenza — *to be ashamed.*
   Tengo vergüenza. *I'm ashamed.*

verde — *green*
   ponerle verde — *to rake someone over the coals.*
   Me puso verde. *He raked me over the coals.*

vestir — *to dress*
   vestir de — *to wear; to be dressed in.*
   Vestía de seda. *She was wearing (was dressed in) silk.*

la vez — *time*
   a la vez — *at the same time.*
   Cantaba y trabajaba a la vez. *She was singing and working at the same
    time.*

a su vez — *in turn.*
Todos probaron el vino a su vez. *Everybody in turn tasted the wine.*

a veces — *at times.*
A veces toma un trago. *At times he takes a drink.*

alguna vez — *ever.*
¿Ha visto alguna vez un alacrán? *Have you ever seen a scorpion?*

alguna vez que otra — *occasionally.*
Tomamos café al aire libre alguna vez que otra. *We have coffee in the open air occasionally.*

algunas veces — *sometimes.*
Viene algunas veces a comer con nosotros. *He sometimes comes to eat with us.*

cada vez más — *more and more.*
Se ponía cada vez más pálida. *She was getting paler and paler.*

de una vez — *and be done with it.*
Tómelo de una vez. *Take it and be done with it.*

de una vez por todas (de una vez y para siempre) — *once and for all.*
Lo terminaron de una vez por todas (y para siempre). *They ended it once and for all.*

de vez en cuando — *from time to time.*
De vez en cuando hacen un viaje a México. *From time to time they take a trip to Mexico.*

en vez de — *instead of.*
En vez de ir, se quedó. *Istead of going, he remained.*

hacer las veces de — *to act as.*
Ella hace las veces de madre. *She acts as a mother.*

las más (la mayoría de las) veces — *most of the time.*
Las más (La mayoría de las) veces hay agua caliente. *Most of the time there's hot water.*

muchas veces — *often.*
Muchas veces viene solo. *He often comes alone.*

ni una sola vez — *not even once; not a single time.*

Ni una solo vez me vino a ver. *Not even once (Not a single time) did she come to see me.*

otra vez — *again.*
Tuve que decirlo otra vez. *I had to say it again.*

otras veces — *on other occasions; other times.*
Otras veces iba a algún concierto. *On other occasions (Other times) she would go to a concert.*

para otra vez — *for another (a later) occasion.*
Lo dejaremos para otra vez. *We'll leave it for another (a later) occasion.*

por primera (última) vez — *for the first (last) time.*
Lo hizo por primera (última) vez. *He did it for the first (last) time.*

raras (contadas) veces — *rarely; seldom.*
La vi raras (contadas) veces. *I rarely (seldom) saw her.*

repetidas veces — *repeatedly.*
Me lo dijo repetidas veces. *He told me (so) repeatedly.*

tal vez — *perhaps; maybe.*
Tal vez vengan. *Perhaps (Maybe) they're coming.*

tantas veces — *so often.*
Nos llama tantas veces que nos molesta. *She calls us so often that it's a nuisance (bother).*

una vez (dos veces) — *once (twice).*
Una vez (Dos veces) vino a vernos. *Once (Twice) she came to see us.*

---

el viaje — *trip*
¡Buen viaje! — *Bon voyage!*

el viaje de ida y vuelta — *the round trip.*
El viaje de ida y vuelta dura cuatro horas. *The round trip lasts four hours.*

estar de viaje — *to be on a trip.*
Están de viaje. *They're on a trip.*

hacer (realizar) un viaje — *to take a trip.*
Hicieron (Realizaron) un viaje. *They took a trip.*

---

salir de viaje — *to leave on a trip.*

Mañana salimos de viaje. *Tomorrow we're leaving on a trip.*

---

la vida — *life*

amargarle la vida — *to make life miserable for (make one's life miserable).*

No hace más que amargarme la vida. *She does nothing but make life miserable for me (make my life miserable).*

darse buena vida — *to live it up; to enjoy life.*

Le gusta darse buena vida. *He likes to live it up (enjoy life).*

echarse (lanzarse) a la vida — *to take to the streets; to become a prostitute.*

Se echó (Se lanzó) a la vida. *She took to the streets (became a prostitute).*

en su vida — *never in one's life.*

En mi vida he comido una sopa tan sabrosa. *Never in my life have I eaten such delicious soup.*

en una sola vida — *in a single lifetime.*

En una sola vida no se puede hacer mucho. *In a single lifetime you can't do much.*

en vida — *while one was alive; during one's lifetime.*

En vida siempre leía mucho. *While he was alive (During his lifetime) he always used to read a lot.*

ganarse la vida — *to earn one's living.*

Se gana la vida tocando la guitarra. *He earns his living (by) playing the guitar.*

jugarse (arriesgarse) la vida — *to risk one's life.*

Se jugó (Se arriesgó) la vida. *He risked his life.*

la vida y milagros — *the life and doings.*

Es una revista que cuenta la vida y milagros de las estrellas del cine. *It's a magazine that tells all about the life and doings of the movie stars.*

llevar (hacer) una vida . . . — *to lead a . . . life.*

Lleva (Hace) una vida muy tranquila. *He leads a very quiet life.*

Los gatos tienen siete vidas. — *Cats have nine lives.*

viejo — *old*
  un viejo verde — *a dirty old man.*
  Es un viejo verde. *He's a dirty old man.*

el viento — *wind*
  contra viento y marea — *against all odds.*
  Triunfó contra viento y marea. *He triumphed against all odds.*

el vigor — *vigor, force*
  entrar en vigor — *to go into effect.*
  La ley entró en vigor el mes pasado. *The law went into effect last month.*
  estar en vigor — *to be in effect.*
  La ley está en vigor. *The law is in effect.*
  poner en vígor — *to put into effect.*
  Pusieron en vigor varias restricciones. *They put several restrictions into effect.*

vilo
  en vilo — *(up) in the air.*
  Levantó al niño en vilo. *He lifted the child (up) in the air.*
  tenerle en vilo — *to keep someone up in the air.*
  Díganoslo en seguida, no nos tenga en vilo. *Tell us right away, don't keep us up in the air.*

el vinagre — *vinegar*
  hecho un vinagre — *in a very sour tone.*
  Se lo dijo hecho un vinagre. *He said it to her in a very sour tone.*

la virtud — *virtue*
  en virtud de — *by virtue of.*
  Lo decretó en virtud de su autoridad. *He decreed it by virtue of his authority.*

la visita — *visit*
  devolverle la visita — *to repay (to return) one's visit.*

Me devolverán la visita. *They'll repay (return) my visit.*

hacerle una visita — *to pay one a visit.*
Me hizo una visita. *He paid me a visit.*

la víspera — *eve*
estar en vísperas de — *to be about to; to be on the eve of.*
Estaban en vísperas de casarse. *They were about to get married (were on the eve of getting married).*

la vista — *sight, view*
a primera vista — *at first sight.*
Se enamoraron a primera vista. *They fell in love at first sight.*

andar mal de la vista — *to have poor eyesight.*
Andaba mal de la vista. *She had poor eyesight.*

con vistas a — *with a view to.*
Compré el libro con vistas a regalárselo a mi esposa. *I bought the book with a view to presenting it to my wife.*

conocer de vista — *to know by sight.*
Se conocen de vista. *They know each other by sight.*

corto de vista — *near-sighted.*
Es un poco corto de vista. *He's a little near-sighted.*

estar a la vista — *to be in sight.*
El policía no estaba a la vista. *The policeman wasn't in sight.*

hacer la vista gorda — *to look the other way; to pretend not to notice.*
Hizo la vista gorda. *He looked the other way (pretended not to notice).*

Hasta la vista. — *So long!; See you later.*

levantar la vista — *to raise one's eyes; to look up.*
No levantó la vista. *He didn't raise his eyes (look up).*

no echarle la vista encima — *not to lay eyes on someone.*
No le he echado la vista encima. *I haven't laid eyes on him.*

perder de vista — *to lose sight of.*
Los perdimos de vista. *We lost sight of them.*

saltar a la vista — *to be obvious (self-evident).*
Los errores saltan a la vista. *The errors are obvious (self-evident).*

---

el vistazo — *glance, look*
  echar (dar) un vistazo — *to take a look at; to glance at.*
  Le echó (dio) un vistazo. *He took a look at it (glanced at it).*

---

visto — *seen*
  por lo visto — *apparently.*
  Por lo visto no hay nadie aquí. *Apparently there is nobody here.*

---

vivir — *to live*
  viva — *long live; hurrah for.*
  ¡Viva el presidente! *Long live (Hurrah for) the president!*

---

vivo — *alive, lively*
  a lo vivo — *vividly.*
  Habla muy a lo vivo de su estancia en Chile. *He speaks very vividly about his stay in Chile.*

  asarse vivo — *to be burning up; to be roasting.*
  Me asaba vivo. *I was burning up (roasting).*

  tocar en lo vivo — *to hurt one deeply.*
  Lo que le dijeron le tocó en lo vivo. *What they said to him hurt him deeply.*

---

la voluntad — *will*
  depender de su santa voluntad — *to be entirely up to one.*
  Eso depende de su santa voluntad. *That's entirely up to him.*

  ganarse la voluntad de — *to win the favor (affection) of.*
  Se ganó la voluntad del rey. *She won the favor (affection) of the king.*

  por propia voluntad — *of one's own free will.*
  Volvió por propia voluntad. *He came back of his own free will.*

---

volver — *to return*
  volver a — *to . . . again.*

Volvió a decirlo. *He said it again.*

volver en sí — *to come to.*
Parecía ofuscada cuando volvió en sí. *She appeared dazed when she came to.*

---

la voz — *voice*

a una voz — *with one voice.*
Dijeron a una voz que no. *With one voice they said no.*

a voz en cuello — *at the top of one's voice.*
Cantaba a voz en cuello. *She was singing at the top of her voice.*

apagar la voz — *to lower one's voice.*
Apagó la voz. *She lowered her voice.*

correr la voz — *to be rumored.*
Corre la voz de que van a casarse. *It is rumored that they are going to get married.*

dar voces — *to shout.*
Daban voces. *They were shouting.*

en voz alta — *out loud; aloud.*
Nos lo leyó en voz alta. *He read it to us out loud (aloud).*

en voz baja — *in a low (soft) voice.*
Lo dijeron en voz baja. *They said it in a low (soft) voice.*

llamarle a voces — *to shout to someone.*
Me llamaban a voces. *They were shouting to me.*

---

el vuelco — *overturning, upset*

dar un vuelco — *to turn over.*
El corazón le dio un vuelco. *Her heart turned over.*

---

el vuelo — *flight*

alzar el vuelo — *to take wing.*
El pájaro alzó el vuelo. *The bird took wing.*

---

la vuelta — *turn; return*

buscarle las vueltas — *to get around someone; to find someone's weak spot.*

Para conseguirlo hay que buscarle las vueltas. *In order to get it you've got to get around him (find his weak spot).*

dar media vuelta — *to turn halfway around.*
Dio media vuelta. *He turned halfway around.*

dar una vuelta — *to go for a walk.*
Vamos a dar una vuelta. *Let's go for a walk.*

dar (la) vuelta a — *to walk around.*
Da (la) vuelta a la manzana. *He walks around the block.*

dar vueltas — *to toss and turn.*
Daba vueltas en la cama. *I was tossing and turning in bed.*

dar vueltas en redondo — *to go around in circles.*
Daban vueltas en redondo. *They were going around in circles.*

darle vuelta — *to turn something over.*
Le da vuelta. *He turns it over.*

estar de vuelta — *to be back.*
Ya están de vuelta. *They're back already.*

estar de vuelta de todo — *to have been around; to know what the score is.*
Está de vuelta de todo. *He's been around (knows what the score is).*

No hay que darle vueltas. — *There are no two ways about it; There's no use talking about it (discussing it).*

sin más vueltas — *without question.*
Sin más vueltas, ella es la más bonita. *Without question she is the prettiest.*

tomar la vuelta de — *to start back to.*
Tomó la vuelta del lago. *He started back to the lake.*

ya — *already, now*
   ya no — *no longer; not any more.*

Ya no llueve. *It's no longer raining (not raining any more).*

ya que — *since.*
Ya que está aquí, quédese a comer. *Since you're here, stay to eat.*

ya . . . , ya . . . — *now . . . , now. . . .*
Le traían ya carne, ya verduras. *They would bring him now meat, now vegetables.*

yo — *I*
yo que usted — *if I were you.*
Yo que usted, no lo hacía. *If I were you, I wouldn't do it.*

Z

la zaga — *rear*
no ir en zaga — *to be not far behind; to be just as good.*
Tiene un gran talento para los idiomas, y su hermano no le va en zaga. *He has a great talent for languages, and his brother is not far behind (is just as good).*

la zancadilla — *act of tripping someone, trick*
ponerle (hacerle, echarle) la zancadilla — *to trip someone.*
Le puse (Le hice, Le eché) la zancadilla. *I tripped him.*

Zamora — *proper name*
No se ganó Zamora en una hora. — *Rome wasn't built in a day.*

Spanish Pronunciation Guide

Letter	Approximate Pronunciation	English Equivalent
VOWELS		
a	*ah*	father
e	*eh*	net
i (and y meaning "and")	*ee*	machine
o	*oh*	note
u	*oo*	flute
DIPTHONGS		
ai, ay	*I*	by
au	*ow*	cow
ei, ey	*ay*	day
eu	*eh-oo*	net
I (followed by another vowel)	*y*	yet
oi, oy	*oy*	boy
CONSONANTS		
b, f, k, l, m, n, p, s, t, v, x, y	same as English	
ce, ci	*seh, see*	cent (Hispanic America)
	th	thin (Spain)
ca, co, cu	*kah, koh, koo*	cat
ch	*ch*	chin
d	*th*	them
ge, gi	*heh, hee*	heat
gue, gui	*u* is silent	
güe, güi	*gweh, gwee*	Gwen
h	always silent	
j	*h*	hat
ll	*y*	yet
ñ (a separate letter of the alphabet in Spanish)	*ny*	canyon

Letter	Approximate Pronunciation	English Equivalent
que, qui	*k* (*u* is silent)	kite
r	*r* (rolled or trilled)	roll
z	*s*	say (Hispanic America)
	th	thin (Spain)

STRESS

Spanish words that have a written accent mark are stressed (accented) on the syllable that has the accent mark, as in *pájaro* (PAH-ha-roh).

A word that has no written accent and ends in **n**, **s**, or a vowel is stressed on the first or next to the last syllable, as in *joven* (HOH-ben) or *harina* (ah-REE-nah).

A word that has no written accent and ends in anything other than **n**, **s**, or a vowel is stressed on the last syllable, as in *calor* (kah-LOHR).

Guía de Pronunciación del Inglés

Letra o Combinación de Letras	Pronunciación Aproximada	Ejemplo en Inglés	Equivalente en Español
a	a	bat	papa
a	e	any	pero
a	ei	may	seis
au	o	nautical	nombra
aw	o	saw	no
e	e	get	mete
ea	i	seal	risa
ee	i	feet	sin
i	i	hit	niño
i	ai	site	hay
o	o	sonic	sonido
o	a	come	cama
o	ou	bone	bondad
oa	ou	boat	botar
oo	u	boot	común
ou	u	youth	yuca
ow	ou	know	*(inexistente)*
u	u	rule	mula
u	uh	but	*(inexistente)*
u	yu	cute	yunque
ur	er	curtain	mercurio
uy	ai	buy	naipe
b	b	bold	baño
c	k	car	casa
c	c	city	cinta
ch	ch	change	chino
d	d	doll	dato
f	f	fine	fino
g	g	goat	gordo
g	j	germ	gime
h	j	hard	jardín
h	(muda)	hour	hora
j	j	jam	como la "y" de reyes
k	k	keep	kilo
l	l	lost	lino

Letra o Combinación de Letras	Pronunciación Aproximada	Ejemplo en Inglés	Equivalente en Español
m	m	mix	mala
n	n	no	no
ny	ñ	canyon	cañón
p	p	pit	pala
q	ku	quick	quántum
r	r	rest	marca
s	s	sea	sol
sh	ch	show	*(inexistente)*
t	t	mat	tiene
th	s	third	como la "d" de todo
v	v	volt	aviso
w	u + vocal	West	*(inexistente)*
x	ax	experto	
y	y	yes	yeso
z	z	zebra	zapato

Abbreviations — Spanish-English

Abbreviation	Meaning	English Equivalent	English Abbreviation
A			
ab.	abril	April	Apr., Apl.
A. de C.	antes de Jesucristo	Before Christ	B.C.
admor.	administrador	administrator	adm., admin.
afmo.	afectísimo	yours truly	yrs. trly.
agr.	agricultura	agriculture	agric.
agto.	agosto	August	Aug.
a.m.	de la mañana	in the morning	A.M., a.m.
art.	artículo	article	art.
Arzbpo.	Arzobispo	Archbishop	Arch.
apdo.	apartado	post office box	P.O. Box
atto.	atento	yours truly	yrs. trly.
av.	avenida	avenue	Av., Ave.
B			
Br.	Bachiller	Bachelor (academic)	B., b.
C			
c.	centígrado	centigrade	c., cent.
c.a.	corriente alterna	alternating current	a.c.
cap.	capítulo	chapter	ch., chap.
Cap., capn.	Capitán	Captain	Capt.
c.d.	corriente directa	direct current	d.c.
c.f., c. de f.	caballo de fuerza	horsepower	hp., h.p.
cg.	centigramo	centigram	cent.
Cía.	Compañía	Company	Co.
cm.	centímetro	centimeter	cm.
Cnel.	Coronel	Colonel	Col.
C.P.T.	Contador Público Titulado	Certified Public Accountant	C.P.A.
c/u	cada uno	each	ea.
D			
D.; Da.	Don; Doña	(titles of respect; no English equiv.)	
D. de C.	Después de Cristo	Anno Domini	A.D.

294

Abbreviation	Meaning	English Equivalent	English Abbreviation
der., dra(-o).	derecha(-o)	right	r., rt.
D.F.	Distrito Federal	Federal District	F.D.
dic.	diciembre	December	Dec.
dls.	dólares	dollars	dls.
dom.	domingo	Sunday	Sun.
Dr.	Doctor	Doctor	Dr.

E

EE.UU.	Estados Unidos	United States	U.S.(A.)
en.	enero	January	Jan.
etc.	etcétera	and so on	etc.
E.U.(A.)	Estados Unidos (de América)	United States (of America)	U.S.(A.)
Exca.	Excelencia	(Your) Excellency	Exc.

F

F°	Fahrenheit	Fahrenheit	F°
f.a.b.	franco a bordo	free on board	fob.
facta., fra.	factura	invoice	inv.
F.C.	ferrocarril	railway; railroad	ry.; rr., R.R.
feb.	febrero	February	Feb.

G

g(r).	gramo	gram	gr.
gnte., gte.	gerente	manager	mgr.
gob.	gobierno; gobernador	government; governor	govt.; gov.
Gral.	General	General	Gen.

H

h.	hijo; hora	son; Junior; hour	Jr., h.
hect.	hectárea	hectare	ha.
Hnos.	Hermanos	Brothers	Bros.
hosp.	hospital	hospital	hosp.

I

ib.	ibídem	in the same place	Ibid.
id.	ídem	the same	id.
Ilmo(-a)	Ilustrísimo(-a)	Most Illustrious	Mt. Illus.
impr.	imprenta	publishing house	pub., publ.

Abbreviation	Meaning	English Equivalent	English Abbreviation
Ing.	Ingeniero	engineer	engr.
ingl.	inglés	English	Eng., Engl.
izq.	izquierda	left	l.

J

J.C.	Jesucristo	Jesus Christ	J.C.
jue.	jueves	Thursday	Thur., Thurs.

K

kg.	kilogramo	kilogram	kilo.
km.	kilómetro	kilometer	km., kilom.
kv.	kilovatio	kilowatt	kw.
k.p.h.	kilómetros por hora	kilometers per hour	k.p.h.

L

l.	litro	liter	lit.
L.A.B.	libre a bordo	free on board	fob.
lb(s).	libra(s)	pound(s)	lb(s).
Lic.	Licenciado	Licentiate	Lic., L.
lun.	lunes	Monday	Mon.

M

mar.	martes	Tuesday	Tu., Tue., Tues.
med.	medicina	medicine	med.
mg.	miligramo	milligram	mg.
miérc.	miércoles	Wednesday	Wed.
mm.	milímetro	millimeter	mm.
m/n	moneda nacional	national currency	
Mons.	Monseñor	Monsignor	Msgr., Monsig.
mrz., mzo.	marzo	March	Mar.
m.p.h.	millas por hora	miles per hour	m.p.h.

N

n.	nacido	born	b.
nac.	nacional	national	nat., natl.
No., núm.	número	number	no.
nov.	noviembre	November	Nov.

Abbreviation	Meaning	English Equivalent	English Abbreviation
N.S.	Nuestro Señor	Our Lord	

O

Abbreviation	Meaning	English Equivalent	English Abbreviation
oct.	octubre	October	Oct.
(O)NU	(Organización de) Naciones Unidas	(Organization of) United Nations	U.N.
onz., on(s).	onza(s)	ounce(s)	oz(s).

P

Abbreviation	Meaning	English Equivalent	English Abbreviation
pág(s).	página(s)	page(s)	p., pp.
P.D., P.S.	Posdata	postscript	P.S.
p.ej.	por ejemplo	for example	e.g.
pl.	plural	plural	pl., plu.
p.p.	porte pagado	postage paid	p.p., P.P.
ppdo.	próximo pasado	last	
P.R.	Puerto Rico	Puerto Rico	P.R.
pral.	principal	principal	pral.
prof.	profesor	professor	prof.
pta(s).	peseta(s)	peseta(s)	

Q

Abbreviation	Meaning	English Equivalent	English Abbreviation
Q.E.P.D.	que en paz descanse	(May he) Rest in Peace	R.I.P.

R

Abbreviation	Meaning	English Equivalent	English Abbreviation
Rep.	República	Republic	Repub.
r.p.m.	revoluciones por minuto	revolutions per minute	r.p.m.

S

Abbreviation	Meaning	English Equivalent	English Abbreviation
S.	San(to); Santa	Saint	St.
S.A.	Sociedad Anónima	Corporation	Corp., Inc.
sáb.	sábado	Saturday	Sat.
S.A. de C.V.	Sociedad Anónima de Capital Variable	Corporation with variable capital	
sept.	septiembre	September	Sep., Sept.
S.M.	Su Majestad	His (Her) Majesty	H.M.
Sr(es)	Señor(es)	Sir, Mister; Sirs, Gentlemen	Mr.; Messrs.
Sra(s).	Señora(s)	Madam, Mrs.; Mesdames, Ladies	Mrs., Ms.

Abreviatura	Significado	Equivalente en Español	Abreviatura en Espzñol
Srta(s).	Señorita(s)	Miss(es)	Miss, Ms.
sria.	secretaria	secretary	sec., secy.
sría.	secretaría	Office of the Secretary	
S.S.	seguro servidor	Yours truly	yrs. trly.
S.S.S.	su seguro servidor	Yours truly	yrs. trly.

T

t(on).	tonelada	ton	t.
TNT	trinitrotolueno	trinitrotoluene	TNT
Tte., Tente.	Teniente	Lieutenant	Lt., Lieut.

U

U., Ud.	usted	you (polite sing. or pl.)	
U.R.S.S.	Unión de Repúblicas Socialistas Soviéticas	Union of Soviet Socialist Republics	U.S.S.R.

V

V., Vd.; Vds.	usted; ustedes	you (polite sing.); you (pl.)	
v.	verbo	verb	v., vb.
v.gr.	verbigracia	for example	e.g.
vier.	viernes	Friday	Fri.
V.M.	Vuestra Majestad	Your Majesty	
vol.	volumen	volume	vol.

Y

yd(a).; yd(as).	yarda(s)	yard(s)	yd(s).

Abreviaturas — Inglés-Español

Abreviatura	Significado	Equivalente en Español	Abreviatura en Español
A			
A.B.	Bachelor of Arts	Bachiller en Artes	
a.c.	alternating current	corriente alterna	c.a.
A.D.	Anno Domini	Después de Cristo	D. de C.
ADC	aide-de-camp	ayudante de campo; edecán	
ad lib	at will; without restraint	a libertad	ad lib.
Ala., AL	Alabama	Alabama	
Alas., AK	Alaska	Alaska	
A.M., a.m.	ante meridiem; before noon	de la mañana	a.m.
anon.	anonymous	anónimo	X.
Apr.	April	abril	ab.
apt.	apartment	apartamento	
Ariz., AZ	Arizona	Arizona	
Ark., AR	Arkansas	Arkansas	
assn.	association	asociación	
asst.	assistant	asistente; ayudante	
att(n).	(to the) attention (of)	atención	
atty.	attorney	abogado	
at. wt.	atomic weight	peso atómico	p.a.
Aug.	August	agosto	agto.
Av., Ave.	Avenue	avenida	Av., avda.
AWOL	absent without official leave	ausente sin licencia	
B			
b.	born	nacido	n.
B.A.	Bachelor of Arts	Bachiller en Artes	
B.C.	Before Christ	antes de Jesucristo	A. de C.
B.D.	Bachelor of Divinity	Bachiller en divinidad	
bldg.	building	edificio	
Blvd.	Boulevard	bulevar	
Br.	British	Británico	
B.S.	Bachelor of Science	Bachiller en Ciencias	

Abreviatura	Significado	Equivalente en Español	Abreviatura en Español

C

Abreviatura	Significado	Equivalente en Español	Abreviatura en Español
C.A.	Central America	Centro América	C.A.
Calif., Cal., CA	California	California	
Can.	Canada	Canadá	
Capt.	Captain	Capitán	Cap., Capn.
cf.	compare	compárese	comp.
ch., chap.	chapter	capítulo	capo., cap.
cm.	centimeter	centímetro	cm.
c/o	in care of	casa de	a/c, c/de
Co.	Company	compañía	Cía., C.
C.O.D.	Collect (or Cash) on Delivery	cóbrese al entregar	C.A.E
Col.	Colonel	Coronel	Cnel.
Colo., CO	Colorado	Colorado	
Comdr.	Commander	Comandante	Cdte.
Conn., Ct., CT	Connecticut	Connecticut	
Corp.	Corporation	Sociedad Anónima	S.A.
C.P.A.	Certified Public Accountant	Contador Público Titulado	C.P.T.
cr.	credit	crédito	
cu.	cubic	cúbico	cú.
C.Z.	Canal Zone	Zona del Canal	

D

Abreviatura	Significado	Equivalente en Español	Abreviatura en Español
D.A.	District Attorney	Fiscal de Distrito	
d.c.	direct current	corriente directa	c.d.
D.D.	Doctor of Divinity	Doctor en Divinidad	D.D.
dec.	deceased	difunto	
Dec.	December	diciembre	dic.
Del., DE	Delaware	Delaware	
dept.	department	departamento	dpto.
dist.	district	distrito	d.
do.	ditto	lo mismo	do.
doz.	dozen	docena	dna., doc.
Dr.	Doctor	doctor	Dr.

E

Abreviatura	Significado	Equivalente en Español	Abreviatura en Español
ea.	each	cada uno	c/u.
ed.	editor	redactor	red.
ed(s).	edition(s)	edición(es)	ed(s).

Abreviatura	Significado	Equivalente en Español	Abreviatura en Español
e.g.	for example	por ejemplo	p. ej.
enc.	enclosure	incluso	incl.
Eng.	England; English	Inglaterra; inglés	
Esq.	Esquire	Señor	Sr.
et al.	and others	y otros	et al.
etc.	and so forth; etcetera	etcétera	etc.
ext.	extension	extensión	ext.

F

Abreviatura	Significado	Equivalente en Español	Abreviatura en Español
F°	Fahrenheit	Fahrenheit	F°
F.B.I.	Federal Bureau of Investigation	Oficina Federal de Investigaciones	
Feb.	February	febrero	feb.
fed.	federal	federal	
fem.	feminine	femenino	fem.
fig.	figurative; figure	figurativa; figura	fig.
fl.	fluid	fluido	
Fla., FL	Florida	Florida	
F.M.	Frequency Modulation	modulación de frecuencia	m.f.
f.o.b.	free on board	franco a bordo	f.a.b.
for.	foreign	extranjero	
Fri.	Friday	viernes	vier.
ft.	foot; feet	pie(s)	

G

Abreviatura	Significado	Equivalente en Español	Abreviatura en Español
Ga., GA	Georgia	Georgia	
gen.	gender	género	gen.
Gen.	General	General	Genl., Gral.
Ger.	Germany; German	Alemania; Alemán	
govt.	government	gobierno	gob.
gr.	gram	gramo	g.; gr.
GB	Great Britain	Gran Bretaña	
gro. wt.	gross weight	peso bruto	p.b.

H

Abreviatura	Significado	Equivalente en Español	Abreviatura en Español
hdqrs., HQ	headquarters	dirección general	D.G.
H.I., HI	Hawaiian Islands	Islas Hawaianas	
H.M.	Her (His) Majesty	Su Majestad	
H.M.S.	Her (His) Majesty's Ship		
Hon.	(The) Honorable	honorable	

Abreviatura	Significado	Equivalente en Español	Abreviatura en Español
HP	horsepower	caballo de fuerza	HP, c.f., c. de f.
hr.	hour	hora	h.

I

Abreviatura	Significado	Equivalente en Español	Abreviatura en Español
Ia., IA	Iowa	Iowa	
id.	the same	lo mismo	id.
Ida., ID	Idaho	Idaho	
i.e.	that is	esto es	i.e.
Ill., IL	Illinois	Illinois	
in(s).	inch(es)	pulgada(s)	pulg(s).
Inc.	incorporated	sociedad anónima	S.A.
Ind., IN	Indiana	Indiana	
Inst.	Institute	instituto	
I.O.U.	I owe you	vale	
I.Q.	intelligence quotient	cociente intelectual	c.i.
It.; Ital.	Italy; Italian	Italia; italiano	ital.
ital.	italics	itálica; bastardilla	

J

Abreviatura	Significado	Equivalente en Español	Abreviatura en Español
Jan.	January	enero	en.
Jap.	Japan	Japón	
J.C.	Jesus Christ	Jesucristo	J.C.
J.P.	Justice of the Peace	juez de paz	
Jr.	Junior	menor; hijo	h.
Jul.	July	julio	jul.
Jun.	June	junio	jun.

K

Abreviatura	Significado	Equivalente en Español	Abreviatura en Español
Kan(s)., KS	Kansas	Kansas	
kg.	kilogram	kilogramo	Kg.
km.	kilometer	kilómetro	Km.
kw.	kilowatt	kilovatio	Kv., Kw.
Ky., KY	Kentucky	Kentucky	

L

Abreviatura	Significado	Equivalente en Español	Abreviatura en Español
La., LA	Louisiana	Louisiana	
lab.	laboratory	laboratorio	
lat.	latitude	latitud	lat.
Lat.	Latin	latín	
lb(s).	pound(s)	libra(s)	lib(s).

Abreviatura	Significado	Equivalente en Español	Abreviatura en Español
l.c.	lower case	caja baja	c.b.
L.C.	Library of Congress	Biblioteca del Congreso	
Lieut., Lt.	Lieutenant	Teniente	Tte., Tente.
Lit. D.	Doctor of Letters	Doctor en Letras	Dr. en Let.
LL.D.	Doctor of Laws	Doctor en Leyes	Dr. en L.
loc. cit.	in the place cited	loco citado	loc. cit.
long.	longitude	longitud	long.
Ltd.	Limited	Limitada	Ltda.

M

Abreviatura	Significado	Equivalente en Español	Abreviatura en Español
M.A.	Master of Arts	Maestro en Artes	A.M.
Maj.	Major	Comandante	
Mar.	March	marzo	mrz., mro.
masc.	masculine	masculino	m.
Mass., MA	Massachusetts	Massachusetts	
M.C.	Master of Ceremonies	Maestro de Ceremonias	
Md., MD	Maryland	Maryland	
M.D.	Doctor of Medicine	Doctor en Medicina	
Me., ME	Maine	Maine	
Messrs.	plural of Mr.	Señores	Sres.
Mex.	Mexico; Mexican	México; mexicano	Méx.; mex.
mfg.	manufacturing	fabricación	
mfr.	manufacturer	fabricante	
mg.	milligram	miligramo	mg.
Mgr.	Monsignor	monseñor	Mons.
Mich., MI	Michigan	Michigan	
min.	minute	minuto	m.
Minn., MS	Minnesota	Minnesota	
misc.	miscellaneous	misceláneo	
Miss.	Mississippi	Mississippi	
mm.	millimeter	milímetro	mm.
mo(s).	month(s)	mes(es)	m(s).
Mo., MO	Missouri	Missouri	
Mon.	Monday	lunes	lun.
Mont., MT	Montana	Montana	
M.P.	Military Police	Policía Militar	P.M.
m.p.h.	miles per (or an) hour	millas por hora	m.p.h.
Mr.	Mister	Señor	Sr.
Mrs.	Mistress, Mrs.	Señora	Sra.
Ms.	Miss or Mrs.	no Spanish equivalent	

Abreviatura	Significado	Equivalente en Español	Abreviatura en Español
ms.	manuscript	manuscrito	ms.
M.S.	Master of Science	Maestro en Ciencias	
Mt.	Mount; mountain	monte; montaña	

N

n.	number; noun	número; sustantivo	n.
N.A.	North America	Norteamérica	
nat., nat'l.	national	nacional	nac.
N.C., NC	North Carolina	Carolina del Norte	
N.D., ND	North Dakota	Dakota del Norte	
N.E.	New England	New England	
Neb., NE	Nebraska	Nebraska	
neut.	neuter	neutro	neut.
Nev., NV	Nevada	Nevada	
N.H., NH	New Hampshire	New Hampshire	
N.J., NJ	New Jersey	New Jersey	
N. Mex., N.M., NM	New Mexico	New Mexico	
No.	number	número	n°.; núm.
Nov.	November	noviembre	nov.
nt. wt.	net weight	peso neto	no. n°.
N.Y., NY	New York	Nueva York	

O

Oct.	October	octubre	oct.
O.K.	all right	visto bueno	V°.B°.
Okla., OK	Oklahoma	Oklahoma	
Ore., OR	Oregon	Oregon	
Oxf.	Oxford	Oxford	
oz(s).	ounce(s)	onza(s)	on(s). onz.

P

p.	page	página	pág.
Pa., PA	Pennsylvania	Pennsylvania	
Pac.	Pacific	Pacífico	
Pan.	Panama	Panamá	
par.	paragraph	párrafo	
p.c.	per cent	por ciento	p.c.
pd.	paid	pagado	

Abreviatura	Significado	Equivalente en Español	Abreviatura en Español
Pfc.	Private first-class	soldado de primera	
Ph.D.	Doctor of Philosophy	Doctor en Filosofía	
Phila.	Philadelphia	Philadelphia	
P.I.	Philippine Islands	Islas Filipinas	
pl., plu.	plural	plural	pl.
P.M., p.m.	post meridiem; in the afternoon	de la tarde	p.m.
P.M.	Postmaster	Administrador de Correos	
P.O.	post office	oficina de correos	
P.O. Box	Post Office Box	apartado	apdo.
pp.	pages	páginas	págs.
ppd.	prepaid	prepagado	p.p.
p.p.	parcel post	paquetes postales	
pr.	pair	par	
P.R.	Puerto Rico	Puerto Rico	P.R.
pres.	present	presente	pres.
Prof.	Professor	profesor	prof.
pron.	pronoun	pronombre	pron.
P.S.	Postscript	posdata	P.D., P.S.
pt.	pint	pinta	
pvt.	private	soldado raso	
POW	Prisoner of War	prisionero de guerra	
pub., publ.	publisher	publicador	publ.

Q

qt(s).	quarts	cuarto(s) de galón	
Que.	Quebec	Quebec	

R

R.A.F.	Royal Air Force	Real Fuerza Aérea	
R.C.	Roman Catholic	católico romano	
Rd.	road	camino	
ref.	reference	referencia	ref.
reg.	registered	registrado	reg.
regt.	regiment	regimento	
Rep.	Representative	representante	
Rep.	Republic	república	rep.
Rev.	Reverend	reverendo	R.; Rdo.
Rev.	Revolution	revolución	

Abreviatura	Significado	Equivalente en Español	Abreviatura en Español
R.I., RI	Rhode Island	Rhode Island	
riv.	river	río	
R.N.	Registered Nurse	Enfermera Titulada	
r.p.m.	revolutions per minute	revoluciones por minuto	r.p.m.
R.R.	Railroad	ferrocarril	f.c.
Ry.	Railway	ferrocarril	f.c.
R.S.V.P.	Please answer	Sírvase responder	R.S.V.P.

S

Abreviatura	Significado	Equivalente en Español	Abreviatura en Español
S.A.	South America	América del Sur	
Sat.	Saturday	sábado	sáb.
S.C., SC	South Carolina	South Carolina	
Scot.	Scotland	Escocia	
S.D., SD	South Dakota	Dakota del Sur	
sec.	second; section	segundo; sección	
secy.	secretary	secretario	secret^{o}.; srio.
Sen.	Senator	Senador	Sen.
Sept.	September	septiembre	sept^{e}.; set^{e}.; se^{bre}.
Sgt.	Sergeant	sargento	sgto.
sing.	singular	singular	
So.	South	sur	
Soc.	Society	sociedad	soc.
Sp.	Spain; Spanish	España; español	
sq.	square	cuadrado	cuad.
Sr.	Sister	hermana	
S.S.	steamship	vapor	
St.	Saint	San; Santo (-a)	S.; Sto.; Sta.
St.	Street	calle	
subj.	subject	sujeto	
Sun.	Sunday	domingo	dom^{o}.
supp.	supplement	suplemento	
Supt.	Superintendent	superintendente	supert^{le}.

T

Abreviatura	Significado	Equivalente en Español	Abreviatura en Español
tbs.	tablespoon	cuchara grande	
tel.	telephone; telegram	teléfono; telegrama	tel.; TLF
Tenn., TN	Tennessee	Tennessee	
Test.	Testament	Testamento	Test^{mto}.

Abreviatura	Significado	Equivalente en Español	Abreviatura en Español
Tex., TX	Texas	Texas	
Thur(s).	Thursday	jueves	juev.
TNT	trinitrotoluene	trinitrotuoleno	TNT
trans.	transitive; transportation	transitivo; transporte	
tsp.	teaspoon	cucharita	
Tue(s).	Tuesday	martes	mart.
TV	Television	televisión	T.V.

U

U., Univ.	University	universidad	
u.c.	upper case	caja alta	
U.K.	United Kingdom	Reino Unido	R.U.
U.N.	United Nations	Naciones Unidas	O.N.U.
U.S.A.	United States of America	Estados Unidos de América	E.U.A.
U.S.A.	United States Army	Ejército de los Estados Unidos	
U.S.A.F.	United States Air Force	Fuerzas Aéreas de los Estados Unidos	
U.S.N.	United States Navy	Marina de Guerra de los Estados Unidos	
U.S.S.R.	Union of Soviet Socialist Republics	Unión de Repúblicas Socialistas Soviéticas.	U.R.S.S.
Ut., UT	Utah	Utah	

V

v.	verb; volt	verbo; voltio	v.
Va., VA	Virginia	Virginia	
V.D.	venereal disease	enfermedad venérea	
Ven.	Venerable	venerable	
Visc.	Viscount	vizconde	
viz.	namely	a saber	v.g., v.gr.
vol.	volume	tomo; volumen	t.; vol.
V.P.	Vice President	vice presidente	
vs.	versus; against	contra	
Vt., VT	Vermont	Vermont	

W

w.	watt	vatio, watio	v., w.

Abreviatura	Significado	Equivalente en Español	Abreviatura en Español
Wash., WA	Washington	Washington	
W.C.	water closet	servicio higiénico	serv.
Wed.	Wednesday	miércoles	miérc.
Wisc., WI	Wisconsin	Wisconsin	
wk(s).	week(s)	semana(s)	
wt.	weight	peso	p°.
W. Va., WV	West Virginia	West Virginia	
Wyo., WY	Wyoming	Wyoming	

Y

yd(s).	yard(s)	yarda(s)	yd(a).
yr(s)	year(s)	año(s)	

Z

Z.	Zone	zona	

Weights and Measures

Medidas Métricas		(Metric Measures)	

PESOS
(Weights)

Tonelada	2204.6 lb.	Ton	2204.6 lbs.
Kilogramo	2.2046 lb.	Kilogram	2.2046 lbs.
Gramo	15.432 granos	Gram	15.432 grains
Centigramo	0.1543 granos	Centigram	0.1543 grains

LINEALES
(Linear)

Kilómetro	0.62137 millas	Kilometer	0.62137 miles
Metro	39.37 pulgadas	Meter	39.37 inches
Decímetro	3.937 pulgadas	Decimeter	3.937 inches
Centímetro	0.3937 pulgadas	Centimeter	0.3937 inches
Milímetro	0.03937 pulgadas	Millimeter	0.03937 inches

CAPACIDAD
(Capacity)

Hectolitro	2.838 bushels	Hectoliter	2.838 bushels
o	26.418 galones	or	26.418 gallons
Litro	0.9081 cuarto de galón (áridos)	Liter	0.9081 dry qt.
o	1.0567 cuarto de galón (líq.)	or	1.0567 liq. qts.

VOLUMEN
(Cubic)

Metro cúbico	1.308 yardas^3	Cubic meter	1.308 cu. yards
Decímetro cúbico	61.023 pulgadas^3	Cubic decimeter	61.023 cu. inches
Centímetro cúbico	0.0610 pulgadas^3	Cubic Centimeter	0.0610 cu. inches

SUPERFICIE
(Surface)

Kilómetro cuadrado	247.104 acres	Sq. kilometer	247.104 acres
Hectárea	2.471 acres	Hectare	2.471 acres
Metro cuadrado	1550 pulgadas^2	Square meter	1550 sq. inches
Decímetro cuadrado	15.50 pulgadas^2	Square decimeter	15.50 sq. inches
Centímetro	0.155 pulgadas^2	Square centimeter	0.155 sq. inches

Pesos y Medidas

U.S. Measures   (Medidas de E.U.A.)

WEIGHTS
(Pesos)

Ounce (avoirdupois)	28.35 grams.	Onza (avoirdupois)	28.35 gms.
Pound	0.4536 kgs.	Libra	0.4536 kgs.
Long ton	1.0161 met. tons.	Tonelada larga	1.0161 ton. met.
Short ton	0.9072 met. tons.	Tonelada corta	0.9072 ton. met.
Grain	0.0648 grams.	Grano	0.0648 gms

LINEAR
(Lineales)

Mile	1.6093 kms.	Milla	1.6093 kms.
Naut. mile	1.853 kms.	Milla marina	1.853 kms.
Yard	0.9144 ms.	Yarda	0.9144 ms.
Foot	0.3048 ms.	Pie	0.3048 ms.
Inch	2.54 cms.	Pulgada	2.54 cms.

CAPACITY
(Capacidad)

Liquid quart	0.9463 liters	Cuarto del gal. (líq.)	0.9463 litros
Dry quart	1.101 liters	Cuarto de gal. (áridos)	1.101 litros
Gallon	3.785 liters	Galón	3.785 litros
Bushel	35.24 liters	Bushel	35.24 litros

CUBIC
(Volumen)

Cubic inch	16.387 cu. cm.	Pulgada cúbica	16.387 cm.^{3}
Cubic foot	0.0283 cu. ms.	Pie cúbico	0.0283 m.^{3}
Cubic yard	0.7646 cu. ms.	Yarda cúbica	0.7646 m.^{3}

SURFACE
(Superficie)

Acre	0.4453 hectares	Acre	0.4453 hectáreas
Square mile	259 hectares	Milla cuadrada	259 hectáreas
Square yard	0.8351 sq. meters	Yarda cuadrada	0.8361 m.^{2}
Square foot	929.03 sq. cms.	Pie cuadrado	929.03 cms.^{2}
Square inch	6.4516 sq. cms.	Pulgada cuadrada	6.456 cms.^{2}

Common English Idioms

The Spanish words in parentheses indicate the entry word under which you will find the English idiom.

A

to . . . again 286 (*volver*)
A bad penny always turns up. 135 (*hierba*)
a baker's dozen 95 (*docena*)
A barking dog never bites. 208 (*perro*)
a bed of roses 152 (*lecho*)
a bird in the hand is worth two in the bush. 192 (*pájaro*)
a blind alley 45 (*callejón*)
a chip off the old block 194 (*palo*)
a dead end 45 (*callejón*)
a diamond in the rough 92 (*diamante*)
a dirty old man 284 (*viejo*)
to a great extent 197 (*parte*)
a house of cards 53 (*castillo*)
a long time 265 (*tiempo*)
A man is known by the company he keeps. 227 (*quién*)
a mile off 152 (*legua*)
a real he-man 205 (*pelo*)
a short time ago 133 (*hacer*)
a tempest in a teapot 261 (*tempestad*)
a war of nerves 130 (*guerra*)
a week (*two weeks*) from today 91 (*día*)
a white elephant 99 (*elefante*)
A word to the wise is sufficient. 102 (*entendedor*)
above all 268 (*todo*)
according to 8 (*acuerdo*)

to acquire a liking for 131 (*gusto*)
across country 47 (*campo*)
across from 120 (*frente*)
to act as 281 (*vez*)
to add fuel to the flames 153 (*leña*)
after a fashion 175 (*modo*)
after a while 42 (*cabo*)
after all 117 (*fin*)
against all odds 284 (*viento*)
against one's will 122 (*fuerza*)
against one's will 128 (*grado*)
to agree to 226 (*quedar*)
ahead of time 19 (*antemano*)
to aim too high 210 (*picar*)
all along 220 (*principio*)
all dressed up 223 (*punta*)
All hell is going to break loose. 94 (*Dios*)
All that glitters is not gold. 191 (*oro*)
all joking aside 39 (*burla*)
all of a sudden 127 (*golpe*)
all over 149 (*lado*)
all the livelong day 91 (*día*)
to amount to 232 (*reducir*)
An eye for an eye and a tooth for a tooth. 189 (*ojo*)
an ivory tower 270 (*torre*)
an occasional 274 (*uno*)
an old salt 155 (*lobo*)
and as if that weren't enough 215 (*poco*)
and be done with it 281 (*vez*)
any old way 274 (*tuntún*)
any time now 176 (*momento*)

312

at top speed 68 (*correr*)

At your service. 250 (*servir*)

to attract attention 26 (*atención*)

to avoid someone's glance 173 (*mirada*)

B

to back up 165 (*marcha*)

be careful 78 (*cuidado*)

to be . . . years old 21 (*año*)

to be a babe in arms 194 (*pañal*)

to be a dime a dozen 176 (*montón*)

to be a fan of 9 (*aficionado*)

to be a fiend for 116 (*fiera*)

to be a horse of another color 134 (*harina*)

to be a matter of 271 (*tratar*)

to be a minor 98 (*edad*)

to be a part of 197 (*parte*)

to be a question of 78 (*cuestión*)

to be a sorry sight 151 (*lástima*)

to be a stab in the back 225 (*puñalada*)

to be a tough nut to crack 139 (*hueso*)

to be a wet blanket 116 (*fiesta*)

to be a wise old owl 208 (*perro*)

to be about 271 (*tratar*)

to be about to 109 (*estar*)

to be afraid 171 (*miedo*)

to be all dolled up 13 (*alfiler*)

to be all ears 188 (*oído*)

to be all right 108 (*estar*)

to be all the same 174 (*mismo*)

to be another story 48 (*cantar*)

to be as cool as a cucumber 121 (*fresco*)

to be as crazy as a loon 42 (*cabra*)

to be as deaf as a post 259 (*tapia*)

to be as easy as pie 269 (*torta*)

to be as nutty as a fruitcake 42 (*cabra*)

to be as poor as a church mouse 230 (*rata*)

to be as solid as a rock 43 (*cal*)

to be as thick as thieves 275 (*uña*)

to be ashamed 280 (*vergüenza*)

to be at a loss 51 (*carta*)

to be at death's door 274 (*último*)

to be at one's service 95 (*disposición*)

to be back 288 (*vuelta*)

to be becoming to 145 (*ir*)

to be beside oneself 122 (*fuera*)

to be bordered by 154 (*limitar*)

to be born lucky 211 (*pie*)

to be born with a silver spoon in one's mouth 13 (*algodón*)

to be brimming with 232 (*rebosar*)

to be burning up 286 (*vivo*)

to be careful 79 (*cuidado*)

to be child's play 71 (*coser*)

to be conspicuous by one's absence 27 (*ausencia*)

to be cut out for 159 (*madera*)

to be daydreaming 184 (*nube*)

to be down on all fours 202 (*pata*)

to be dressed fit to kill 13 (*alfiler*)

to be dressed to the nines 13 (*alfiler*)

to be driving at 219 (*pretender*)

to be drunk as a lord 75 (*cuba*)

to be dying to 177 (*morir*)

to be eaten up with envy 103 (*envidia*)

to be enough to make one laugh 234 (*reírse*)

to be equal to (up to) 16 (*altura*)

to be even 203 (*paz*)

to be expected to 131 (*haber*)

to be fed up with 134 (*harto*)

to be fit to be tied 80 (*chispa*)

to be flat broke 33 (*blanca*)

to be forced to 279 (*ver*)

to be freezing to death 139 (*hueso*)

to be getting at 219 (*pretender*)

to be good for one 278 (*venir*)

to be hand in glove 275 (*uña*)

to be hanging by a hair 41 (*cabello*)

to be hanging by a thread 135 (*hilo*)

to be hanging on one's words 148 (*labio*)

to be hard for one 270 (*trabajo*)

to be hopping mad 80 (*chispa*)

to be hungry 134 (*hambre*)

to be ill at ease 94 (*disgusto*)

to be in (out of) one's right mind 8 (*acuerdo*)

to be in a foul mood 151 (*leche*)

to be in a good mood 38 (*bueno*)

to be in a hurry 221 (*prisa*)

to be in a rush 221 (*prisa*)

to be in a sad state 151 (*lástima*)

to be in charge of 50 (*cargo*)

to be in command 160 (*mando*)

to be in doubt 96 (*duda*)

to be in effect 284 (*vigor*)

to be in favor of 198 (*partidario*)

to be in full swing 7 (*actividad*)

to be in good form 152 (*lechuga*)

to be in mourning 157 (*luto*)

to be in no mood for jokes 37 (*broma*)

to be in one's bad books 226 (*quedar*)

to be in one's element 99 (elemento)

to be in one's glory 126 (*gloria*)

to be in one's hands 216 (*poder*)

to be in one's right mind 40 (*cabal*)

to be in one's shoes 205 (*pellejo*)

to be in seventh heaven 126 (*gloria*)

to be in sight 285 (*vista*)

to be in style 174 (*moda*)

to be in the family way 108 (*estado*)

to be in the habit of 72 (*costumbre*)

to be in the limelight 48 (*candelero*)

to be in the right 231 (*razón*)

to be in the same boat 271 (*trance*)

to be in the way 252 (*sobra*)

to be in vogue 35 (*boga*)

to be just the thing 207 (*perla*)

to be late 158 (*llegar*)

to be left holding the bag 178 (*muerto*)

to be left without a penny to one's name 45 (*calle*)

to be like one of the family 9 (*adentro*)

to be lucky 256 (*suerte*)

to be meant to be 93 (*Dios*)

to be no genius 217 (*pólvora*)

to be no laughing matter 147 (*juego*)

to be nobody's fool 204 (*pelo*)

to be nothing but skin and bones 139 (*hueso*)

to be of age 98 (*edad*)

to be off like a shot 29 (*bala*)

to be on a diet 92 (*dieta*)

to be on duty 274 (*turno*)

to be on edge 48 (*canto*)

to be on firm ground 118 (*firme*)

to be on good terms with 108 (*estar*)

to be on one's knees 240 (*rodilla*)

to be on pins and needles 24 (*ascua*)

to be on the fence 10 (*agua*)

to be on the house 76 (*cuenta*)

to be on the lookout 172 (*mira*)

to be on time 265 (*tiempo*)
to be on to someone 147 (*juego*)
to be one's business (*one's affair*) 70 (*cosa*)
to be one's turn 267 (*tocar*)
to be opposed to 190 (*oponer*)
to be out of print 9 (*agotado*)
to be out on a spree 147 (*juerga*)
to be put on sale 278 (*venta*)
to be red in the face 36 (*brasa*)
to be right 231 (*razón*)
to be right where one belongs 55 (*centro*)
to be rolling in money 93 (*dinero*)
to be rumored that 114 (*fama*)
to be run-of-the-mill 274 (*uno*)
to be scared stiff 244 (*sangre*)
to be scared to death 257 (*susto*)
to be set on 54 (*ceja*)
to be short of 105 (*escaso*)
to be short-tempered 223 (*pulga*)
to be sick and tired of 134 (*harto*)
to be sick in bed 45 (*cama*)
to be soaked to the skin 139 (*hueso*)
to be soft-hearted 67 (*corazón*)
to be sold on oneself 192 (*pagado*)
to be something to write home about 70 (*cosa*)
to be sound asleep 273 (*tronco*)
to be stark raving mad 155 (*loco*)
to be supposed to 131 (*haber*)
to be taken in 212 (*píldora*)
to be the land of milk and honey 146 (*Jauja*)
to be the limit 58 (*colmo*)
to be the scapegoat 202 (*pato*)
to be the spitting image of one's . . . 105 (*escupir*)
to be thirsty 246 (*sed*)
to be time to 138 (*hora*)
to be to blame for 79 (*culpa*)
to be to one's liking 9 (*agrado*)

to be to the point 53 (*caso*)
to be too bad 151 (*lástima*)
to be too much for one 123 (*fuerza*)
to be too smart for one's own good 199 (*pasar*)
to be two of a kind 258 (*tal*)
to be unaware of 11 (*ajeno*)
to be up in the clouds 28 (*Babia*)
to be up to one 75 (*cuenta*)
to be up to one's old tricks 257 (*suyo*)
to be up-to-date 91 (*día*)
to be up-to-date on 69 (*corriente*)
to be very close 63 (*confite*)
to be warming up 44 (*calor*)
to be well along in years 21 (*año*)
to be well thought of 173 (*mirar*)
to be well-heeled 239 (*riñón*)
to be wild about 28 (*baba*)
to be willing to 95 (*disponer*)
to be within (out of) one's reach 12 (*alcance*)
to be worth one's weight in gold 275 (*valer*)
to be worth the trouble 206 (*pena*)
to be written all over one's face 121 (*frente*)
to keep in mind 76 (*cuenta*)
to bear fruit 121 (*fruto*)
to bear in mind 219 (*presente*)
to beat it 211 (*pie*)
to beat around the bush 239 (*rodeo*)
to beat up 217 (*polvo*)
to become of 249 (*ser*)
to bell the cat 125 (*gato*)
to bend an elbow 57 (*codo*)
to bite one's tongue 148 (*labio*)
to bite the hand that feeds one 77 (*cuervo*)
to bleed white 277 (*vena*)
to block the way 201 (*paso*)
to blow one's brains out 259 (*tapa*)
to bother to 175 (*molestar*)

315

to break off with 240 (*romper*)

to break someone's heart 67 (*corazón*)

to break someone's neck 31 (*bautismo*)

to break the ice 134 (*hielo*)

to breathe down someone's neck 253 (*sol*)

to breathe one's last 256 (*suspiro*)

to bring someone up-to-date (on) 69 (*corriente*)

to bring up 242 (*sacar*)

to build castles in the air (castles in Spain) 53 (*castillo*)

to burn one's bridges behind one 181 (*nave*)

to burn the midnight oil 54 (*ceja*)

to burst out laughing (crying) 240 (*romper*)

to butt in 75 (*cuchara*)

to butter someone up 146 (*jabón*)

to buy a pig in a poke 55 (*ciego*)

to buy for a song 204 (*pedazo*)

the beaten path 46 (*camino*)

because of 54 (*causa*)

behind . . . 's back 106 (*espalda*)

behind closed doors 222 (*puerta*)

behind the scenes 30 (*bastidor*)

behind the times 184 (*noticias*)

Better late than never. 275 (*valer*)

Between the devil and the deep blue sea. 106 (*espada*)

the black sheep of the family 191 (*oveja*)

The blind leading the blind. 55 (*ciego*)

Birds of a feather flock together. 93 (*Dios*)

Bon voyage! 282 (*viaje*)

both . . . and . . . 259 (*tanto*)

bound for 90 (*destino*)

by chance 54 (*casualidad*)

by degrees 129 (*grado*)

by dint of 122 (*fuerza*)

by hand 161 (*mano*)

by heart 168 (*memoria*)

by hook or by crook 115 (*fas*)

by mistake 104 (*equivocación*)

by mutual agreement 8 (*acuerdo*)

by no means 175 (*modo*)

by that time 103 (*entonces*)

by the day 91 (*día*)

by the handful 224 (*puñado*)

by the hundreds 55 (*centenar*)

by the light of the moon 157 (*luz*)

by the skin of one's teeth 205 (*pelo*)

by the way 221 (*propósito*)

by virtue of 284 (*virtud*)

by way of 130 (*guisa*)

C

to call a spade a spade 194 (*pan*)

to call foul 102 (*engaño*)

to call one's attention to 26 (*atención*)

to call roll 155 (*lista*)

to call up 261 (*teléfono*)

to carry a lot of weight 276 (*vara*)

to carry coals to Newcastle 153 (*leña*)

to carry off 50 (*cargar*)

to carry out 42 (*cabo*)

to cast doubt on 96 (*duda*)

Cast your bread upon the waters. 227 (*quién*)

Cats have nine lives. 283 (*vida*)

to catch in a lie 169 (*mentira*)

to catch in the act 118 (*flagrante*)

to catch on (to) 75 (*cuenta*)

to catch one's breath 14 (*aliento*)

to catch red-handed 162 (*mano*)

to catch up with 12 (*alcance*)

to change one's mind 141 (*idea*)

to cheer up 18 (*ánimo*)

to clean out 47 (*camisa*)
to clear the table 170 (*mesa*)
to clear up 57 (*claro*)
to clip one's wings 11 (*ala*)
to close all avenues to someone 222 (*puerta*)
cock and bull story 77 (*cuento*)
the cock of the walk 124 (*gallito*)
to come down in the world 278 (*venir*)
to come down to 232 (*reducir*)
to come face to face with 100 (*encararse*)
Come in! 8 (*adelante*)
to come to 287 (*volver*)
to come to a head 23 (*arder*)
to come to an agreement 8 (*acuerdo*)
to come to blows 163 (*mano*)
to come to mind 171 (*mientes*)
to come to terms 7 (*acuerdo*)
to come to that 106 (*eso*)
to confide in 62 (*confidencia*)
to consent to 64 (*consentir*)
to consist of 65 (*constar*)
to cost a fortune 188 (*ojo*)
to cost an arm and a leg 188 (*ojo*)
to cost one dearly 71 (*costar*)
cost what it may 72 (*costar*)
to cough up 35 (*bolsillo*)
to count on 65 (*contar*)
crocodile tears 149 (*lágrima*)
to cuss a blue streak 245 (*sapo*)
to cut class 57 (*clase*)

D

to dance attendance 9 (*agua*)
to deal with 271 (*tratar*)
to depend on 87 (*depender*)
to die laughing 239 (*risa*)
to die like flies 80 (*chinche*)
to do halfway 167 (*medio*)

to do one good 278 (*venir*)
to do one's utmost to 90 (*desvivirse*)
to do without 199 (*pasar*)
don't get the wrong idea 73 (*creer*)
Don't look a gift horse in the mouth. 40 (*caballo*)
Don't mention it. 132 (*haber*)
down the street 45 (*calle*)
to draw someone out 153 (*lengua*)
to dream about 254 (*soñar*)
to drink (to) . . . 's health 243 (*salud*)
to drink like a fish 108 (*esponja*)
to drive crazy 52 (*casilla*)
to drive someone to distraction 227 (*quicio*)
drop by drop 127 (*gota*)
to drop someone a line 154 (*línea*)
during the week 247 (*semana*)

E

To each his own. 43 (*cada*)
The early bird catches the worm. 93 (*Dios*)
to earn one's living 283 (*vida*)
to ease up 238 (*rienda*)
the eighth wonder of the world 164 (*maravilla*)
either . . . or . . . 185 (*o*)
to end up by 6 (*acabar*)
the ends of the earth 42 (*cabo*)
to enjoy oneself 199 (*pasar*)
even so 267 (*todo*)
Every cloud has a silver lining. 160 (*mal*)
every little while 200 (*paso*)
every living soul 32 (*bicho*)
Every man for himself! 244 (*salvar*)
every once in a while 135 (*higo*)
every other 251 (*sí*)

317

every so often 43 (*cada*)

Everyone to his own taste. 131 (*gusto*)

to excess 86 (*demasía*)

F

face down (up) 34 (*boca*)

face to face 120 (*frente*)

to face up to 120 (*frente*)

the fact is 52 (*caso*)

the fact is 86 (*dejar*)

to fail to 86 (*dejar*)

to fall flat 43 (*caer*)

to fall ill 43 (*caer*)

to fall in love at first sight 118 (*flechazo*)

to fall into line 23 (*aro*)

to fall into the clutches of 124 (*garra*)

to fall into the hands of 161 (*mano*)

to fall into the trap 270 (*trampa*)

to fall like a bombshell 35 (*bomba*)

to fall on one's face 38 (*bruces*)

to fall out of favor with 128 (*gracia*)

to fall to one's lot 256 (*suerte*)

to fall upon 232 (*recaer*)

to fancy oneself as 98 (*echar*)

far from it 169 (*menos*)

farther on 8 (*adelante*)

to feather one's nest 239 (*riñón*)

feel free 62 (*confianza*)

to feel like 124 (*gana*)

to feel one's way along 265 (*tienta*)

to feel right at home 210 (*pez*)

to fight in hand-to-hand combat 77 (*cuerpo*)

to find a way 143 (*ingeniar*)

to find fault 151 (*leche*)

to find out about 102 (*enterar*)

to find someone's weak spot 287 (*vuelta*)

Fine feathers don't make fine birds. 176 (*mona*)

to fire on 94 (*disparar*)

flesh and blood 50 (*carne*)

to foam at the mouth 108 (*espumarajo*)

to follow the crowd 69 (*corriente*)

to foot the bill 125 (*gasto*)

for all one is worth 216 (*poder*)

for example 99 (*ejemplo*)

For heaven's sake! 93 (*Dios*)

for instance 99 (*ejemplo*)

for lack of 113 (*falta*)

for sure 116 (*fijo*)

for the benefit of 32 (*beneficio*)

for the first (last) time 282 (*vez*)

for the time being 221 (*pronto*)

Forewarned is forearmed. 136 (*hombre*)

from A to Z 203 (*pe*)

from bad to worse 160 (*mal*)

from hand to hand 162 (*mano*)

from now on 22 (*aquí*)

from one end to the other 42 (*cabo*)

from time to time 281 (*vez*)

from top to bottom 24 (*arriba*)

The fur is going to fly. 94 (*Dios*)

G

to gain ground 263 (*terreno*)

to get a breath of (fresh) air 121 (*fresco*)

to get a lump in one's throat 184 (*nudo*)

Get a move on! 27 (*avío*)

to get ahead of 86 (*delantera*)

to get along 85 (*defender*)

to get along well with 159 (*llevar*)

to get along with 226 (*quedar*)

to get along without 199 (*pasar*)

to get by 145 (*ir*)

to get carried away 162 (*mano*)

to get dark 183 (*noche*)

to get dead drunk 178 (*muerte*)

to get down on one's knees 240 (*rodilla*)

to get down to business 26 (*asunto*)

to get even with someone 192 (*pagar*)

to get gooseflesh 50 (*carne*)

to get hold of 133 (*hacer*)

to get in touch with 65 (*contacto*)

to get into it 100 (*emprender*)

to get it into one's head 41 (*cabeza*)

to get off the track 46 (*camino*)

to get off to a good start 211 (*pie*)

to get on one's feet again 119 (*flote*)

to get one's own way 243 (*salir*)

to get out in the sun 253 (*sol*)

Get out of here! 150 (*largo*)

to get rattled 110 (*estribo*)

to get red in the face 203 (*pavo*)

to get rid of 89 (*deshacer*)

to get the jump on someone 7 (*acción*)

to get to sleep 256 (*sueño*)

to get to the point 129 (*grano*)

to get tongue-tied 153 (*lengua*)

to get under way 165 (*marcha*)

to get up from the table 170 (*mesa*)

to get up on the wrong side of the bed 149 (*lado*)

to get used to 133 (*hacer*)

to get what is coming to one 170 (*merecido*)

to give a dressing-down 271 (*trapo*)

to give birth to 157 (*luz*)

to give free rein to 238 (*rienda*)

Give him an inch and he'll take a mile. 211 (*pie*)

to give one an appetite 21 (*apetito*)

to give or take a few 215 (*poco*)

to give rise to 156 (lugar)

to give someone a dressing-down 44 (*calada*)

to give someone a light 122 (*fuego*)

to give something everything one's got 34 (*bofe*)

to give up 278 (*vencer*)

to give up the ghost 108 (*espíritu*)

to go abroad 112 (*extranjero*)

to go after 145 (*ir*)

to go ahead with 158 (*llevar*)

to go back to one's old ways 18 (*andadas*)

to go by 26 (*atenerse*)

to go crazy 155 (*loco*)

to go Dutch 105 (*escote*)

to go fifty-fifty 167 (*medio*)

to go for a walk 200 (*paseo*)

to go from one extreme to the other 112 (*extremo*)

to go hungry 133 (*hambre*)

to go in one ear and out the other 188 (*oído*)

to go looking for trouble 210 (*pie*)

to go on a diet 233 (*régimen*)

to go out of style 174 (*moda*)

to go out on a spree 196 (*parranda*)

to go out on strike 139 (*huelga*)

to go overboard 51 (*casa*)

to go shopping 60 (*compra*)

to go through hell 43 (*Caín*)

to go to bed with the chickens 123 (*gallina*)

to go to one's head 41 (*cabeza*)

to go to the expense 124 (*gasto*)

to go to the trouble of 268 (*tomar*)

to go too far 230 (*raya*)

to go up in smoke 140 (*humo*)

to go without saying 84 (*decir*)

Good heavens! 93 (*Dios*)

Good riddance! 140 (*humo*)

the great beyond 16 (*allá*)

to grasp at a straw 40 (*cabello*)

to grin and bear it 243 (*saliva*)

H

half . . . and half . . . 103 (*entre*)

halfway through 174 (*mitad*)

to handle with kid gloves 14 (*algodón*)

hard cash 65 (*contante*)

to have a lot of pull 42 (*cabida*)

to have a drink 270 (*trago*)

to have a falling-out 94 (*disgusto*)

to have a good ear 188 (*oído*)

to have a good eye 189 (*ojo*)

to have a good time 230 (*rato*)

to have a grudge against 228 (*rabia*)

to have a hard time 22 (*apuro*)

to have a heart of gold 194 (*pan*)

to have a little fling 47 (*cana*)

to have a lot of nerve 177 (*morro*)

to have a lot of pull 13 (*aldaba*)

to have a narrow escape 172 (*milagro*)

to have a nerve 146 (*jeta*)

to have a notion to 20 (*antojarse*)

to have a run of bad luck 160 (*malo*)

to have a run of bad luck 229 (*racha*)

to have a screw loose 269 (*tornillo*)

to have a way with people 96 (*don*)

to have an ax to grind 144 (*intención*)

to have an iron constitution 244 (*salud*)

to have at one's fingertips 84 (*dedillo*)

to have bats in the belfry 192 (*pájaro*)

to have been around 288 (*vuelta*)

to have designs 173 (*mira*)

to have had it up to here 176 (*moño*)

to have it out with 132 (*haber*)

to have just 6 (*acabar*)

to have left 226 (*quedar*)

to have no rhyme or reason to it 211 (*pie*)

to have nothing to do with 24 (*arte*)

to have on 262 (*tener*)

to have on one 158 (*llevar*)

to have on the tip of one's tongue 223 (*punta*)

to have one foot in the grave 110 (*estribo*)

to have one's eye on 188 (*ojo*)

to have one's hair stand on end 204 (*pelo*)

to have one's head in the clouds 156 (*luna*)

to have one's nerves on edge 182 (*nervio*)

to have one's hands tied 163 (*mano*)

to have pull 193 (*palanca*)

to have the bright idea of 187 (*ocurrencia*)

to have the floor 193 (*palabra*)

to have the nerve to 88 (*descaro*)

to have to 262 (*tener*)

to have to do with 262 (*tener*)

to have under one's thumb 225 (*puño*)

to have winning ways 96 (*don*)

He who laughs last laughs best. 233 (*reír*)

head first 41 (*cabeza*)

Heads or tails. 48 (*cara*)

to hear of 188 (*oír*)

to heave a sigh of relief 256 (*suspiro*)

321

in the daytime 83 (*de*)
in the distance 152 (*lejos*)
in the family circle 114 (*familia*)
in the first place 156 (*lugar*)
in the least 172 (*mínimo*)
in the long run 150 (*largo*)
in the meantime 258 (*tanto*)
in the middle of 167 (*medio*)
in the moonlight 157 (*luna*)
in the near future 123 (*futuro*)
in the open air 11 (*aire*)
in the open country 87
   (*descampado*)
in the shape of 119 (*forma*)
in the strictest confidence 236
   (*reserva*)
in the twilight 157 (*luz*)
in the twinkling of an eye 189 (*ojo*)
in time to 59 (*compás*)
in turn 281 (*vez*)
in two 174 (*mitad*)
in vain 276 (*vano*)
in writing 105 (*escrito*)
inch by inch 193 (*palmo*)
inside and out 87 (*dentro*)
to insist on 100 (*empeñar*)
insofar as possible 217 (*posible*)
instead of 281 (*vez*)
to intend to 144 (*intención*)
into the bargain 221 (*propina*)
It all depends. 247 (*según*)
It can't be helped. 234 (*remedio*)
It doesn't ring a bell. 254 (*sonar*)
it so happens that 54 (*casualidad*)
It'll all come out in the wash. 58
   (*colada*)
It's a deal! 271 (*trato*)
it's a good thing 160 (*mal*)
It's about time! 137 (*hora*)
It's all fallen through. 128 (*gozo*)
It's an ill wind that blows nobody
   good. 160 (*mal*)

It's as plain as day. 10 (*agua*)
It's better than nothing. 13 (*algo*)
It's easier said than done. 91
   (*dicho*)
It's gone down the drain. 128
   (*gozo*)
It's like carrying coals to
   Newcastle. 135 (*hierro*)

J

Jack of all trades, master of none.
   22 (*aprendiz*)
to join the ranks 15 (*alta*)
judging by 148 (*juzgar*)
to jump for joy 128 (*gozo*)
to jump for joy 243 (*salto*)
to jump out of the frying pan and
   into the fire 130 (*Guatemala*)
to jump to conclusions 61
   (*conclusión*)
just a step away 201 (*paso*)
just a stone's throw from 200
   (*paso*)
just any old way 93 (*Dios*)
just because 251 (*sí*)
just for a change 276 (*variar*)
just in case 7 (*acaso*)
just like everybody else 135 (*hijo*)
just like that 180 (*nada*)
just plain 246 (*seco*)
just the opposite 237 (*reverso*)
just yesterday 174 (*mismo*)

K

to keep at a safe distance 95
   (*distancia*)
to keep in line 231 (*raya*)
to keep in mind 219 (*presente*)
to keep one's figure 154 (*línea*)
to keep one's mouth shut 34 (*boca*)

to keep one's word 192 (*palabra*)
to keep posted 69 (*corriente*)
to keep someone up in the air 284 (*vilo*)
Keep your chin up. 67 (*corazón*)
to kick the bucket 202 (*pata*)
to kill the goose that laid the golden eggs 124 (*gallina*)
to kill time 230 (*rato*)
to kill two birds with one stone 192 (*pájaro*)
to knock at the door 223 (*puerta*)
to knock on wood 159 (*madera*)
to know a thing or two 58 (*colmillo*)
to know backwards and forwards 84 (*dedillo*)
to know by sight 285 (*vista*)
to know how to roll with the punches 254 (*son*)
to know what one is doing 64 (*conocimiento*)
to know what the score is 288 (*vuelta*)

L

later on 8 (*adelante*)
to laugh at 233 (*reír*)
to laugh till one cries 239 (*risa*)
to lay a hand on 163 (*mano*)
to lay it on thick 161 (*mano*)
to lay waste 122 (*fuego*)
Leave well enough alone. 38 (*bueno*)
to lead a . . . life 283 (*vida*)
to lead one to 159 (*llevar*)
to learn at one's mother's knee 151 (*leche*)
to leave high and dry 246 (*seco*)
to leave in the lurch 214 (*plantar*)
to leave no stone unturned 212 (*piedra*)

to leave word 92 (*dicho*)
to lend a hand 136 (*hombro*)
to lend someone a hand 162 (*mano*)
The lesser of two evils. 159 (*mal*)
The leopard can't change his spots. 125 (*genio*)
to let it drop 66 (*conversación*)
to let . . . stew in one's own juice 243 (*salsa*)
to let someone alone 203 (*paz*)
to let the cat out of the bag 163 (*manta*)
Let the dead bury the dead. 178 (*muerto*)
Let them talk. 93 (*Dios*)
Let's get to work! 163 (*mano*)
Let's see. 279 (*ver*)
like a fish out of water 123 (*gallina*)
Like father, like son. 123 (*galgo*)
like manna from heaven 55 (*cielo*)
Like water off a duck's back. 227 (*quien*)
to listen to reason 231 (*razón*)
to live from hand to mouth 91 (*día*)
to live it up 283 (*vida*)
to live on 14 (*alimentar*)
to lock in 158 (*llave*)
long live 286 (*vivir*)
to look after 187 (*ocupar*)
to look askance 235 (*reojo*)
to look at everything through rose-colored glasses 59 (*color*)
to look favorably on 189 (*ojo*)
Look before you leap. 52 (*casar*)
to look like 195 (*parecer*)
look out 78 (*cuidado*)
to look out for 173 (*mirar*)
to look out for number one 185 (*número*)
to look out for oneself 30 (*barrer*)
to look the other way 285 (*vista*)

Look who's talking! 227 (*quién*)
to look up 285 (*vista*)
loose ends 42 (*cabo*)
to lose count (track) 76 (*cuenta*)
to lose ground 263 (*terreno*)
to lose one's head 41 (*cabeza*)
to lose one's mind 250 (*seso*)
to lose sight of 285 (*vista*)
to lose the thread (of the conversation) 135 (*hilo*)
to lose touch with 65 (*contacto*)

M

mad as a hornet 123 (*furia*)
to make a clean breast of it 62 (*confesar*)
to make a clean sweep 245 (*santo*)
to make a fool of oneself 268 (*tonto*)
to make a great show of 12 (*alarde*)
to make a hit 123 (*furor*)
to make a killing 9 (*agosto*)
to make a note of 184 (*nota*)
to make a nuisance of oneself 151 (*lata*)
to make a scene 104 (*escándalo*)
to make a virtue of necessity 182 (*necesidad*)
to make as if to 8 (*ademán*)
to make available 113 (*facilitar*)
to make common cause 54 (*causa*)
to make do 21 (*apañar*)
to make faces 126 (*gesto*)
to make friends with 17 (*amigo*)
to make fun of 39 (*burlar*)
to make love 17 (*amor*)
to make mincemeat out of someone 210 (*picadillo*)
to make one mad 228 (*rabia*)
to make one's mouth water 10 (*agua*)

324

to make one's way 201 (*paso*)
to make one's way 46 (*camino*)
to make peace 203 (*paz*)
to make sense 248 (*sentido*)
to make someone toe the line 55 (*cintura*)
to make the best of things 265 (*tiempo*)
to make up 17 (*amistad*)
to make use of 250 (*servir*)
to make way 201 (*paso*)
Man overboard! 136 (*hombre*)
Man proposes, God disposes. 136 (*hombre*)
to meddle in other people's business 171 (*meter*)
to meet one's match 138 (*horma*)
to melt in one's mouth 10 (*agua*)
The moon is out. 156 (*luna*)
Money makes the world go round. 40 (*caballero*)
more and more 281 (*vez*)
more or less 70 (*cosa*)
most of 197 (*parte*)
most of the time 281 (*vez*)
to move heaven and earth 55 (*cielo*)
to move into 143 (*instalar*)
Much ado about nothing. 241 (*ruido*)
Mum's the word. 34 (*boca*)
to my way of thinking 279 (*ver*)

N

to neglect to 88 (*descuido*)
neither . . . nor . . . 182 (*ni*)
never in one's life 283 (*vida*)
next door 148 (*lado*)
next to 148 (*junto*)
to nip in the bud 229 (*raíz*)
no buts about it 208 (*pero*)
no doubt 96 (*duda*)

no end of 117 (*fin*)
No indeed! 106 (*eso*)
no longer 288 (*ya*)
no sooner . . . than 32 (*bien*)
No sooner said than done. 83
    (*decir*)
not . . . at all 180 (*nada*)
not any more 288 (*ya*)
not at all 175 (*modo*)
not by a long shot 178 (*mucho*)
not even 182 (*ni*)
not for love or money 266 (*tiro*)
not for nothing 13 (*algo*)
not only 253 (*sólo*)
not only that 165 (*más*)
not to amount to anything 55 (*cero*)
not to be able to care less 206
    (*pepino*)
not to be able to go on 216 (*poder*)
not to be able to help 216 (*poder*)
not to be able to see past the end of
    one's nose 181 (*nariz*)
not to be able to stand 216 (*poder*)
not to be able to stand the sight of
    216 (*poder*)
not to be able to stomach 270
    (*tragar*)
not to be on speaking terms 133
    (*hablar*)
not to be out of place 165 (*más*)
not to be worth a damn 59
    (*comino*)
not to change the subject 196
    (*párrafo*)
not to get anywhere 197 (*parte*)
not to give a damn about 33
    (*bledo*)
not to have a penny to one's name
    179 (*muerto*)
not to have a penny to one's name
    74 (*cuarto*)
not to have the heart to 67
    (*corazón*)

not to know where to turn 171
    (*meter*)
not to lift a finger 127 (*golpe*)
not to mention 84 (*decir*)
not to mince words 205 (*pelo*)
not to sleep a wink 189 (*ojo*)
not to understand a thing 194
    (*papa*)
not yet 267 (*todavía*)
Nothing ventured, nothing gained.
    164 (*mar*)
now . . . now . . . 190 (*ora*)
now then 10 (*ahora*)
Now's the time. 10 (*ahora*)

O

to object to 190 (*oponer*)
of course 256 (*supuesto*)
of one's own free will 286
    (*voluntad*)
of tender years 98 (*edad*)
old wives' tale 77 (*cuento*)
on a large scale 104 (*escala*)
on account of 178 (*motivo*)
on all fours 125 (*gatas*)
on credit 115 (*fiar*)
on duty 130 (*guardia*)
on one's back 78 (*cuesta*)
on one's guard 130 (*guardia*)
on pins and needles 36 (*brasa*)
on purpose 222 (*propósito*)
on the average 263 (*término*)
on the contrary 66 (*contrario*)
on the defensive 86 (*defensiva*)
on the dot 224 (*punto*)
on the high seas 164 (*mar*)
on the occasion of 178 (*motivo*)
on the one hand; on the other 149
    (*lado*)
on the other hand 197 (*parte*)
on the point of 223 (*punto*)
on the side 149 (*lado*)

325

to put on a pedestal 15 (*altar*)
to put on airs 268 (*tono*)
to put one's cards on the table 51 (*carta*)
to put one's foot in one's mouth 202 (*pata*)
to put one's hands on one's hips 146 (*jarra*)
to put one's shoulder to the wheel 136 (*hombro*)
to put out to sea 164 (*mar*)
to put someone on bread and water 194 (*pan*)
to put something over (*gato*)
to put the cart before the horse 228 (*rábano*)
to put to the test 222 (*prueba*)
to put two and two together 42 (*cabo*)
to put up with 63 (*conformar*)

Q

quite a few 75 (*cuatro*)

R

to rack one's brains 250 (*seso*)
to rain cats and dogs (pitchforks) 48 (*cántaros*)
to raise objections to 185 (*objeción*)
to raise one's eyebrows 54 (*ceja*)
to rake over the coals 271 (*trapo*)
to reach an agreement 8 (*acuerdo*)
to read between the lines 154 (*línea*)
to refrain from 130 (*guardar*)
to refresh someone's memory 168 (*memoria*)
to refuse to 182 (*negar*)
to resign oneself to 63 (*conformar*)

to rest assured 247 (*seguridad*)
to rest on one's laurels 151 (*laurel*)
to retrace one's steps 201 (*paso*)
to revolve around 269 (*torno*)
to ride bareback 204 (*pelo*)
to ride horseback 40 (*caballo*)
right and left 92 (*diestro*)
right away 246 (*seguida*)
right from the start 220 (*principio*)
right here 22 (*aquí*)
right now 11 (*ahora*)
right off the bat 38 (*bueno*)
right offhand 175 (*momento*)
right to one's face 29 (*barba*)
right under one's nose 181 (*nariz*)
right-hand man 36 (*brazo*)
rightly so 231 (*razón*)
to rise to the occasion 16 (*altura*)
to risk one's life 283 (*vida*)
to risk one's neck 205 (*pellejo*)
Rome wasn't built in a day. 289 (*Zamora*)
to rob Peter to pay Paul 245 (*santo*)
to run into 81 (*dar*)
to run like a deer 153 (*liebre*)
to run smoothly 241 (*rueda*)
to run the risk of 238 (*riesgo*)
to run things (the show) 31 (*batuta*)

S

safe and sound 244 (*sano*)
the same old 251 (*siempre*)
to save one's skin 206 (*pellejo*)
to save time 264 (*tiempo*)
to say nothing of 84 (*decir*)
to say the first thing that comes into one's head 268 (*tonto*)
to see fit to 262 (*tener*)
to see stars 109 (*estrella*)
to see the point of 75 (*cuenta*)

327

to see the world 179 (*mundo*)

to see through someone 147 (*juego*)

to see what someone is up to 279 (*ver*)

See you later. 156 (*luego*)

See you tomorrow. 164 (*mañana*)

Seeing is believing. 279 (*ver*)

to sell for a song 278 (*vender*)

to send about one's business 200 (*paseo*)

to send packing 43 (*caja*)

to separate the wheat from the chaff 129 (*grano*)

to serve someone right 100 (*emplear*)

to set a trap 151 (*lazo*)

to set an example 99 (*ejemplo*)

to set fire to 122 (*fuego*)

to set one's sights on 173 (*mira*)

to set out 100 (*emprender*)

to set out after 217 (*pos*)

to set the table 170 (*mesa*)

to set up housekeeping 51 (*casa*)

to settle accounts 75 (*cuenta*)

to shake hands with 162 (*mano*)

to shake like a leaf 28 (*azogado*)

to shed bitter tears 150 (*lágrima*)

to show one's hand 99 (*embozo*)

to show one's teeth 92 (*diente*)

to show signs of 179 (*muestra*)

to show signs of life 248 (*señal*)

to show someone up 111 (*evidencia*)

to shower someone with 58 (*colmar*)

to shrug one's shoulders 136 (*hombro*)

to side with 231 (*razón*)

since the world began 179 (*mundo*)

to sit down 25 (*asiento*)

to sit up 142 (*incorporarse*)

sky high 184 (*nube*)

to slam the door in someone's face 222 (*puerta*)

to sleep it off 176 (*mona*)

to sleep like a log 273 (*tronco*)

to sleep on it 15 (*almohada*)

to slip away 39 (*bulto*)

to slip one's mind 168 (*memoria*)

so far 134 (*hasta*)

so far as I know 242 (*saber*)

So much the better. 168 (*mejor*)

So much the worse. 206 (*peor*)

so to speak 84 (*decir*)

so what? 225 (*qué*)

to soft-soap someone 57 (*coba*)

some . . . or other 242 (*saber*)

to some extent 224 (*punto*)

some time back 265 (*tiempo*)

something else 70 (*cosa*)

sooner or later 261 (*tarde*)

The sooner the better. 19 (*antes*)

to spare no effort 106 (*esfuerzo*)

to speak of 84 (*decir*)

to speed up 201 (*paso*)

to split the difference 93 (*diferencia*)

to stand in line 58 (*cola*)

to stand on one's own (two) feet 11 (*ala*)

to stand up to 101 (*enfrentar*)

to stare at 136 (*hito*)

stark naked 77 (*cuero*)

to start a tempest in a teapot 276 (*vaso*)

to start out 47 (*camino*)

to starve to death 133 (*hambre*)

to stay afloat 118 (*flote*)

to stay in bed 46 (*cama*)

step by step 201 (*paso*)

to stick one's head in the lion's mouth 34 (*boca*)

to stick out one's tongue 153 (*lengua*)

to stick to one's guns 272 (*trece*)

to stick to one's ribs 239 (*riñón*)

stick to someone like a leech 148 (*ladilla*)

stoop to 231 (*rebajar*)

stop beating around the bush 239 (*rodeo*)

op right there! 15 (*alto*)

ictly speaking 238 (*rigor*)

strike it rich 36 (*bota*)

strike up a friendship with 17 (*amistad*)

suck up to 205 (*pelota*)

sugar-coat the pill 212 (*píldora*)

suit the action to the word 7 (*acción*)

suit to a T 18 (*anillo*)

sum up 76 (*cuenta*)

swallow it hook, line, and sinker 20 (*anzuelo*)

swear a blue streak 245 (*sapo*)

sweat blood 127 (*gota*)

ll it to the marines. 208 (*perro*)

anks to 128 (*gracia*)

hat depends. 247 (*según*)

at is 249 (*ser*)

at is to say 84 (*decir*)

at very thing 174 (*mismo*)

hat will do! 38 (*bueno*)

nat's water over the dam. 9 (*agua*)

nat's his problem. 131 (*haber*)

hat's out of the question! 206 (*pensar*)

hat's right! 106 (*eso*)

at's why 106 (*eso*)

here are no two ways about it. 288 (*vuelta*)

here's many a slip twixt cup and lip. 214 (*plato*)

nere's more here than meets the eye. 125 (*gato*)

There's no hurry. 221 (*prisa*)

there's no telling 94 (*Dios*)

There's no use crying over spilt milk. 203 (*pecho*)

There's something fishy here. 125 (*gato*)

There's trouble brewing! 38 (*bueno*)

this very day 138 (*hoy*)

this way 23 (*aquí*)

through and through 273 (*tuétano*)

throughout the length and breadth of (*largo*)

tied to the apron strings of 113 (*falda*)

Time will tell. 120 (*freír*)

to take a (little) nip 32 (*beso*)

to take a dislike to 54 (*ceja*)

to take a fancy to 219 (*prendar*)

to take a liking to 128 (*gracia*)

to take a stand 198 (*partido*)

to take a trip 282 (*viaje*)

to take a turn for the better 126 (*giro*)

to take a walk 200 (*paseo*)

to take advantage of 22 (*aprovechar*)

to take after one's . . . 202 (*pasta*)

to take amiss 268 (*tomar*)

to take an interest in 144 (*interesar*)

to take aside 158 (*llevar*)

to take by surprise 255 (*sorpresa*)

to take care of 79 (*cuidar*)

to take charge of 101 (*encargar*)

to take for 268 (*tomar*)

to take for granted 247 (*sentar*)

to take French leave 120 (*francés*)

to take heart 14 (*aliento*)

to take into account 77 (*cuenta*)

to take it into one's head 82 (*dar*)

to take it the wrong way 159 (*mal*)

to take lightly 239 (*risa*)

U

331

Y

Index (Indice)

A

Indice

Indice

337

Indice

C

Indice

Indice

Indice

Indice

E

Indice

351

Indice

Indice

Indice

357

Indice

J

L

Ll

M

361

N

Indice

Indice

Indice

Índice

Indice

377

Indice

KOHALA HIGH SCHOOL